Managing Networks in
Project-Based Organisations

Managing Networks in Project-Based Organisations

Stephen Pryke

University College London
London

WILEY Blackwell

Registered Offices
John Wiley & Sons, Inc., 111 River Street, Hoboken, NJ 07030, USA
John Wiley & Sons Ltd, The Atrium, Southern Gate, Chichester, West Sussex, PO19 8SQ, UK

Editorial Office
9600 Garsington Road, Oxford, OX4 2DQ, UK

For details of our global editorial offices, customer services, and more information about Wiley products visit us at www.wiley.com.

Wiley also publishes its books in a variety of electronic formats and by print-on-demand. Some content that appears in standard print versions of this book may not be available in other formats.

Library of Congress Cataloging-in-Publication data applied for

ISBN: 9781118929926

Cover Design: Wiley
Cover Image: Karen Rubin/Balamurugan Soundaraj

Set in 10/12pt Warnock by SPi Global, Pondicherry, India
Printed and bound in Malaysia by Vivar Printing Sdn Bhd

10 9 8 7 6 5 4 3 2 1

Dedication

This book is dedicated to Karen whose love has been unwavering and who encouraged me to make the time to share my work through the publication of this book.

It is also dedicated to my mother Betty, who has endured the hardships and indignities of old age with stoicism and cheerfulness.

Bless you both

Contents

List of Figures

About the Author

Dr Stephen Pryke is a Senior Lecturer in Project Management at the Bartlett School of Construction and Project Management, University College London. He is the Director of Studies for the MSc Project and Enterprise Management programme and Director of Postgraduate Teaching and Learning for the school. Stephen is founder and Managing Director of CONA – the Centre for Organisational Network Analysis (CONA@UCL). He has published four texts for Wiley Blackwell: *The Management of Projects: A Relationship Approach* (with Smyth), *Collaborative Relationships in Construction* (with Smyth), *Supply Chain Management in Construction* and most recently *Social Network Analysis in Construction*. He is a series editor of the RICS/Wiley Blackwell Innovation in Construction series and has contributed to *Advanced Research Methods in the Built Environment* (Knight and Ruddock (eds), 2008) and *Managing the Professional Practice in the Built Environment* (Smyth (ed.), 2011), both also published by Wiley Blackwell. He has published a number of papers in leading research journals dealing with supply chain management, social network analysis and the legal aspects of procurement reforms in the UK. His work has been presented to a number of international research conferences and his work on procurement and project management systems in France and China has been published by RICS. Most recently Stephen was commissioned by RICS to write a report on the links between transport hub evolution and property, entitled *The Hub and the Place*. Stephen is a reviewer for a number of leading academic journals and EPSRC. He is an RICS APC panel member for the RICS Project Management Faculty. He sits on the Infrastructure Supply Chain Management Roundtable for RICS and his work is also disseminated through Infrastructure UK (IUK). He has provided project management training and consultancy to a number of major European companies. He was a consultant to Durland Consulting in Chicago, USA. Prior to entering academia in the mid 1990s he held senior project management positions in both the public and private sectors within the UK. He is currently working with Crossrail, Transport for London and the Spanish contractor Drogados – applying social network analysis to major complex rail infrastructure schemes.

Preface

This book builds upon the ideas developed and presented in *The Management of Projects: A Relationship Approach, Collaborative Relationships in Construction* and more recently *Supply Chain Management in Construction* and *Social Network Analysis in Construction* (all published by Wiley Blackwell). My thinking on the management challenges facing those dealing with complex construction and engineering projects increasingly moves away from traditional ideas about projects and their management.

The book responds to requests from industry and the publisher to operationalise and apply the theory developed in *Social Network Analysis in Construction*. The centre I established at University College London to exploit and disseminate my research work in the area of social network analysis (SNA) and its application, particularly, to project environments in the construction and engineering fields, builds on the premise that there are gaps in what we know and discuss about organisational structures, procurement and systems. We procure resources and hope that those resources will organise themselves into systems that deliver excellent projects. Yet we understand very little about how those systems evolve and decay, and how they are managed. Most of all, I became disillusioned about the idea that delivering great projects could be achieved by assembling an array of discrete systems dedicated to the management of value or cost or design, and so on – what must surely comprise a 'disintegrated' approach to project management.

So much of our thinking in management and project management has been constrained by the terminology that has prevailed and our reluctance to eschew the rather hierarchical, quasi-military models of organisational structures and their management. The Centre for Organisational Network Analysis (CONA@UCL – see http://www.ucl.ac.uk/cona) has engaged with a number of organisations in its short life so far; these have included Crossrail, Transport for London, the California High Speed Railway Group and Infrastructure UK (IUK), as well as Price Waterhouse Coopers and Deloittes. The recent bias toward rail infrastructure has reflected the prominence of rail infrastructure spending prevailing at the time that this book was being conceived and written. Earlier work using SNA on project case studies involved property developers and public sector clients. In fact, many of the challenges are the same whether you are building a leisure centre, commercial office space or rail infrastructure. The challenge fundamentally is to understand how people collaborate to deliver excellent projects; to make interventions where they don't; and to replicate the best network configurations and behaviour over time.

The aim of the book was to challenge some of the traditional thinking on the conceptualisation of projects and their management and to bring human behaviour into more prominence in our ideas about successful delivery of projects. The aim was also to synthesise some of my thoughts on collaborative relationships. If we can express collaborative relationships as networks of actors, each with project function-related roles, linked to others with needs and resources, then we can understand how our projects solve problems, overcome adversarial behaviour, create value, and innovate, as well as reducing time, cost and carbon emissions.

This book reflects the journey I have made as a practitioner from managing complex projects for demanding clients, over a period of 20 years, to doctoral research and the development of theory in the areas of collaborative relationships, supply chains and their management, and the conceptualisation of the project as a network of relationships. It has been a career of two halves – half in industry dealing with the issues on a daily basis; half in academia looking for theory and creative methods to understand those issues.

I have been very fortunate to have been based in the Bartlett School of Construction and Project Management at University College London for the last decade or more. The plethora of talented academics is too large to mention here but I have greatly benefitted from the exchange of knowledge that inevitably results from being based in such an environment. During my time at UCL I have led the master's course in project management – MSc Project and Enterprise Management. This course, and others at UCL and the University of Cambridge, has benefitted from the ongoing research work that I have undertaken and I hope that those students have enjoyed the discussions around the ongoing research work. But I want to thank the students as well for challenging the new ideas – in a sense they acted as a test bed for many of the ideas that subsequently went into print or were implemented through training programmes and research bids. Teaching those bright young people from around the world has been a constant joy to me.

The perfect book, like the perfect PhD, is probably never finished and it is therefore almost inevitable that in publishing this book I have left stones unturned and questions unanswered. But I hope that you the reader will see this as a positive thing. The publication of the book is the beginning of a discussion and debate that will increase the depth of our knowledge in the application of social network analysis to the understanding of projects, but fundamentally will provide a framework for the management of project-focused networks.

I sincerely hope that you enjoy reading this book and that you find something that challenges your thinking or helps you manage networks effectively. I have enjoyed putting the book together and capturing some of my thoughts in this important area of study.

S.D.P.
London, UK
December 2016

Acknowledgements

My thanks to each of the organisations that allowed me to work with them exploring the use of social network data to understand project networks. In particular I thank the team working on the Bank Station upgrade scheme, which was the subject of a Knowledge Transfer Partnership awarded to UCL, comprising Simon Addyman and Ed Watson at Transport for London (TfL), Dr Sulafa Badi, my colleague at UCL, and Balamurugan Soundaraj (Bala), the research associate for the Knowledge Transfer Partnership (KTP) with TfL. My thanks also to the team from Drogados and those co-located staff from consultants and subcontractors working on the £600M scheme. Some of the findings of the KTP have made their way into this book and it has served to provide a vehicle for the use of SNA on a mega ($1BN+) project.

Thanks to Infrastructure UK, in particular to Miles Ashley and Simon Murray for expressing an interest in my work on social network analysis and supply chain management maturity models. Both RICS and ICE have helped to publicise the importance of SNA in project team analysis.

Sincere thanks to the Bartlett School of Construction and Project Management at University College London for effectively sponsoring this book. My thanks also go to the Dean of the Faculty of the Built Environment, Professor Alan Penn, who took a personal interest in the work of CONA.

Finally, this book would not have happened without the long-term support and encouragement I have been most fortunate to receive from Karen Rubin. Karen convinced me of the pressing need to get the book published; produced and revised a large number of figures; and edited the manuscript prior to submission to the publishers.

Thank You

1

Introduction

Project management theory, and to some extent practice, have tended to focus on process, systems and documents. But projects are instigated, designed and delivered by human beings. This book focuses on the people involved in projects. It conceptualises the project as a social network, or more accurately, multiple layers of social networks, each network dedicated to the delivery of a particular project function. One of the exciting discoveries during the research that this book draws upon was the importance of self-organising project networks, particularly in complex projects. In this book, I explore some of the factors that affect the behaviour of individuals as project actors, including game theory and personality type. I also consider the environmental and personal attributes that might enable networks to function more effectively, particularly in the context of the project. I look at Building Information Modelling (BIM), because there is an important link between the efforts being made in relation to BIM, and social networks. Finally, the book presents some case study material related to a two-year research project which I led involving the Centre for Organisational Network Analysis and Transport for London.

The previous book in this series – *Social Network Analysis in Construction* (Pryke, 2012) – presented social network analysis (SNA) as an innovative method for the analysis of project organisations. It rationalised the SNA approach, looked at the importance of collaborative relationships in project organisations and proposed a theoretical framework to support the conceptualisation of the project as a network of relationships – contracts, information flows and financial incentives. The book proposed a model for the use of SNA which others might adopt in their research and presented four case studies, comparing collaborative, relationship-based procurement and traditional strategies for procurement. The book provided an insight into the interpretation of network data derived from project-based organisations and finally took a somewhat speculative look at how networks might be managed.

It was the chapter on managing networks that was in my view the most innovative, and *Managing Networks* aims to develop that theme using case study material gathered from recent research carried out at the Centre for Organisational Network Analysis at University College London (CONA@UCL). The raison d'être of CONA is to explore the void that is evident between procurement, systems and organisational hierarchies.

In our projects, we set about procuring resources, place those resources in structures that are often expressed either hierarchically or to a high level of abstraction, and then try to manage the self-organising networks of human relationships that evolve, without conceptualising those relationships as networks. It is little wonder that we often find it difficult to analyse why some projects seem to be successful and others less so. A small group of those associated with CONA@UCL set about trying to classify, and to some extent quantify, organisationally, the 'good' projects and the 'bad' projects, using the language of the social network analysts. Examples of this work are: Badi and Pryke (2006), Badi *et al.* (2014), Badi *et al.* (2016a and 2016b), Doloi *et al.* (2016), Pryke *et al.* (2017), Pryke *et al.* (2015a and 2015b), Pryke (2014), Pryke *et al.* (2014), Pryke *et al.* (2013), Pryke and Badi (2013), Shepherd and Pryke (2014), El-Sheikh and Pryke (2010), Pryke (2005a and 2005b), Pryke and Pearson (2006).

So, this book aims to respond to the needs of several groups: those who ask what the social network theory of project organisations is; the practitioners who ask 'how can I use social network analysis to run smarter projects'; the students who ask how we can start teaching project management in a way that helps them to identify network and actor characteristics – to classify project coalition activity and the actors involved in network terms and to start to build toward defining management in a project-based environment in network terms.

The analysis and representation or visualisation of project-focused activity has involved task-dependency-based approaches, structural analysis (hierarchical) and process mapping, all of which fail to reflect the relationships that deliver our projects – relationships that we can classify by project function.

Structure of the Book

Chapter 2: Theoretical Context This chapter locates the concept of managing networks within a context of managing projects and their supply chains. A number of assumptions have been made about the nature of projects around which procurement and project management practices have evolved. I argue in Chapter 2 that our choice of procurement and the subsequent project management strategies applied have not kept pace with the complexity of many projects. It is also argued that at the point where procurement is completed (and resources identified and secured) a transition occurs where those resources have to configure themselves into systems that will deliver a successful project. We know little of how these self-organising systems evolve. Our lack of awareness means that we typically do not facilitate or manage these systems.

The chapter reflects on the vestiges of scientific management that still remain in project management research and practice. The fact that our projects are delivered by unpredictable, sometimes irrational, imperfect human beings seems sometimes to be ignored in our discussion about programming, risk management and the whole range of sub-systems that we typically bring together in project management. The chapter concludes by pointing to the fact that our highly-connected lives no longer rely on distinguishing task and social structure. Human beings essentially get things done through links to other human project actors. The idea that everything that does not constitute a formal direction or instruction under the terms of the contract should be classified as 'informal' is firmly rejected. There has, perhaps, been some confusion between informal and recreational ties. Although recreational ties are undoubtedly fascinating and important, this book does not deal with them.

The chapter provides a context and perhaps rationale for the chapters that follow. The key themes are developed in more depth in these subsequent chapters.

Chapter 3: Networks and Projects This chapter starts with the reflection that the last fifty years have brought only modest progress in our understanding of 'systems… functions…interrelationships, and the location and prominence of…control and coordination centres' (Higgin and Jessop, 1965: 56). In fact many of the techniques that we use to manage projects seem to ignore all of these issues. The chapter makes a start on the formulation of sub-systems that might be studied to enable a better understanding of how projects are *really* managed. The concepts of ritualistic behaviour and routines are introduced and I reflect on the fact that individuals are attracted to routines because they provide consistency and stability, and reduce mental effort (Becker, 2004).

This chapter refers to Morris' (2013) discussions about the maturity of project definition, or more accurately the tendency for project definition frequently to be insufficiently mature at the point of transition between pre- and post-contract stages. The idea that this uncertainty, exacerbated by continually increasing complexity, leads to project actors forming networks to secure information, solve problems and disseminate processed information is introduced and rationalised. It is argued that at the transition from resource procurement to project delivery, routines are not adequate in the face of complexity in both task and structure. I ask the reader to move on from discussions about the 'iron triangle' for the reasons that: it is very difficult to define client needs at a stage early enough to use procurement successfully; it is difficult to avoid agency problems in procurement and delivery; and, arguably, change in project definition *improves* value to client and end-users, rather than the reverse. It is not possible to allocate project and supply chain roles accurately and to maintain these roles as a constant throughout the entire project design and delivery period. Project systems are iterative and transient and this is to a great extent not reflected in the contractual relationships established through many procurement approaches.

The chapter provides an introduction to project actor characteristics (drawn from Pryke, 2012), and an overview is given of network characteristics (path lengths and density) and linkage characteristics (tie strength or value and direction). The chapter ends with a reflection on the question posed – why networks? – and makes a link to Chapter 4. The chapter concludes that the identification and analysis of interaction networks between the individuals engaged to deliver a project is the only way to observe the self-organising, complex project function-related networks that hold the key to understanding successful and unsuccessful project delivery. If we can understand and map these networks, we can define the actor roles and network configurations that constitute successful project delivery and begin to replicate and eventually to manage these networks.

Chapter 4: Why Networks? The chapter starts with some discussion about the origins of SNA and references to Nohria and Eccles' (1992) work on rationalising the use of SNA in organisations. I emphasise that in a project environment it is important to distinguish between the two types of actors: individuals and firms. Contracts are established between *firms* and projects are delivered through relationships between *individuals*. I discuss some of the issues to be considered when applying SNA to project and supply chain research – the quantitative/interpretative paradigm; the issue of causality and the complexity of SNA as an analytical approach; the importance of precise network classification; and the limitations arising from sampling. Studying and managing projects that are highly complex in terms of technical content, as well as process, inevitably leads to complexity in both analysis and management approaches.

Some basic SNA terminology is discussed as a preamble to the analysis and discussion in later chapters. A structure for the analysis of projects (and in particular construction and engineering projects) is introduced. I suggest that while traditional project management analytical tools and management approaches essentially pursue the 'iron triangle' of cost, time and quality, clients' and stakeholders' needs are sophisticated and complex, requiring a more finely-grained approach to both analysis and management.

I end this chapter with a call for more research using SNA in projects and provide some details about suitable software and the identification of network boundaries for research.

Chapter 5: Self-Organising Networks in Projects In this chapter I further develop the theme that procurement and project management strategies have not kept pace with rapidly increasing complexity in projects. I discuss the increased prevalence of temporary, project-related organisation forms in a range of industries. Film and software tend to be highly creative but construction and engineering are perceived to be more routine-based. Yet this is contentious and many involved in major construction and engineering projects would emphasise the need for creativity in finding design solutions and in problem-solving. The chapter considers what clients want from projects and although many clients may not express it in those terms, 'completeness' is felt to be of primary concern to most clients. I assert that the previous focus on the iron triangle in the context of financial incentive for designers and constructors is dysfunctional in terms of the client's needs and leads to ritualistic behaviour by project actors. In this context, the chapter moves on to focus upon what I refer to as some 'dangerous assumptions'.

These dangerous assumptions move in chronological order through project procurement and delivery, starting with the definition of client needs. The definition of clients' needs, the difficulty of achieving an accurate representation of those needs in documentary form by human or technological means, the fact that changes in project definition have been regarded as undesirable, and the accuracy and sustainability of role allocation in a long-term, uncertain project environment, are all discussed as possible reasons for our misunderstanding the reasons for failure in project design and delivery.

The discussion turns to the evolution of project management over time and I move through production orientation, functional management, information processing and my own work with Smyth on the relationship approach (Pryke and Smyth, 2006). I ask the question that I frequently put to practising project managers and postgraduate students – 'why does it matter how we conceptualise the project?' I emphasise the need to find a means of understanding the 'non-linear, complex, iterative and interactive' processes that projects constitute (Pryke, 2012). If we can be clear how we conceptualise projects, we can be clear about the way in which we understand and monitor projects and formulate an effective means of managing those projects.

The chapter closes with some case study findings which conclude that:

- Self-organising networks form quickly when project actors are under pressure to gather and disseminate information
- Some actors place themselves into prominent positions for personal reasons that are detrimental to the delivery of the project

- Although at contract placement stage, typically the client formally enters a lump-sum contract, much of the design of the construction project has still to be done, which carries uncertainty (and particularly financial uncertainty) for the client
- Short path lengths between the client and Tier 2 subcontractors are useful in terms of managing design evolution and maintaining knowledge transfer
- Large, confident clients will internalise risk if this is the most effective way to deal with risk, not hesitating to involve themselves with Tier 2 subcontractors to resolve design issues and minimise risk.

Finally, I suggest that we will manage projects more effectively if we conceptualise them as networks of actor relationships.

Chapter 6: Game Theory and Networks The chapter starts with a discussion of the transition between resource acquisition and project delivery. Roles are allocated to individuals as project actors through contracts, but as soon as work starts, whether it is design or production of some sort, actors acquire roles that are related to their network position and network role (for more detail on the latter refer to Chapter 9, Pryke, 2012). The behaviour of individuals as project actors is a function of their network role. Project actors are also influential in network terms – their behaviour affects the way in which the network functions and modifies the behaviour of other project actors.

Social network analysts frequently place relatively low emphasis on the characteristics of human actors, preferring to map network configurations and characteristics alongside the characteristics of the links between actors. In this chapter I remind the reader that human beings are more than simply 'human resources' to be placed within a system. Game theory helps us to understand how human actors behave in certain environments – with their behaviour being perhaps unpredictable or even irrational.

Chapter 6 provides a little history about game theory and then reviews the research carried out on the application of game theory to construction projects. The chapter looks at the definition of game theory and discusses case study material which illustrates the way that actors (or in the game theory context, 'players') make decisions in relation to the risk context in which they find themselves. The subjects of 'payoff' and completeness of knowledge about the game and the players are discussed, and it is noted that the study of game theory environments involving low levels of knowledge about the structure of the game and the payoff is developing into a field of study in its own right. Finally, the link between the behaviours of individuals and the theory is made. Cooperative or collaborative game theory is distinguished from non-cooperative or competitive game theory – and perhaps this distinction sits at the heart of the difference between collaborative project behaviours and opportunistic project behaviour.

I discuss some of the benefits of applying game theory to project networks. These include: the importance of finding some sort of equilibrium following adaptations to environmental factors; the fact that decisions made by individuals reflect past decisions by other actors; and the operation of incentive design in encouraging self-interested human beings to behave in a way that maximises the benefit that a given network might have in delivering a given project. Complexity and rationality are important factors in this discussion about game theory and networks.

I apply game theory to the information exchange network and its evolution and decay. We also return to the five dangerous assumptions put forward in a previous chapter to see how game theory might be used in that context. I conclude the chapter by asserting that game theory is relevant to the concept of managing networks in a project context through:

- Calculation of payoff and self-interests
- The accuracy of knowledge about the game, the players and the environment
- The identity and behaviour of all other players
- Games played in low levels of knowledge
- The rationality of players
- The importance of the external environment and the fact that this does not prevent players from selecting a particular strategy.

Chapter 7: Network Roles and Personality Types Little has been written about personality type in the context of networks (with the possible exception of Mehra *et al.* (2001), which took a rather specific aspect of personality type). Very little indeed appears to have been written linking project networks with personality type. Chapter 7 was intended as a thought-provoking and speculative discussion about the topic of network roles and personality type, with a view to developing some theory and an agenda for future research.

The chapter recaps on the main actor types found in projects (these were dealt with in more detail in Pryke (2012)). I then outline the aspects of personality identified in personality trait theory.

The discussion turns to the use of humour in networks. Long and Graesser (1988) offered a classification of humour based upon an analysis of television shows and the audience reaction to them. They offer the following classifications: irony, satire, sarcasm, overstatement and understatement, self-deprecation, teasing, replies to rhetorical questions, clever replies to incongruous statements, double entendres, transformation of frozen expressions, and puns. Having explored the terminology of humour, the discussion turns to an exploration of the ways in which humour might help in project-based networks. I ask why humour is associated with leisure and not work, despite findings from Martin's (2007) research that humour results in higher levels of happiness and better health, creative thinking and problem-solving in the workplace. I conclude that more work needs to be done to establish the effects of humour in the workplace and specifically in the project network environment.

There is a discussion about cohesiveness and humour; specifically how humour might build better links between actors in project networks over time. Conversely the subversive effect of negative or critical humour is discussed. Dwyer (1991) noted that the relative power of an individual is reflected by who the joke teller is, who the target of the joke is and who laughs.

I offer a formulation of a 'network person' – behaviours that enable networks to function well.

I then review the behaviours in the context of the personality traits identified earlier in the chapter and particularly in relation to the main project network actor types. I conclude that personality type and behaviour are not commonly associated with network analysis but suggest that the combination could be important in understanding how it is that some project networks appear to be very effective, while others appear to find difficulty in delivering successful projects.

Chapter 8: Network Enabling The chapter starts with a reflection on the types of relationships that we find in the project environment – essentially interpersonal relationships within the firm and between firms, and inter-organisational relationships which in the project context tend to be dyadic contractual relationships. While the sister publication to this book (Pryke, 2012) covered both interpersonal and inter-organisational relationships, this book focuses on *interpersonal* relationships within and between firms.

The case is made for consideration to be given to the environment in which the networks being studied are operating. Although environmental issues potentially represent unwanted variables in the context of the analysis of network data, if we are to use SNA to deliver better projects, these environmental issues need to be considered. The chapter suggests that alongside the environmental issues noted above, certain factors influence the evolution, maintenance and eventual decay of interpersonal networks. These factors are:

- Trust – the existence and maintenance of trust
- Empathy – the ability to place ourselves in the position of others and to relate to that position and the constraints and anxieties associated with it
- Reciprocity – the extent to which individuals are willing and able to respond to efforts made by others, to provide advice or project information, for example
- Favours – the willingness to grant favours to others, regardless of previous reciprocal activity
- Generosity – the context for reciprocity and the granting of favours.

Set against these positive influential factors are: competitiveness, narcissism and egotism. These are frequently present in networks that appear to operate inefficiently for otherwise inexplicable reasons.

The chapter looks at the environmental conditions affecting interpersonal networks and reflects on the factors that have a positive impact on network evolution, maintenance and decay, as well as those factors having a negative impact. I conclude that good network behaviour is contagious. The pursuit and encouragement of behaviour that promotes trust, empathetic behaviour, reciprocity and generosity are fundamental to improving network performance. Ironically, behaviour that tends to improve career advancement, including appointment to organisations, is the very behaviour that creates difficulty in forming and maintaining communication networks.

Chapter 9: Project Networks and BIM In Chapter 9 I acknowledge that only weak links exist between organisational network analysis and building information modelling, both in terms of research and practice. The chapter links back to the 'five dangerous assumptions' identified earlier in the book. In particular, it is noted that projects do not always accurately interpret clients' wishes, for a range of reasons.

The chapter deals with a brief history of the term 'building information modelling' from its early beginnings in the mid-1980s. The development of software providing the third dimension alongside the first two dimensions and subsequently adding cost and time is discussed. BIM is discussed alongside its more generic cousin, information management, and I reflect on the location of highly specialised design expertise associated with technically complex projects and the effect that this relocation of knowledge and expertise has upon the procurement of design and the systems through which we monitor and manage design.

The chapter moves on to consider liability for and ownership of design, and responsibility for design coordination. Intellectual property rights are also identified as an important factor in the successful implementation of BIM. The effect of organisational structure and information technologies are dealt with through reference to the work of Whyte and Levitt (2010). Coordination is clearly an issue and social interactions are an important aspect of this coordination. BIM is frequently regarded as a 'clash detection' system, ignoring its potential for managing and modelling design along with cost and time parameters. The question is raised as to the potential effect of the full implementation of BIM on contractual 'completeness' and the consequent effects on contractual disputes and their resolution. The question whether BIM is an artefact in the context of the project or the system through which the project is designed is raised.

I conclude the chapter by suggesting that SNA and BIM are theoretically complementary. I acknowledge the work of Al Hattab and Hamzeh (2015) but suggest that research is needed on nodal characteristics; network actor roles; comparison between the three types of centrality measures for project actors; network topography; and, finally, cluster identification. This chapter aims to promote discussion and develop a research agenda in this area, given the relatively little research that currently exists.

Chapter 10: Introduction to the Case Studies This chapter provides a description of the project from which the three case studies were taken. The project comprises a rail infrastructure interchange upgrade costing approximately £600 M at the time of going to press. The chapter deals with some of the particular challenges of gathering network data in a busy design project environment.

Chapter 11: Case Study 1 This case study principally dealt with the application of community detection in social networks – relatively small clusters of actors with relatively high density, embedded within a network context of lower levels of network density. This approach to the analysis of a large and complex project – complex both technically and organisationally – challenged some of the traditional views about how projects should be procured and how they proceed. The research found, inter alia, that decision-making and problem-solving are important in the way in which project actors execute their design roles. In particular the coordination function is prominent when we look at actor relationships in the design phase. The chapter concludes that there is a gap between what is routinely procured in terms of roles and the roles that are acquired through project actors' network positions.

Chapter 12: Case Study 2 This case study looks at the concept of 'dysfunctional prominence'. The data were gathered from the same large rail infrastructure project used in Case Study 1. I discuss the relative merits of point, eigenvector and betweenness centrality in analysing complex projects. The comparison of the values for centrality generated by using these three measures enables us to identify actors who hoard information unnecessarily in information exchange networks. In this case the dysfunctional prominence was identified coincidentally with management interventions to resolve matters. A study carried out at an earlier stage in the project could have identified the trend toward the inappropriate hoarding of project information and enabled earlier intervention. I argue that dysfunctional prominence is a risk to all information exchange project networks and is related to personality type.

Chapter 13: Case Study 3 In the third and final case study I reflect upon the static nature of the roles and responsibilities allocated through project procurement. I consider the cost of network evolution over time and suggest that this is an aspect of project networks that is in its infancy. The case study took the Barabási and Albert (1999) and Erdös and Rényi (1960) models for network evolution and applied these to the case study project using data on actor cost per day. The chapter concluded that it is potentially very useful to profile network evolution and decay costs in the project context. There is a period in the evolutionary cycle of a project network between 2 and 20 actors where scaling costs are disproportionately high. This suggests that project managers should consider network interventions in those early stages of network evolution to enable connections to be formed quickly and effectively, thus helping to reduce the disproportionate cost of network evolution. I suggest the establishment of a network broker team, whose role it would be to facilitate information exchange linkages and to diffuse disputes over role negotiation between project actors.

Chapter 14: Summary and Conclusions In the final chapter I synthesise the twelve preceding chapters and draw out the key arguments and conclusions developed in this book. The theory is developed and some speculative discussion associated with future research agendas is set out. I reflect on the three case studies, which provide a small sample of some of the findings of a two-year research project which was completed just before publication of this book.

I hope that this overview of the book will encourage the reader to dip into particular areas of interest. For those with no background in social networks, the previous book, *Social Network Analysis in Construction* (Pryke, 2012), is recommended as a precursor to this book.

2

Theoretical Context

This chapter is aimed at establishing a context for the conceptualisation of the project as a network of relationships. The purpose of the chapter is not to build a theoretical framework for the analysis later in the book. Rather, it is to locate this book within the context of the study of project management. Some might argue this is exactly what a theoretical framework does. But I will build some theory later in the book that explains the relevance of social network analysis, and then move toward some network theories relating to the management of project-based networks.

Management Context

Projects are delivered in a 'project environment'. The project environment will have a range of characteristics that will differ between projects but that may include: external threats imposed by government, the economy, overseas competitors and changes brought about by a rapidly developing technological context; the extent of interdependencies in relationships, which will vary with the complexity of the project specification and process; previous experience within identical coalitions or those with common membership; pressure of time at design stage, tender stage and during delivery; lack of certainty about scope of task, project and/or programme.

The contracting process has evolved in a context of increasing complexity in projects and it is argued here that the assumptions that we make and on which much of current procurement and project management thinking is based are becoming increasingly irrelevant. Later in the book I look at some of the assumptions that are made when procuring and delivering projects – the five dangerous assumptions (see Chapter 5). The case study material in Chapters 10–13 contains evidence that the social networks that perform the main functions of project management are essentially self-organising and frequently perform roles that are not procured through the contracting system. This is contentious and threatens much of our traditional theory and practice in this area. This self-organisation is a function of the transition between the pre- and post-contract phases of projects. But although there is governance in place within the context of the organisations delivering projects (the resources procured to deliver the project), once these individuals become full-time or part-time members of the temporary project organisation, there is relatively little governance of the project delivery.

Managing Networks in Project-Based Organisations, First Edition. Stephen Pryke.
© 2017 John Wiley & Sons Ltd. Published 2017 by John Wiley & Sons Ltd.

Later I will argue that individuals are driven by the need to acquire and disseminate project information – they are driven into forming networks through a range of relationships in pursuit of a range of objectives.

Project Transitions

Transitions are an essential element of the temporary organisation (Jacobsson *et al.*, 2013) and both internal (endogenous) and external (exogenous) environments affect the way in which project 'routines' are established and evolved (Billinger and Becker, 2014). Some of these routines are codified and quite explicit. In this book I want to look at those routines that are *not* codified and that come about through project role-holding actors striving to fulfil their roles efficiently. We need to take an interest in the project governance arrangements that evolve and the transactional structures associated with this governance (Jones and Lichtenstein, 2008; Winch, 2014) in our study of more effective project management.

Project Management as Practice

There is a need for a more fine-grained approach to understanding our projects, linking more closely to the 'project management as practice' school of thought (Lalonde *et al.*, 2012). Winter *et al.* (2006) suggest that project management research should refocus away from the highly conceptual theoretical position toward a more practice and practitioner focus. Real projects are increasingly perceived to be more complex, unpredictable and 'multidimensional' than the project management literature, based upon a rational and deterministic premise, would suggest. Winter *et al.* (2006) suggest that we need new ways of looking at projects that take account of the complexity of social interaction within a context of politics and power. Ika and Hodgson (2010) argue that power, domination, manipulation and exploitation are important underlying concepts in understanding temporary organisations. So perhaps we should move from the question 'what is a project' toward 'what do we do collectively when we have a role in a project' (Hodgson and Cicmil, 2006). This is a question that is at the heart of the material presented in this book – what do people do when they design and deliver projects? This information is not currently visible to those who commission and manage projects.

The extent to which organisational theory helps us with the formulation of theory that relates to project management is an interesting point. We clearly need better-developed theory relating to projects (Monsanto *et al.*, 2013). Borg and Söderlund (2014) recognised that temporary project organisations are 'embedded' within organisational theory. They also refer to the importance of 'qualitative' studies into the 'real life' of project management and into the practices that are associated with the 'social processes' inherent in complex projects. Burger and Sydow (2014) call for research that explores the relationship between the permanent and temporary aspects of projects and the dynamic, transient and time-defined nature of organisation in temporary organisations. Pryke (2012) also emphasised the importance of understanding the relationships in temporary project organisations as *transient*. Our procurement practices do not envisage any change in roles and responsibilities throughout the entire post-contract phase of a project. The transient nature of projects represents a source of potential risk to project clients – understanding the nature of this transience is a first step toward managing those transient networks of relationships hidden from view in our projects.

Systems Theory and Networks

So, we have moved a long way forward since the early days of 'Taylorism' (Taylor, 1911), and the other scientific management school protagonists (see also Weber (1946) and Fayol (1919), for example). Following this scientific school, management thinking moved on to what was referred to as the 'informal' aspects of projects. At this time Maslow (1943) and others seemed to regard social interaction as 'informal' rather than as being at the very core of what humans do, whether in pursuit of friendship or love, or simply the attempt to earn a living within a project organisation. By the middle of the twentieth century, systems theory had taken hold, principally through the work of von Bertalanffy (1979) and Boulding (1956). Systems theory was embraced by academics but was typically presented at too high a level of abstraction for the practitioner. Although social network analysis (SNA) was being discussed in some circles – most notably by sociologists and mathematicians – it had not been married with systems theory. This is a pity because SNA and systems thinking make very happy bedfellows. Much later Walker (2015) explored in some detail the idea that projects need to be open systems (and/or perhaps sub-systems of client systems) to deal with the continually changing environment in which all but the very simplest projects are designed and delivered. Although Walker's work on open systems in projects was well received, some would claim that this new framework typically did little to improve the success of projects (see Flyvberg *et al.*, 2003; Crawford and Helm, 2009, among others). Denis *et al.* (2012) offered a process philosophy whereby the project organisation is a product of the social environment within which it functions.

Transient Relationships

This book pursues an understanding of the transient, dynamic and temporary characteristics of project networks. Engwall (2003) linked projects to 'history' (in the broadest sense) and the 'context' of the project. His work posed a question about methods, structures and processes and how these are derived. Manning's (2005) use of structuration theory proposed that organisation structure in projects relates to the structural properties of the systemic context – task, time and team all being relevant here. Winch (2010), Pryke and Smyth (2006) and Pryke (2012) have looked at relationships between project actors and Winch has a particular interest in the relationships that the client has with the project team (Winch, 2014). Winch questions the tendency for clients to cast themselves in the role of 'purchasers of services'. Pryke's (2012) work identified two main types of client for construction projects: those that saw themselves as having an active role in managing their supply chains; and those that regarded the management of the supply chain as the responsibility of Tier 1 contractors. In some cases those clients who recognised the importance of engaging with the supply chain but who lacked the knowledge, expertise or resources to behave proactively might employ a supply chain manager – either in the form of a consultant or a contractor with the brief to intensively manage Tier 2 and below (see Holti *et al.*, 2000).

Müller *et al.*'s (2013) work on governance identified the need for predictability and consistency in project delivery. They recognised the corporate governance context and the relevance of contracts between the parties forming the project coalition. A theme running through the research supporting my book is that project governance has very little connection with either corporate governance or contract documentation. Project governance is a function of the networks of relationships between the role-holding actors in the project. Prominence within these networks is acquired by actors rather than imposed by contracts and organisational protocols. The need for self-organising networks is reinforced by the idea of what Pitsis *et al.* (2003) refer to as an 'imagined future' – the idea that projects are delivered under high levels of uncertainty and therefore need to accommodate that uncertainty routinely and effectively to be successful. Pitsis and Gudergan (2010) suggest that construction provides a useful context in which to study inter-organisational collaboration because of the typically high levels of uncertainty, compared to other sectors. They go on to suggest that everyday organisational life is where the key to more successful projects lies, rather than in a study of the documentation and codification of protocols.

Dyadic Contractual Relationships and Structure

The previous book in this series – *Social Network Analysis in Construction* (Pryke, 2012) – made the case (inter alia) that contractual relationship networks have quite different structures from the communication exchange structures in construction projects. In particular, interdependencies between project actors could usefully be studied using social network analysis – and these interdependencies and the manner in which networks respond dynamically to transient interdependencies are important in our pursuit of more effective ways of managing design and project delivery post-contract. Ruuska *et al.* (2011) also concluded that we will understand our projects better if we focus less on dyadic contractual relationships (a feature of a 'contract management' approach to managing projects) and more on relationships and self-regulation. They also recognised that project actors are fundamentally managing their own firms and the supply chains supporting them. Although the project is the focus of the interests of the client, the stakeholders and the project managers, it is merely the vehicle through which workload is received by the firms engaging with the project. Many firms engaging with project clients have attempted to respond to the environment for project delivery by organising themselves into matrix structures. These structures attempt to provide a 'vertical axis' hierarchy by which to manage the firm, alongside a 'horizontal axis' project management structure – an attempt to provide a project-structured interface with clients and stakeholders. Engagement with the supply chain including procurement tends to be a 'y axis' (vertical) function.

Structure has interested economists too. Jacobides and Winter (2012) looked at agency and its relationships with structure. They linked organisational capability and structure through transaction cost economics. They emphasised the importance of

structure and suggested that 'belonging' to a particular firm is of relatively minor importance in trying to understand performance. The recognition that 'agents' are located or
embedded within a network of relationships is important in terms of opening a dialogue
with those who come from a network analysis position. Easley and Kleinberg (2010)
looked at modelling network traffic using game theory and concluded that adding
capacity to networks does not necessarily increase the speed of flow around the network. Individuals must continually reappraise the path that they choose for sending or
receiving information (to illustrate with an example that relates to the context here)
based upon an ever-changing pattern of congestion. In construction project terms this
congestion could be the appearance of one or more gatekeeper actors on a path that
previously had none. This highlights a basic problem with one of the assumptions (see
'Dangerous Assumptions', Chapter 5) that we make about projects – that once we allocate roles these remain static for the duration of the project phase. This leads us to
consider the basis of the contracts that we form in our projects. Should these contracts
be outcome-based, or should they relate to behaviours? The construction industry has
embraced 'partnering' – the pursuit of relationships between clients and Tier 1 organisations (contractors and consultants) that endure beyond the duration of individual
contracts (projects) (Smyth and Pryke, 2008 and Pryke, 2009). The interesting point
here is that a lot of energy was put into partnering, particularly 'post-Latham' (Latham,
1994), and the outcome typically was a formal contract for a project lying alongside a
relational contract focused upon the collaborative behaviour of actors. Only the bravest
of clients committed wholeheartedly to the spirit of partnering (particularly following
the Egan Report, 1998) and moved away from formal contracts for projects. The construction industry has effectively remained in transition – recognising the need for
flexible and collaborative day-to-day relationships but not feeling confident in casting
aside the comfort (albeit arguably illusory) that a formal project-based contract
provides. It is in this context that the discussion about networks of relationships sits.

Permanent and Temporary Organising

The relationship between the permanent and temporary organisations that faces those
awarded project-based contracts has fascinated a number of commentators (Jacobsson
et al., 2013; Bakker and Leiter, 2010; Sydow *et al.*, 2004; Winch, 2014). Whether the
project is a 'transitory unit' of the permanent organisation (Bakker and Leiter, 2010) or
whether a 'transition' (Winch, 2014) takes place is a moot point. From a network perspective all that matters are relationships. We have actors (nodes) and linkages between
them. As we shall see later, attempting to overlay an institutional perspective is actually
quite limiting and restricts our understanding of relationship structures. I argue here
that trying to classify firms and the relationship that their employees have with other
individuals when a firm is awarded a project-based contract is of limited value. There is
no boundary between the temporary and permanent organisations – the matrix over-
lies two quite different and potentially conflicting sets of relationships. Blomquist and
Lundin (2010) suggest that there has been an overly scientific and rational analysis of
projects in the past, and propose a practice-based approach looking at 'what is actually
being done' (2010: 13). Going back to 1973, Geertz (1973) suggested that before we try
to define what project management is, we need to find out *what project managers do*.

We therefore need to focus upon actors and their behaviour rather than models and their application (Blomquist and Lundin, 2010: 7).

The idea that we all understand the socially constructed term 'project', what a project comprises and how we set about managing projects is therefore not entirely useful. It is clear that designing and delivering a project which is complex in a context which is uncertain and transient presents problems that previous 'project management' and 'management of projects' approaches have not adequately addressed.

Structure and Networks

Projects have predetermined goals, finite time and scope, finite resources and some means of organisation and coordination. This book and the associated research programme focus on information processing referencing Galbraith (1974) but also acknowledge the findings in previous texts that the primary activity of the project coalition is the processing and exchange of project-related information. Walker and Rowlinson (2007) argued that organisational structure is an important factor in the successful management of projects. This structure influences project performance and is linked to behaviour, decision-making processes and the external (business) environment. But, so often, these structures are represented as authority relationships – who reports to whom in a permanent organisation. Even in the case of a permanent organisation, those representing the organisation as a hierarchy of authority relationships cannot resist showing information exchange as a number of non-hierarchical links superimposed upon a strangely incompatible hierarchy of authority relationships. Back in 1967 Perrow argued that we needed to think about two aspects of structure: task structure and social structure. Try telling a young person organising a party or a construction project with their mobile phone that two structures are at play (task and social) and they simply will not understand how humans could organise and coordinate in a non-social way. I argue that social structure responds to task, rather than task being a structure. Whyte and Levitt (2011) recognised that information and communication technologies shape the structures that we use in projects. Winch (2001) suggested that the project is an 'information-processing system' and that the flows between the actors are directed and enabled by structure.

Information Classification

Senescu (2011) argues that information exchange involves three types of information: product, organisation and process. My (Pryke, 2004a, 2012) work in the construction field classified information exchange into the following categories:

- Information originated by the client relating to project scope and end-user requirements
- Design information, regardless of whether this was 'primary' design or coordinated 'secondary' information produced following a number of iterations between interdependent systems within the project
- Programme and progress information

- Financial information – relating to client budgets and costs to client
- Project delivery process.

These might be summarised as the following five classifications of information exchange:

- briefing
- design
- progress
- financial
- process.

So, the relationship between information exchange studies and networks goes back to Galbraith (1974) and subsequently involved Huber (1990) and Levitt *et al.* (1999). Borgatti and Foster (2003) argue that social capital rests upon the prominence of actors within a network, measured by the number of links to each actor in comparison with the maximum number of links possible. In alliance research the ties between the actors are seen to be a function or outcome of some sort of organisational process.

Nodes and Linkages

Networks, in SNA terms, comprise nodes and links. The nodes each represent an actor and the actor has attributes and can instigate flows of various kinds between actors, and the actor can respond to flows and affect those flows arriving from other actors in the network. The links between the actors comprise a conduit or pipe through which something or some things can flow, in two directions simultaneously. These flows have characteristics that are quantifiable – speed, volume and quality. These characteristics are frequently expressed in terms of value as perceived by the actors at either end of the flow. The characteristics of the actors include personality traits and behaviour types and I will discuss proposed classifications of both later. The flows between the actors are influenced by attitudes that actors have toward other actors in the network and their perceptions about the configuration of the network and the context in which the network is located. Later in the book I will consider 'network currency' factors – the effect that trust, empathy, reciprocity, generosity and reputation have upon flows within a project-based network. Projects involve multiple layers of networks dealing with the project functions associated with the five classifications of information exchange listed above (Pryke, 2012). Network analysis and network theory are closely linked (Borgatti and Foster, 2003). Some criticise social network analysis as merely a research method. Even a cursory look at the depth and breadth of network theory (look at the work of Bavelas, Berkowitz, Borgatti, Burt, Everett, Faust, Freeman, Granovetter, Mizruchi, Wasserman, to name but a small sample from this highly specialised field) should dispel this view.

There is a difference in the way in which network theory is applied in the physical sciences and the social sciences (see Pinheiro (2011), whose work in telecommunications crossed the boundaries of physical and social sciences). Yet I would argue that social network analysis (SNA), and in particular the application of a range of algorithms that provide numerical values for density and various centrality measures, have no place in the physical sciences. This is contentious and there are those who, for example, have used SNA to map transatlantic aircraft movements, who consider that they have applied SNA appropriately. But, in my view, for the application of the SNA to be valid and rigorous, the nodes must be able to influence the flows between the nodes in some way. In a proper network, content flows and their differing natures can affect the outcomes for the actors (Lin, 1999). The variation in the content of the flows affects the rate of flow (Borgatti, 2005). When we represent nodes in a network graphically, we usually codify in some way to provide a classification for the nodes. Hence in construction projects we might show different colours for nodes based upon whether they might be classified as client, consultant, Tier 1 or Tier 2; alternatively, for representing nodes in journals that only use monochrome for illustrations, different node types might have different shapes. Frequently the prominence (centrality) will be indicated by the size of the node. Nodes which are large relative to other nodes indicate prominence.

The links can and almost always in project-based studies *will* have direction of flow. In project information exchange situations we are interested in direction of flow and prominence based upon 'in' flows and 'out' flows. These are simply indicated using arrow heads at either end of the links. These work well enough in colour or monochrome until the networks become large – perhaps in excess of 100 nodes. At this point (and very much depending upon the size at which the diagram is reproduced) the arrow heads become contiguous around the node and difficult to understand. Links can also be valued – perhaps using the Likert scale to give value to frequency or importance. These values can usefully be represented by the thickness of the line; we might also use dots and varying lengths of dashes. Network density, actor prominence and the values associated with links can all be expressed numerically. Frequently, given the small size of figures in various media, numerical values are important to support analysis of networks for publication.

Summary

I started with a reference to the issue of assumptions that we make when we use a contracting system. I argued that lump-sum contracts, and their procurement, relate to a context of relatively low complexity. The presence of complexity raises the question as to whether the contracting system, as currently constituted, continues to be relevant and viable. The transition that must occur for the resources, through the establishment post-contract of dyadic contractual relationships, to deliver a complex project requires routines which are not visible to the client and project manager(s). These interdependent actor relationships – their identification, analysis and management – are important. So I am proposing a move from relatively abstract conceptualisation of project activities to a much more finely-grained approach, looking at relationships between individuals working in project function delivery clusters. Power, manipulation and exploitation are important issues in understanding the operation of these hidden networks.

We have moved a long way since those early scientific management approaches to management. And yet in project management we still see vestiges of this scientific school heritage. I am proposing we move on and make our focus the multi-layered networks that relate to management systems and ultimately deal with the main project functions. I make the point that understanding the demand for flexibility of project definition and transience of project function networks are important in delivering better projects. Ultimately, although the project is the vehicle which provides workload to Tier 1 and its supply chain, the project tends to focus upon cost, time and quality rather than on the transient systems and networks that I argue hold the key to delivering better outcomes for clients and stakeholders.

Structure has always been of interest, but the hierarchy of authority relations represented in the typical organogram has little relevance in the management of projects. So the transition between permanent and temporary organising remains a conundrum. Our highly connected lives no longer seek or maintain a distinction between task and social structure; the formal/informal paradigm no longer serves a purpose in examining the innermost workings of our projects and supply chains. So, the focus on actors and their linkages in networks classified by project function and quantified by actor prominence and the direction and value of flow in the linkages provides a very rich framework within which to fully understand our projects. In this way we can begin to manage the networks that emerge and ultimately to design networks for project delivery that build on an understanding of those examined networks.

3

Networks and Projects

The purpose of this chapter is to explore the context of the book and to provide justification for the conceptualisation of temporary project organisations as networks of project function-related systems. The chapter starts with the reflection that in the half-century since the publication of the Tavistock Institute's seminal work on construction, we have moved very little closer to understanding 'systems...functions...interrelationships and the location and prominence of...control and coordination centres...' (Higgin and Jessop, 1965: 56). This might, arguably, be sufficient justification for the exploration of the relationship networks that follows in this chapter. The chapter looks initially at the evolution of network theory and the early beginnings of social network analysis associated with Gestalt theory and the group at Harvard in the USA. I then return to the Tavistock Institute's work and highlight the two main themes of their study from 1965 – interdependence and uncertainty. I look at the behaviour of project actors in this environment of interdependence and uncertainty and reflect on the problems associated with ritualistic behaviour and routines. I ask the question whether networks are a response to uncertainty in project activities and the problems faced when we try to replicate systems between projects. The chapter finishes with a discussion of the 'iron triangle' as a basis for project governance and the extent to which the study of project networks enables analysis, presentation and ultimately management of networks in projects, providing a better basis for modelling and management.

Social network analysis (SNA) is the product of an unlikely collaboration between mathematicians, anthropologists and sociologists. But we should not allow the word 'social' to discourage us from using the method to explore what might initially appear to be the non-social aspects of the project environment. All interactions between human beings are 'social'. We should not confuse 'informal', extra-contractual interactions with 'recreational' interactions. Recreational networks may have an effect on informal and formal interactions in organisations and projects. Recreational interactions are not the focus of this book, however.

SNA is essentially a form of structural analysis, allowing mathematical and graphical analysis of what otherwise might be regarded as essentially qualitative data. SNA can be employed to investigate organisational issues as diverse as contractual relationships and problem-solving clusters.

Managing Networks in Project-Based Organisations, First Edition. Stephen Pryke.
© 2017 John Wiley & Sons Ltd. Published 2017 by John Wiley & Sons Ltd.

Definition

Social network analysis involves the representation of organisational relationships as a system of nodes or actors linked by precisely classified connections, along with the mathematics that defines the structural characteristics of the relationship between the nodes. Wasserman and Faust (1994) define a social network in even simpler terms as:

> a finite set or sets of actors and the relation or relations (between them).

Research into project systems and their effectiveness has in the past frequently relied upon what might be regarded as positivist approaches. Although viewed by some as robust, these approaches try to explain what comprises a complex social arrangement (Morris, 1994) through methods that essentially have their origins in natural science (Pryke, 2004b). Project management researchers have increasingly looked to the social science disciplines to explain and understand the key issues and problems faced in the management of projects (Bresnen *et al.*, 2005). Some have argued for a need to bridge positivist and interpretivist approaches with more qualitative methods (Lin, 1998) and Loosemore (1998) has argued that SNA is a quantitative tool capable of being applied within an interpretative context in construction research. Loosemore (1998) questions the association of quantitative and qualitative methods with causality and the production of universal models, but feels that both quantitative and qualitative methods (jointly) have a part to play in understanding social roles, positions and behaviour in the project environment. Others have argued that qualitative and quantitative approaches can be integrated using critical realism (Smyth *et al.*, 2007) and that combining extensive and intensive methods is more important than a quantitative–qualitative dichotomy. The main critique of positivism from the critical realist viewpoint is that explanations are both general and particular/context dependent; this position may be appropriate when considering issues associated with the complexity of projects (Smyth and Morris, 2007).

SNA is proposed, therefore, on the basis that it is not used as a method to the exclusion of other methods. I am keen that actors and linkages are very precisely classified and that the context for each network is also clearly defined. Qualitative contextual data is particularly important in the context of complex projects since repeatability is very limited. Most projects are unique and their uniqueness, in part, contributes to their classification as 'projects'.

Origins and History of the Concept of Social Networks and their Analysis

Scott (2012: 7) describes the evolution of modern network theory through three main schools of academic endeavour. During the 1930s, a team working in the United States on cognitive and social psychology were wrestling with the problems of sociometry and group dynamics. This fascination with the structural aspects of human thought and processes owed much to the work of Wolfgang Köhler's Gestalt theory (Scott, 2012). The team was essentially interested in group structure and information flows. The second group described by Scott might be referred to as the 'Harvard Group': a group of anthropologists and sociologists developing some of the ideas of British anthropologist Radcliffe-Brown. The emphasis of their work was informal communications and social systems in the workplace. Finally, a team at the University of Manchester was looking at the analysis of conflict and contradiction, principally in relation to African tribal societies.

It was not until the 1960s that SNA developed into a coherent body of theory, although an important contribution to the mathematics of social networks was provided by Bavelas as early as 1948 (Bavelas, 1948, 1950). Those influential in the development of SNA theory included Harrison White from Harvard. His work on the analysis of kinship relationships (White, 1963) provided a breakthrough that was complementary to the work of the academics in Manchester, who placed great emphasis upon the informal side of communications. White's work was joined, during this period, by important work from Blau and Duncan (1967) on organisational structure, and work by Buckley (1967), Homans (1961) and Milgram (1967), the latter's work being concerned with the sociological aspects of social networks. Meanwhile Barnes' (1974) work on graph theory and Kruskal's (1964a and 1964b) work on multi-dimensional scaling made major contributions to the development of the mathematics of SNA (Scott, 2012).

During the following two decades, the SNA theory and method found critical mass through the work of a large group of emerging social network academics. Atkin (1974, 1977, 1981), Barnes (1974) and Barnes and Harary (1983) made major contributions to the mathematical side of social network theory. Along with this came work from emergent leading lights such as Bonacich (1972, 1987; Bonacich and McConaghy, 1980) and Everett (1982, 1983a, 1983b, 1984). Everett later joined forces with Borgatti to form an important intellectual partnership combining the mathematics and IT skills of Everett with the IT and sociological interests of Borgatti (Borgatti and Everett, 1989; Borgatti *et al.*, 1989). Social theory was covered during this period by important offerings from Burt (1976, 1977a, 1977b, 1979, 1980, 1982, 1983, 1987, 1988), whose work on structural holes was ground-breaking. Laumann (1966), Laumann and Pappi (1973, 1976) and Laumann *et al.* (1983, 1989) made their contribution in the area of boundary specification (the definition of network area) – a particular problem in social networks. Wellman (1982, 1985, 1988) was interested primarily in social structure and was the founder of the International Network of Social Network Analysts (INSNA). White's work on social structure spanned four decades (1963, 1976 (with Boorman and Breiger), 1970, 1992a, 1992b, 1993). The work of Erickson (1978), Erickson and Nosanchuck (1983), Erickson *et al.* (1981) and Frank (1978, 1979a, 1979b, 1988) dealt with gathering and understanding network data. Freeman and Granovetter became very prominent in their field through their work on centrality (Freeman, 1978, 1980, 1983, 1996) and tie strength (Granovetter, 1973, 1976, 1977, 1979, 1982).

The 1980s and 1990s brought important work in the area of network theory from Mizruchi (1982, 1992, 1993, 1994, 1981 (with Bunting), 1994 (with Galaskiewicz), 1987 (with Schwartz)), Nohria and Eccles (1992), and Scott (1986, 1990, 1991, 1996, 1997, 2012). Wasserman and Faust (1994) produced an important text which comprises an encyclopaedia of social network terminology and formulae. To avoid confusion, the main definitions and terminology in that text are adopted throughout this book. A wide range of terminology and definitions are adopted from the field of network theory. This period also brought about a wealth of software programs aimed at the social scientist. A list of such programs is provided in Table 5.1 in Social Network Analysis in Construction (Pryke, 2012). This provides details of features for a range of the most popular software packages in use at the time. Table 5.2 in the same text provides the URL addresses for these software packages. For a more comprehensive and continually updated list of software available see http://insna.org. The drive to produce software enabling the fast calculation of a wide range of social network measures brought with it a growing interest in the visualisation of social network data. Some of the most prominent of this group are Urlik Brandes from the University of Konstanz (see, for example, Brandes *et al.*, 2003; Brandes, 2008) and Prell (2012). Those starting out in the use of SNA will probably be content, initially at least, with the visualisation packages in the basic SNA software.

Problems with Projects

In 1965, following a research programme involving the construction sector, the Tavistock Institute declared that there was an urgent need to:

> find out how the system works, the functions of its different parts, their interre-lationships...the main centres of control and coordination.
>
> *Higgin and Jessop, 1965: 56*

A year later a more detailed report followed which gave further consideration to the analysis and visualisation of project activities (Tavistock, 1966: 22). The interdependence of individual project actors and the uncertainty associated with designing, procuring and delivering complex projects were reflected in the title of the report. There was also some recognition that there was room for 'new forms of organisation in...communication' (Tavistock, 1966: 58). Yet these noble ideas, relating essentially to task dependency analy-sis (Pryke, 2012), were still not applied in the way that was suggested by the Tavistock Institute. In particular, the report recognised that information and communications did not flow linearly in the direction of the hierarchy reflected in contractual conditions. The use of traditional structural analysis, involving 'organograms' or organisational family trees (see for example the work of Franks (1998) and Masterman (2003) concerning the use of structural diagrams to represent procurement strategies) and process mapping (see Curtis *et al.*'s 1991 work on cognitive mapping) added little to our understanding of the way in which project organisations fail or succeed. Linear responsibility analysis (Walker, 2015) provided a classification of responsibilities, in matrix format, related to specific tasks like the preparation of contract documentation, but failed to provide any detail about how the responsibilities were executed by those to whom they were allo-cated. Very few tasks are executed in isolation; most involve engagement in some way with others. Winch and Carr's work on process protocols once again tried to represent the activities of the project actors against some very broad headings for project activities such as 'detailed design' or 'finishing trades' (Winch and Carr, 2001).

It was argued later by Pryke (2012) that project management systems might be the appropriate focus for the study of project activities. These typically include:

- client briefing activity (including ongoing communication throughout the post-contract phase)
- design and specification of the project (all activities which impact upon the quality of the project)

- progress monitoring and control
- financial monitoring and control
- activities associated with the interface between design and production.

Walker (2015) argued that a number of issues needed to be dealt with in the analysis and design of organisational structures (in construction, but also having more generic application):

- operating system
- managing system
- relationship of people in the organisation and their interdependency
- roles of people in the organisation
- position of the decision points and their status
- contribution of people to each decision and their relationships in arriving at decisions.

Walker (2015) was critical of the combination of descriptive text and simple sociograms to model organisations. The search for a meaningful analysis of organisational structures led him to suggest the application of 'transformed relationships evolved from network data' (TREND: Bennigson and Balthasas 1974) and 'linear responsibility charting' (LRC). There is a common theme in the work of both Tavistock and Walker, that of roles – their definition, evolution and interdependencies. In the next section I examine 'actor' roles in more detail.

Actor Role Classification and Ritualistic Behaviour

We traditionally acquire project role-holding actors (RHAs) – individuals who fulfil or help fulfil a project function – through a process of procurement. We create project roles and then write contracts which define these roles and deal with remedies in the case of delay or failure in some way. These actors are a function of a system which involves intensive specialisation in a particular role – typically a role defined by a professional body. In order to practice and earn a living carrying out a given project role, the actors would typically have completed a programme of study and been assessed for entry by one of the professional bodies based upon some predefined sub-role definitions or competencies. Some professional bodies adopt the 'body of knowledge' approach (for example, the Association of Project Managers (APM) and the Institute for Project Management (IPM)); others, the Royal Institution of Chartered Surveyors (RICS), for example, adopt a system of 'competencies'. These bodies of knowledge and competencies are embedded in the education and training of our project role-holding actors. The APM does not assess familiarity with its APM Body of Knowledge (APM, 2012) at the point of entry to the profession, preferring to rely upon a demonstration of relevant experience through documentation showing involvement in relevant projects. RICS, through its Assessment of Professional Competencies (APC), requires evidence of knowledge and experience in a range of relevant competencies, evidenced by a log book and a panel assessment interview.

So, actors are procured according to a definition established by a professional body and/or an experienced client and reinforced by the requirement in many of those bodies to maintain professional indemnity insurance cover. Essentially the insurance industry reinforces the stereotypes established by the professional bodies by requiring experience that falls within the classifications of activity established by the professional bodies. These actors are then faced with a highly complex information-gathering and information-dissemination problem in the context of, typically, a unique project environment. Pressure to be seen to be performing well drives them toward certain routines that provide certainty of behaviour and assurance of income from those behaviours. These actors are not, typically, subject to orientation, training or any other management interventions between project commencement and completion. Typically the project does not provide training. The management of the project is related to project outcomes rather than to the behaviour of project actors individually and collectively.

Routines

Routines are habitual behaviour by groups of people and closely related to the concept of habit in the context of the individual (Becker, 2004). In complex projects, where the product of the project is essentially a prototype (having never been produced before), it would be useful to observe the nature of the relationships arising out of the combination of individual habits, routines and clusters of routines. Financial pressures (the need to deliver project functions at the lowest cost to ensure profitability) and time pressures (driven by the key dates arising out of the programme for the project and its associated critical paths) tend to lead humans to resort to habit and routines. And yet the prototype complex project demands adaptability in these routines. So there is a conflict between the desire of individuals in groups to adopt habitual behaviours in the context of other individuals' habitual behaviour. There is also the pressure to comply with routines imposed by contract conditions and project protocols, these routines being played out in the context of the routines and habits of individuals. There is conflict relating to the time taken to establish and validate routines. Financial and time constraints tend to lead to individuals and groups resorting to familiar routines. Training and experience, along with custom and practice within certain professional and practice groups, together conspire to drive the evolution of standard, lump-sum-based services, or recipes (Spender, 1989), against which milestones can be created and fee income streams generated (see also McSmythurs, 2011). Where the technical and organisational context of a project demands different behaviour there is tension for the project actors between continuing with the familiar, relatively fast and low-cost routines and devising and implementing different routines to deal with the unique demands of a particular project. This 'routinised' behaviour can result in catastrophic systems failure and very poor risk decision-making. Becker (2004) argues that routines provide comfort by virtue of the following:

- coordination and control – derived from: the potential for simultaneity; regularity, unity and their systematic nature; the 'mutual consistency' of group activities; and the provision to each actor of the knowledge of the behaviour, or likely behaviour, of others (ibid. p. 654)
- stability – familiar routines, providing that they are compatible with the strategic objectives of the project, are fast and cheap (ibid, p. 659)
- the reduction of cognitive effort – as these routines become increasingly familiar they become subconscious or perhaps 'automatic' (ibid, p. 662)

- consolidation and codification of knowledge – Becker (2004) claims that routines 'store knowledge' (Becker, 2004: 660). I would dispute whether a routine, either represented by an artefact of some sort (perhaps a procedure manual or contract), or embedded in repetitive human behaviour, can store knowledge. Rather I suggest that codified routines store information (in as much as a process constitutes information and not knowledge) and provide references to the relevant knowledge.

In complex projects there are a number of pressures on the project actors:

1) In order to deliver the role and comply with responsibilities, each individual actor seeks information from a range of sources, most importantly, from other project actors. This data gathering needs to be carried out in the shortest possible time and at the lowest cost.
2) The information gathered from others needs to be processed and disseminated to other actors in a timely fashion.

In order to achieve the first objective above, relationships have to be established and managed over time. In order to achieve the second objective, ambiguities in incoming information must be resolved and problems solved.

Routinised behaviour in a high-risk environment with complex information causes excessive iterations and 'dysfunctional prominence' – the idea that an actor is prominent in a network for negative reasons, which I will expand upon later in the book.

Are Networks a Response to Uncertainty in Projects?

Maturity of project definition (Morris, 2013) is frequently an issue with projects. The lack of development of concept and specification frequently leads to incompleteness in the documents that constitute the contract documents. What follows is financial uncertainty for the client. Some might argue that there is a fundamental flaw in the proposition that it is possible to deliver successful projects through a 'contracting system' (Winch, 2000) whereby an assumption is made that project definition is substantially complete at tender stage.

Although some might regard project management as 'routinised', for example, Shenhar (2001) and Manning and Sydow (2007), recent research relating to construction (Soundararaj *et al.*, 2015; Pryke *et al.*, 2015a, 2015b, 2017) indicates that although the practice of project management appears to be routinised to some extent, the activities of the project actors in solving technical problems and making decisions are not routinised and require prominent actors to form clusters or communities to ensure that these project functions are carried out effectively. In fact Hanisch and Wald (2011) found that the lack of routines in projects poses challenges to project managers. This lack of routines and a context where there is complexity in both structure and task tend to lead to the formation of 'self-organising' networks (Pryke, 2012; Pryke *et al.*, 2015a, 2015b), as those appointed to deliver projects wrestle with the need to gather and disseminate information and to coordinate their activities in circumstances where they are frequently under pressure of time. 'Legally autonomous' firms (Sydow and Staber, 2002) need to evolve systems for project delivery, the combination of interdependence and uncertainty (Tavistock, 1966) providing a particularly challenging environment for success.

Project clients need certainty in order to be confident about the level of risk which they carry and need to manage. Yet some would argue that clients are not always fully aware of the level of incompleteness embedded within the documents that constitute the contract documents; at least they are not fully aware until the lack of completeness manifests itself as a dispute between Tier 1, Tier 2 and/or client at a later stage in project delivery (see Walker and Pryke, 2009, 2011). Unfortunately, accurate, timely project definition is also a challenge which tends to exacerbate the incompleteness. Pryke (2014) identified that the 'agency problem' frequently leads designers to design at a sub-optimum standard in relation to the need to complete accurate documents based upon a complete design. The amount of risk that clients carry forward into the project delivery stage as a result of incomplete design and problem-solving pre-contract sits within a context where consultants acting for clients opt for a 'lump-sum' contract arrangement, as distinct from 'cost-reimbursement'. Whether it is more advantageous for clients to enter a cost-reimbursement contract and try to manage the inevitable uncertainty associated with cost as project definition emerges post-contract, or to proceed with a lump-sum contract arrangement based upon information that is incomplete for the purposes of forming a lump-sum contract, is a dilemma faced by all clients. As Merrow (2011) has identified, different industry sectors have different norms of behaviour – the petrochemical sector, for example, manages cost within a cost-reimbursement contract by using a cost plan as a financial model for project financial management. Elsewhere, client and advising consultants may lean toward lump-sum procurement approaches that do not ultimately best serve the interest of clients.

Temporary Project Systems and their Replication

The project networks that appear post-contract and respond to the need for individual actors to acquire and disseminate information in a context of high levels of incompleteness might be regarded as 'temporary systems'. These temporary systems could potentially be replicable on subsequent projects if we could find a way of graphically representing them and using this information to train and manage the relevant project staff. Social capital can be aggregated between individual projects if the client avoids adopting procurement approaches that disrupt the process (disruption through, for example, continually tendering projects on price alone to Tier 1 and Tier 2 organisations with which they are not familiar). The continual interruption of relationships between project actors and the 'partial uniqueness and novelty' of the majority of projects are critical project success factors (Lundin and Söderholm, 1995; Manning and Sydow, 2011).

Beyond the 'Iron Triangle'

The definition of successful project delivery, ubiquitously, as the achievement of acceptable standards in the three areas of cost, time and quality – the so-called 'iron triangle' (Barnes, 1988) – has served projects well enough over the years. But I would argue that a focus on these three metrics has distracted from a broader, stakeholder-focused agenda and the pursuit of 'customer delight' (Latham, 1994). Much of the ritualistic behaviour we see from project actors, whether they be consultants or contractors and perhaps even clients, arises from the focus upon the interdependent triumvirate of cost, time and quality. It is argued in more detail elsewhere in this book that we make several assumptions when we commit to procuring and delivering a project that are irrational in the context of a lump-sum contract; assumptions that:

- It is possible to accurately define clients' needs at an early stage, before any visualisation is produced of those needs and desires;
- It is possible to accurately interpret clients' wishes, without any corruption of intention through 'agency' (Aoki *et al.*, 1990) and to represent the physical manifestation of those wishes and desires accurately and unambiguously (using a range of digital design files and documents);
- Change in project definition is undesirable;
- It is possible to allocate project actor roles to individuals through contracts executed by the client with the actors' employers that will create temporary communication and information exchange networks that will function to deliver the project effectively without intervention;
- Interdependent project actors' roles will be constant over time.

The contracting system (Winch, 2000) and the various bodies of knowledge (APM (Morris and Pinto, 2004) and PMBok (PMI, 2008)) reflect a linear process of client brief, design, measurement and quantification, followed by a financial bid and contract award. At contract award the assumption is made that the procurement process has effectively defined the roles of project actors in a manner that will endure to contract completion and be unambiguous and complete in its detail. Design 'lock in' is to be avoided and the hope is that the contractual arrangements will facilitate a process of scope development – as an absolute minimum the governance framework needs to have the facility to absorb changes in legislation and the requirements of local authority town planning departments.

I argue that the project is delivered by a network of individuals with reference to a formal set of contract documents but that these documents are peripheral because the project functions are evolved through iterative information exchange relationships in an environment which is essentially transient. These networks need to be flexible and adaptive. Pryke and Smyth (2006) classify the evolution of project management from traditional 'hard' tools and techniques, through a functional project management approach emphasising project definition and delivery through a task-driven agenda, through Winch's information-processing approach, finally arriving at the relationship approach. The latter focuses upon understanding the way in which relationships function between people who hold project roles. The traditional tools and techniques tend to have a production orientation and relate to a scientific management outlook. It is argued that as we have transitioned through functional approaches and into the information-processing model, we have arrived at a position where we are giving more emphasis to the importance of interdependence enabling the 'non-linear, iterative and interactive systems that projects constitute' (Pryke, 2004a). The relevance of the way in which an individual practitioner conceptualises the project relates to the way in which that same individual manages the project. Some wish to model the project as a Gant chart for progress and a cost plan for financial control. Those who conceptualise the project as a network of actor relationships effectively move beyond the management of projects as their focus. Networks enable us to look at actor relationships beyond the boundaries of the project.

Why Networks?

Why is a network perspective of organisational behaviour useful? Let's start with Nohria and Eccles (1992), who made some relevant points in answering this, which I have paraphrased below:

- All human activity comprises the output of human relationships – even solitary activities such as solo sailing around the world require the support of a project management office at base. We need to avoid confusing social relationships in a project or other work-related environments with friendship and kinship networks. These might be referred to as 'recreational networks'.
- Firms operate in an environment comprising a network of other firms. Although much of the discussion in this book will focus upon interpersonal relationships, most project actors are employed by a firm (sole-traders apart – but the principle still applies) and these firms have to survive and generate income and profit in an environment where a network of other firms are operating. Some of these other firms will have a helpful influence; others will have competitive and/or disruptive influence. The social capital associated with groups of individuals and groups of firms collaborating for mutual benefit is an important factor in the success of projects.
- We rarely see the whole picture by observing the activities of one individual or firm – as Nohria and Eccles (1992) noted: 'organisations are suspended in multiple, complex, overlapping webs of relationships and we are unlikely to see the overall pattern from the point of view of one organisation'.
- Actor behaviours are best understood in the context of the network position the actor holds. There is frequently a difference between the role allocated by the contract and that envisaged by overlapping contracts (such as a contract of employment and the contractual conditions under which the organisation itself is employed by the client). This ambiguity is important to our understanding of project networks and their management.
- Network characteristics are an important factor in the comparative analysis of project activities and the formulation of effective network behaviour in the project context.

Resources for projects are procured either by negotiation or some form of competitive bidding process. These resources are placed within a matrix environment with (some might argue) relatively little governance in relation to the project environment flowing from the contract through which the resources are procured. This governance is essentially 'remedy driven' and construction contracts frequently do not describe processes focused upon the delivery of excellent projects. The project then commences and the project role-holding actors commence the ritual of delivering a project, using a number of well-rehearsed routines carried forward from previous project experiences. Some projects have better outcomes than others, despite best efforts in tendering and procurement. We procure resources to a specification deemed appropriate for a given project but 'complementariness' (the extent to which project role-holding actors complement others' skills, knowledge and behaviours) and the potential for reciprocity (the willingness and desire to create and respond to indebtedness in a network) are also very important to the effective functioning of networks. Yet we do not seek or select actors against these two important criteria.

The use of social network analysis to study and evaluate the self-organising networks that develop following commencement of the project implementation stage provides evidence to support the nature of effective and ineffective project delivery networks. The uncertainty arising out of 'incompleteness' (Walker and Pryke, 2008, 2009, 2011) (the fact that typically design is not complete at tender stage) and that arising from uniqueness of, or lack of familiarity with, product or process leads to the formation of networks. Individuals are trying to provide a service or deliver a project function in a context of uncertainty; they also have to gather information from a large group of actors, many of whom they are not linked to contractually. So networks of relationships are established essentially to reduce transaction costs and enable profitable activities.

Powell and Giannella (2010) identify several factors that enable networks to form:

- 'Know-how' – where there is diversity and intensity in knowledge-based activity and exchange of distinctive competencies
- Pressure of time – all projects are constrained by time and there is a statement of 'contract periods' in the contract conditions with penalties for late completion
- Trust – Powell and Giannella argue that networks are more likely to form where individual actors trust each other; homogeneity (the extent to which we perceive others to be similar to ourselves) is a factor in the establishment of trust.

So project actors need to acquire information from other project actors with whom they have no contract. They then need to solve problems and resolve ambiguities within an emerging project definition environment. It is argued that under these circumstances 'self-organising' project role-holding actor networks will emerge as an expedient for the delivery of project functions with a minimum of iterations (the existence and volume of which affect profitability for individual actors and the firms by whom they are employed). These self-organising networks need to establish 'mutual orientation' (Thompson, J. D., 2003) – the focusing of the networks of individuals on common project-orientated behaviour. This is achieved through complementariness and accommodation (reciprocity in exchanges and a desire to help others). 'Mutual orientation' is typically not managed in our projects and it is argued that this has a detrimental effect on projects. I will expand on this later in the book.

Too few projects are successful on the basis of the metrics widely applied – cost, time and quality – despite the focus given to project management and the employment of project managers (Flyvberg *et al.*, 2003, *cf.* Morris and Hough, 1987). If we accept that the assumptions discussed above are accurate, then it is very little wonder that many projects are not successful, although the definition of 'project success' itself is, arguably, problematic (Dvir and Lechler, 2004). The focus on using role-holding actors and their governance through a 'Y-axis governance' approach (contracts for resource provision) rather than the 'X-axis governance' alternative (governance of project delivery) prevents those who would manage projects from providing successful outcomes for clients. It deprives them of the opportunity to understand the effectiveness of the relationships between a large group of individuals engaged in the technically difficult process of delivering a complex project.

We start the project delivery process with procurement based upon an emerging definition of the project. The employer or client enters into contracts with a number of consultants and contractors, depending on the procurement route; the resources to deliver the project are located contractually, but possibly not physically, within firms named in the contract. The employees of these firms are the subject of contracts of employment and are managed by their firms and benefit from the existence, potentially, of mission statements, appraisals and perhaps financial incentive schemes operated by the employers. These individuals become the role-holding actors for the project and are then subject to governance flowing from the project. It is argued in this chapter that the contracts between the client and the project function delivery firms (consultants and contractor(s)) are not necessarily very effective in providing governance of the project activities. So these individuals enter a milieu where they are expected to provide a project function, such as financial management, for example, in a context where governance of the project is weak and there are high levels of uncertainty, not least associated with project definition. It is argued here that this context creates an environment where individual role-holding actors form networks in order to function effectively and to provide a service in a manner that delivers profitability to their employers. These networks have, in the past, been invisible to all but the most 'hands-on' clients and project managers.

Individuals and Firms in Networks

Nohria and Eccles (1992) do not distinguish between two quite different types of actors; these are individuals and firms. Project coalitions involve a range of actor roles being fulfilled by individuals (perhaps the sole trader, professional service provider or subcontractor) and a range of actor roles being fulfilled by firms; an example of the latter might be the client role, where a firm is named as the client actor, but where daily interactions occur with a number of individuals. The question of how data is gathered and analysed in the context of different actor types is an issue that will be discussed in Chapter 4. The decision whether to study inter-firm, intra-firm or intra-coalition interpersonal relationships is an important first step in starting out in SNA-based research. If in doubt, gather data based on relationships between individuals. The data can always be aggregated to represent inter-firm relationships later. Extracting interpersonal relationship data from previously collected inter-firm data is much more difficult and frequently impossible.

Problems Associated with the Use of SNA in Project Research

Some of the limitations of SNA as a method were dealt with in Pryke (2012). These limitations are, in summary:

- It is a quantitative (mathematical) method used within an interpretative context (involving subjective judgments about human characteristics and behaviour) (Loosemore, 1998).
- SNA deals with analysis but does not always provide causality.

- SNA is relatively complex in terms of both theoretical and mathematical bases; complexity creates a barrier to entry – some researchers and most consultants prefer to find simpler ways to gather and analyse data especially when restricted funds and short programmes limit the time available for the assimilation of complex ideas, concepts and techniques. It is necessary to classify each network very precisely and this can lead to a potentially large number of different relationships between a given group of actors. This inevitably creates a very large volume of data.
- Sampling is not effective or appropriate with networks within the boundary drawn for the study. It follows that a 100% response from project actors is the ideal scenario. In the absence of a 100% response, estimations of likely responses are necessary in order to provide more accurate mathematical values.[1]

The chapter started by linking the subjects of networks and projects. By way of building a link, I started by reflecting upon the fact that the Tavistock Institute had, over half a century ago, encouraged the construction industry to develop a closer understanding of systems, functions, interrelationships and the location of control and coordination centres. Little progress seems to have been made so far. I looked at the traditional methods of modelling and monitoring temporary project organisations. I referenced routines and their relevance to the management of temporary projects, and the issue of lump-sum contracting and its inherent lack of flexibility in the face of the inevitable uncertainty associated with emergent project definitions. I suggested that networks form as a response to pressure to deliver a project under conditions of uncertainty, particularly in relation to information timeliness and quality. So, projects and networks are linked through a need to understand exactly what the individual project actors are doing – these complex project function-related systems have been invisible so far.

Summary

All successful projects are delivered through social networks of very specialised project actors, networks which evolve in ways that we do not sufficiently understand as yet. This chapter has linked social network theory back to Wolfgang Köhler's Gestalt theory. The evolution of information technology over the last near century has enabled network theory to evolve alongside complex analysis of human relationships. In this chapter the idea that analysis of relationships in projects could be of value is introduced and I look at some of the problems with projects that social network analysis seems to be particularly well suited to respond to. I consider the concept of uncertainty and the effects that this has upon individuals attempting to execute their responsibilities in a project. I also

---

1 At the time of going to press I have had some lively, but good-natured, exchanges with academic colleagues on the subject of what is an acceptable level of completeness for network data within a given group. Many seem to refer to 70% as a reasonable level for a given network dataset and cite the availability of software which simulates the missing data in support of their claims. My view is that I would be very nervous about settling for a 70%-complete data set in the context of the study of complex projects. If we were studying the spread of disease using SNA, then perhaps 70% coverage might be adequate – I have never been involved with this type of network study. For the study of complex, multi-functional projects, however, I would be very suspicious if the findings of such a study were based upon 70% of the data. I hope that some of the figures in Chapters 10, 11 and 12 might help to illustrate this point.

deal with the challenges of replication of systems between projects and the deficiencies of relying upon simple output-based metrics for managing projects. Nohria and Eccles' (1992) rationalisation for the use of a network approach to understanding organisations is reiterated and subsequently the chapter looks at the limitations of SNA.

The project is a useful construct against which to monitor the delivery of cost, time and quality. But when we turn our attention to value and innovation, we need to look beyond the boundaries of individual projects. We need to understand very clearly how the resources that are procured are being exploited. There is value in understanding the topography of the networks delivering projects and the prominence of individual actors and subgroups of actors within a given network. I return to these points later in the book.

4

Why Networks?

This chapter considers why social network analysis is useful as an analytical method and introduces some of the terminology that will be used later in the book, particularly in the context of the case studies. Having dealt with the main terminology that will enable the reader to understand the material elsewhere in the book, the chapter moves on to specifically consider three measures of centrality. Centrality is a measure of a given actor's prominence within a network and is particularly important in dealing with communication and information exchange networks. There are a wide range of terms in use within the network community and there is no single 'industry standard' for network terminology. For the purpose of this book, the terminology adopted in Wasserman and Faust (1994) is used. The chapter also deals with some actor types that particularly apply to projects. This chapter draws upon some material of mine previously published in Knight and Ruddock (2009) and Pryke (2012).

It is hoped that an understanding of the basic terminology will facilitate the reader's understanding of material later in the book; it is also hoped that this might enable the reader who has previously not read research articles in the field of networks to start enjoying these articles. Finally, it is also hoped that the thinking practitioner might start to use some of the network terminology, and ultimately the principles, in the workplace and in this way both theory and practice will benefit.

As noted in the last chapter, SNA is the product of an unlikely collaboration between mathematicians, anthropologists and sociologists. It is a form of *structural analysis* applied to organisations and is particularly useful when trying to make sense of the temporary project organisation. One of the aims of using SNA in the study of projects is to provide a framework through which the transitory systems that our complex projects comprise can be classified, visualised and analysed. Through appropriate visualisation and analysis, it is possible to move to a situation where we conceptualise projects as networks representing systems, enabling us to build network theory appropriate to projects and ultimately to manage and design project networks that deliver better projects.

One of the aspirations for this book is to broaden interest from and engagement by industry in the adoption of SNA as a tool for use in the delivery of successful projects. At the time of writing, the Centre for Organisational Network Analysis – CONA@UCL (https://www.ucl.ac.uk/cona) based at University College London (UCL) and of which I am director – was actively working with Transport for London (TfL), Drogados (a Spanish contractor working for TfL on the Bank Station upgrade scheme) and Crossrail. At the time of writing, discussions were also underway with High Speed 2

Managing Networks in Project-Based Organisations, First Edition. Stephen Pryke.
© 2017 John Wiley & Sons Ltd. Published 2017 by John Wiley & Sons Ltd.

and the Californian High Speed Railway. Previously, I have worked with two of the UK's largest property development groups, Slough Estates and MEPC, and with the Ministry of Defence and Essex County Council.

Definition

As discussed in Chapter 3, social network analysis involves the representation of organisational relationships as a system of nodes or actors linked by precisely classified connections, along with the mathematics that defines the structural characteristics of the relationship between the nodes. In the interests of completeness for this chapter, Wasserman and Faust's (1994) network definition is restated here:

> a finite set or sets of actors and the relation or relations (between them).

A study of the network context is important and classification of context along with classification and analysis of network data has the potential to provide a richness of analysis for project organisations that can make an important difference to our understanding of the management of projects. It is important not to exclude other methods or become obsessed with the mathematics of SNA alone.[1] Qualitative contextual data is also important. Repeatability in the context of complex projects is very limited.

Why Choose Social Network Analysis?

Building on the work of Nohria and Eccles (1992), the following points provide justification for the use of SNA in looking into project organisations:

- All human activity is 'social' in that it involves interaction. It makes sense, therefore, to classify project organisations in social terms and to analyse that social interaction in order to understand the project functions (Pryke, 2012).
- People and organisations affect and are affected by their social environment. If we really want to understand behaviour in the project organisational environment we need to understand the *network environment* in which individuals or firms must operate.
- Structural position affects and constrains action. Actors have the power to change their structural place or position. Increasingly we see that network position (prominence, for example) must be won or commanded by an individual, rather than allocated by 'superiors' in a hierarchical sense.
- Understanding network properties and individual positions within networks is very important in understanding the effectiveness of our organisations. In the project field a great deal of emphasis has previously been placed upon project definition, procurement, and management of project delivery. Projects are designed and

---

1 Many network scientists will disagree with this. The book is really focusing upon the application that network science and SNA have to the study of projects. Projects are, almost by their very nature, unique and therefore analysis based solely upon the mathematics of network science will provide results that lack the richness that an appreciation of the environment in which the network studies are carried out provides.

delivered by networks of individuals enacting project function-related roles. These networks have not been well documented, understood or managed. These networks, in the absence of effective and explicit governance, are essentially self-organising (see also Chapter 3).

Nohria and Eccles (1992) do not distinguish between two quite different types of actors; these are *individuals* and *firms*. Project coalitions involve a range of actor roles fulfilled by individuals (perhaps the sole trader, professional service provider or sub-contractor) and a range of actor roles fulfilled by firms; an example of the latter might be the client role, where a firm is named as the client actor, but where daily interactions occur with a number of individuals. The question of how data is gathered and analysed in the context of different actor types is an issue that will be discussed later in this chapter. The decision about whether to study *inter-firm*, *intra-firm* or *intra-coalition interpersonal* relationships is an important first step in starting out in SNA-based research. If in doubt, gather data based on relationships between individuals. The data can always be aggregated to represent inter-firm relationships later. Extracting interpersonal relationship data from previously collected inter-firm data is much more difficult and frequently impossible.

Problems Associated with the Use of SNA in Project Research

As mentioned above, the purpose of this chapter is to explain and introduce the use of SNA to students, academics and practitioners working in the project management field. Some of the limitations of SNA as a method were dealt with in Pryke (2012) and summarised briefly in Chapter 3. These limitations are summarised as follows (the italicised text represents a response to each point raised):

- SNA is a quantitative (mathematical) method used within an interpretative context (involving subjective judgments about human characteristics and behaviour) (Loosemore, 1998). *SNA is not alone in relation to this criticism; a similar criticism could be made of most, if not all, statistical analysis. SNA provides very rich data when combined with qualitative material relating to project and actor characteristics. This is an important point in relation to the discussion in this book. Using mathematical algorithms alone in trying to understand human behaviour is, it is argued, somewhat sterile. It is the mix of structural analysis through SNA and qualitative material relating to project context that is important.*
- SNA deals with analysis but does not always provide causality. *If we detect a correlation between project performance and actor roles or network roles, can we prove that the former was caused by the latter? Once again, this limitation is not peculiar to SNA. In addition, causality, in terms of its establishment, must almost inevitably be a problem wherever the analysis of essentially unique projects is concerned.*
- SNA is relatively complex in terms of both theoretical and mathematical bases; complexity creates a barrier to entry – some researchers and most consultants prefer to find simpler ways to gather and analyse data especially when restricted funds and short programmes limit the time available for the assimilation of complex ideas, concepts and techniques. *Yes, SNA is complex both theoretically and as a method.*

Personal investment is required to establish the skills and knowledge to undertake successful research using SNA. This is not necessarily bad but does explain the relatively small number of individuals with expertise in SNA related to the project organisational area. Part of the mission of this book and of the previous book, Social Network Analysis in Construction, *is to build a database of SNA research material related to projects and to disseminate that material.*

- It is necessary to classify each network very precisely and this can lead to a potentially large number of different relationships between a given group of actors. This inevitably creates a very large volume of data. *For example, it is insufficiently rigorous to look at unclassified communications between project team members. We need to understand the mode of communication (face to face, telephone, etc.) and the function or purpose of the interaction (brief definition, conceptual design, etc.). Add to this the frequency of communications and perceived importance on the part of the sender and receiver, and we have created several hundred finely classified networks representing communications between our team. This is worth bearing in mind when designing research programmes using SNA.*

- Sampling is not effective or appropriate with networks within the boundary drawn for the study.[2] It follows that a 100% response from project actors is essential. In the absence of a 100% response, estimations of likely responses are necessary in order to provide more accurate mathematical values. *This aspect of SNA means that great emphasis must be placed upon agreeing access to all project actors before work proceeds. Gaining the support of the client and having the client express this support publicly to the team helps considerably in enabling the process of data gathering. This can prove very challenging, particularly when dealing with groups of individuals who are easily coerced by superiors at work or peer group pressure. In these cases it may be necessary to redraw boundaries to maintain response rate completeness for a given population.*

Concepts and Terminology

A number of social network terms are in common use in the English language. We talk of *webs of relationships, networking, cliques,* individuals who become *isolates* or conversely the *prominence* of individuals, individuals' *centrality,* and *links* between firms and individuals. Telecoms firms refer to issues of *connectivity* for network users. SNA

---

2 This is a contentious point and I have been taken to task on this point at the time of going to press. There are clearly differing views here. Many will apply the '70% rule' – the data set is valid if data is available for 70% of the actors within the boundary defined for the study. I have a problem with data based upon anything less than almost 100% completeness. If we are interested in density, for example, or the prominence of a given actor in the network, clearly using a sample of the data will give values for density and centrality that are not accurate. An inspection of the mathematical formulae must surely lead to this conclusion. We then turn to the issue of the importance, or otherwise, of that inaccuracy. For me the importance is that the missing data is based upon self-selection. Isolated actors who are meant to be quite central under the terms of their employment, and central actors who are not meant to be undertaking quite such a prominent gatekeeping role, for example, might choose not to contribute data. To use links and especially weightings identified by the other contributing half of a dyad is surely to use data that is not triangulated. Network data is gathered and analysed in a surprisingly wide range of fields and certainly there is a different discussion to be had in the context of 'big data'. In the context of projects, however, some caution must be exercised in the use of data sampling.

theory gives very precise meanings to these terms in common use, as well as a large number of other terms, and allocates a formula to each of the terms. With one minor exception, it is not the intention to provide SNA formulae here, partly because those wishing to use SNA will want to use one of the numerous software packages available, and partly because Wasserman and Faust (1994) provide what amounts to an encyclopaedia of both terminology and mathematical formulae. A range of alternative words are frequently used in SNA for the same, most common, terms. For example, the words *links*, *edges*, *curves* and *connections* are variations on the term that describes the connection between two given *nodes* or *actors*. It is worth just repeating here that, for the sake of clarity, this book adheres to the terms used in Wasserman and Faust (1994). Wasserman and Faust (1994) provide a comprehensive list of SNA terms and reference to one source for these terms provides consistency and avoids ambiguity. Let us now turn our attention to a discussion of the main SNA terms.

Social Network

Being clear about boundary definition for any given network is important. Boundary definition may be achieved by specifying the nature of the role of the actors within the boundary and perhaps time parameters. For example, on one particular construction research project the actors falling within the boundary were classified as those attending the site during a three-month period prior to the interview date (as identified by another project actor) and not using hand tools for all or part of their working day (Pryke, 2012).

Actor

Networks comprise *nodes* and connections between those nodes. The node is described as an actor in the network and might be, for example, an individual, a group of individuals, departments within a firm or nations within the world. It is also possible to apply SNA outside of a social context, in which case the nodes might be, for example, computer terminals or railway stations. For the purposes of studying projects, our nodes will normally comprise either individual people or firms. Making the initial decision about whether to measure links between individuals or firms is important, as is consistency of application. If there is homogeneity (similarity) within the members of the group, we refer to the network as being a *one-mode network*.

The actors discussed in this book are firms as well as individuals. There was some discussion in Chapter 3 about the ambiguity associated with procuring resources for projects through contractual relationships between client and contractors. The transition, post-contract, from project resource to efficient project delivery systems is complex. Projects start with an emphasis, pre-contract, on contracts between firms. The project then transitions, post-contract, to self-organising networks comprising individuals exchanging information. Studying this transformation is facilitated by the adoption of SNA.

Actors can perform the role of *transmitters* and *receivers* in a network; an actor who performs both functions at once is defined as a *carrier*. The number of incoming connections to any given actor is measured as the *in-degree* for that actor (expressed as the number of other nodes sending to the given actor). A similar principle applies to the term *out-degree* in relation to an actor.

Ties

Traditionally in SNA, actors were linked to others by social ties. Increasingly, as SNA research explores new applications, these ties have included links that are not defined as 'social'. In Pryke (2005b, 2006, for example) the definition is expanded to include contractual and financial relationships between firms. Figure 4.1 illustrates tie strength and directed graphs.

Some useful examples of the most common types of ties, cited by Wasserman and Faust (1994) are:

- Evaluation of one person by another (expressed friendship, liking or respect)
- Transfer of material resources (for example, business transactions, lending or borrowing money or goods)
- Association or affiliation (for example, jointly attending a social event or belonging to the same social club or networking organisation)
- Behavioural interaction (talking together, sending messages)
- Movement between places or statuses (migration, social or physical mobility)
- Physical connection (a road, river or bridge connecting two points)
- Formal relations (for example, authority)
- Biological relationship (kinship or descent).
  Wasserman and Faust (1994: 18)

Examples of application of these types of ties in construction research might include:

- Payments between actors (Pryke, 2001, 2012)
- Incentives to perform (Pryke, 2005b, 2006, 2012)
- Contractual relationships (Pryke, 2006, 2012, 2014; Pryke and Smyth, 2006; Pryke *et al.*, 2014; Loosemore, 1998)
- Instructions issued (Pryke, 2001)
- Information sent and/or received (Pryke, 2004b, 2005a, 2012; Pryke and Badi, 2013; Pryke, Watson and Badi, 2013; Pryke *et al.*, 2015a, 2015b)

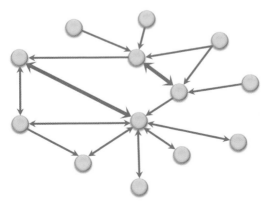

Commentary on Figure 4.1: Tie strength and directed graphs
Look for: thickness or other coding of linkages to reflect tie strength and direction of arrows to reflect direction of flow in the case of information or advice, for example.

Figure 4.1 Tie strength and directed graphs.

- Risk transferred (Pryke and Ouwerkerk, 2003; Loosemore, 1998)
- Knowledge transfer (Conway, 1994, 1997)
- Abuse of power and conflict resolution (Loosemore, 1998).

Validity of Linkages in Networks

An important point to make about the validity of a given relation and the validity of a network based upon such relations is that a connection is only valid if (to use a plumbing analogy) something flows through the connection and the flow type and rate can be influenced by the actors at either end of the connection. A network reflecting contractual relationships is valid ('consideration' on both sides flows between the actors in this typically dyadic relationship); so is a network based upon trust (evaluation by actors of each other). 'Networks' showing actors within a population sharing an actor characteristic are not valid. Hence figures which identify and connect individuals born in the same year or from the same social class, for example, are not networks because the existence of flow is not established until the actors provide evidence of a social connection. This point may be contentious with some. From the point of view of studying organisations and their systems it is not sufficient to record membership of a given group or institution. We are not connected until an interaction is made. We all have email accounts but I am not in your communication network until I send an email to you or receive an email from you.

One-Mode, Two-Mode and Multi-Mode Networks

Many network studies look at relationships between one set of actors and one set of events (for example, the extent to which there are marriage ties in a community) and this is referred to as a *one-mode* network. Others look at the relationship between two sets of actors and one set of events (for example, marriages between white and black South Africans); this is a *two-mode* network. In project terms, relationships between designers involving client requirements would be one-mode. Relationships between designers and cost management consultants involving client requirements, for example, would be regarded as two-mode.

The case studies in this book's sister publication (Pryke, 2012) deal with a number of different types of relationships existing between a group of construction project actors and would be classified as *multi-mode*. These case studies looked at contractual relationships, performance incentives and information exchange (the latter category sub-divided by project function to provide networks related to project sub-systems). The case studies also captured 'instructions', because of the prominence of the instruction in some forms of project contract. The important point here is that the mathematics needs to identify and evaluate each mode separately, even if it is useful or attractive to present different modes in the same network figure through colour-coding, for example. It should, therefore, be possible to establish a correlation or otherwise between the different positions that actors hold in a number of differing networks that relate to one project.

Valued Networks and Tie Strength

Valued networks are important in the study of project organisations. In an organisational setting understanding the performance of networks, and perhaps what interventions to introduce, are linked to tie strength. Research carried out with public and private sector client organisations in construction (Pryke, 2012) and more recently in infrastructure schemes (Pryke *et al.*, 2015a, 2015b; Soundararaj *et al.*, 2015) has shown that tie strength is important in our understanding of project relationships.

Actor Attributes

One of the issues that will be dealt with later in the book (particularly in the case studies – see Chapters 10 to 13) is how actors acquire their roles. In some project contexts, there is an assumption that contracts for the procurement of services accurately specify roles. However, quite commonly roles and responsibilities are not defined very specifically, and roles are acquired through, or allocated by, the relevant networks with which actors are engaged (see Pryke *et al.*, 2015a, 2015b; Soundararaj *et al.*, 2015). One of the key attributes of interest in studying projects (or supply chains, independently of projects) is the role of the actor.

It is, therefore, of fundamental importance to the study of complex projects that the nature of the network (for example, its density and configuration) and the position of a particular actor within a given network *will have the effect of influencing the role of that actor and effectively changing the actor attributes.* In this chapter I stress the need to move toward a *redefinition of project actor roles.* This redefinition reflects the reforms in procurement and management strategies and is expressed in social network terms. In the case of the construction industry it is moving away from defining actor roles using traditional terms like architect, quantity surveyor and main contractor. The industry increasingly refers to roles such as design manager, financial manager and cluster leader. Recent research (Pryke *et al.*, 2015a, 2015b; Soundararaj *et al.*, 2015) shows that roles allocated by procurement contracts are of less importance to the success of projects than the 'network role' acquired and enacted by individual actors in the context of a particular project function-performing network.

Dyads and Triads

These are network configurations involving relationships between two or three actors, respectively. A network of only two or three would scarcely comprise a network at all. Dyads and triads tend, therefore, to apply to clusters or subgroups within the main group. Dyads are particularly important in the context of contractual relationships. Tradition, coupled with the need to specify unambiguous contractual relationships between firms, has led to the almost exclusive use of dyadic contractual relationships in the project context.

Subgroup

Also known as a *clique*, a subgroup (perhaps not surprisingly) is a small group within a larger group. Clusters in construction coalitions (Gray, 1996; Holti *et al.*, 2000) and the relationships between those clusters are analogous with Wasserman and Faust's (1994) *subgroup*. Figure 4.9 below gives an example of the representation of clusters; in this case contractual clusters are shown representing the relationships in a French construction project where two contractors enter into a partnership as main contractors to enable them to carry out work of a higher value than they might be capable of alone (Pryke and Pearson, 2006). The three main network configurations in this figure represent isolates, a single isolated subgroup and the main network.

Network Density

Network density is, in effect, the total number of links between nodes in a given network expressed in relation to the maximum number of links possible for that network. The maximum number of links possible arises where every node is linked to every other node. When this point is reached the density value for a given network is 1.00 (if we choose to use two decimal places and this is usually sufficient for these purposes) and this would represent an unusual situation. Most commonly, the density value would fall between 0 and 1.00.

The implications of the density measure vary depending on which of the project characteristics we are focusing upon. Size and density in relation to contractual and performance-incentive relationships will provide a measure of fragmentation of the project team and the extent to which the team members are connected to each other. Density in relation to information exchange networks might, perhaps, provide a measure of the non-hierarchical nature of information exchanges.

This does, however, need to be considered alongside the configuration of the network as a whole. Traditional projects, where information exchanges correspond to traditional standard forms of contract, will have higher information exchange network densities when compared to projects where collaborative procurement and management practices prevail (all other factors being equal). This assertion is made on the basis that supply chain management, for example, implies a large number of connections between one central actor and each supply chain member but generally *fewer* links *between* members of the supply chain. Figure 4.9 illustrates this point – see isolated subgroup. Actors AGF, ARD, MDI, MTS and SEI represent the ends of the 'spokes' connected to the 'hub' actor SAT. This form of network configuration resembling a 'hub and spoke' or 'star' is common where the client leads in managing the supply chain. The use of cluster leaders, for example, may tend to focus design information exchange around a relatively small group of actors.

The relational basis of collaborative relationships and the totally (and deliberately) non-hierarchical nature of information exchanges associated with the supply chain management and cluster approaches involve smaller, more focused, groups of actors in making decisions.

Density can also be used as a means of establishing a *correspondence* between the network types within a given project. In other words, there is value in the comparison of network configurations involving contractual relationships as against those involving information exchange within a given project case study. For further discussion of this point refer to Pryke (2012).

Barnes' 'socio-centric' approach to the discussion of density in networks is adopted here, rather than the 'ego-centric' approach advocated by Mitchell. For an example of an ego-centric approach see Pryke *et al.* (2011). The concepts associated with both ego-centric and socio-centric approaches are dealt with in some detail by Scott (1991). The socio-centric argument, in essence, is that we focus on the density of the networks as a whole (socio-centric), rather than focusing on networks around particular points of reference. In an ego-centric approach the emphasis is on the formation of networks around the focal agent. As Scott (1991) points out, it is the constraining power of the network over its members through indirect, as well as direct, links that interests us. This *concatenation* (or combination) of indirect linkages needs to feature in our study of the networks, given the interdependent nature of project networks.

Before leaving the subject of density, the issue of comparability of density values between networks and the relevance of the size of the network need to be addressed. If density is an expression of the number of links present, as a proportion of the total number of links theoretically possible, there is an argument that larger networks will have lower densities than smaller networks, all other matters being equal. Density is, therefore, limited in its application where networks are significantly different in size, particularly when the context or function of the network are considered. Hence, for a given project type, size and complexity, a larger network (more actors) would result in a lower network density, unless speed of execution for example (or some other variable, and there could be many) is different.

Actor Centrality

Centrality of a given actor within a network is an expression of prominence and possibly power, depending on the nature of the relationships being measured. The definition of centrality and its application is complex. In simple terms, centrality of an actor refers to the number of links associated with that actor, compared to the total possible number in the context of the network as a whole. At this point the issues of in-degree and out-degree become relevant. In-degree centrality refers to the incoming links, out-degree to the outgoing links. Hence it would be wrong to associate a high level of power within a classic high-centrality star network configuration if the centrality is associated with *outgoing* information or payments (for example) rather than *incoming*. Figure 4.9 illustrates the point of centrality; the actor at the centre of the (relatively small) star, in very simple terms, has a high level of centrality in the network (subgroup) shown. Actor SAT has high centrality within the subgroup comprising actors AGF, ARD, MDI, MTS and SEI.

Point, Betweenness, Closeness or Eigenvector Centrality?

Freeman (1978) referred to three main groups of centrality measures: *degree of points*, *betweenness* and *closeness*. The *degree of points*, or extent to which a given point is connected to other points, provides, typically, a measure used in the analysis of communication or interaction activity of some sort. It is a measure of connectivity. High degree centrality of a given actor within a network implies a high level of prominence in an information exchange network or other type of communication network. Point centrality would provide a measure of the importance of an actor, either because the actor was responsible for the very wide dissemination of information (out-degree) or was responsible for gathering information from a large number of other actors (in-degree). Point or degree centrality is relatively high if a given actor has a relatively large number of *primary* connections.

Betweenness centrality is a measure of 'brokerage' – an index of potential control over communication. Actors with high betweenness indices can restrict flow of information in a network. It therefore relates to the incidence with which a given node falls between two other nodes. Typically an actor with a high value for betweenness centrality has a high level of control over information flowing through them in some way. The actor might typically be acting in a gatekeeper type of role. Betweenness centrality is high if a given node lies on a large number of paths between other actors – it is a measure of the ability to act as a 'bridge' between other actors. Finally, *closeness centrality* involves the measurement of path lengths between two given points. The concept of path length is considered later in this chapter.

Closeness centrality involves consideration of the number of nodes which fall between two given nodes for, typically, some form of interaction network. This latter measure is perhaps the most complex and gives some measure of the independence of a given actor and the efficiency of the organisation (Freeman, 1978). Closeness centrality is high if a given node can communicate with a relatively large number of other actors, including those beyond the primary links. For the examination of project networks, degree of points centrality (commonly referred to as 'degree centrality') provides one of the most useful measures for analysis (Pryke, 2012). In the context of information exchange, betweenness centrality might be important if efficiency of information flows is an issue (Case Study 2, Chapter 12, deals with this issue).

Centrality as a concept was first developed by Bavelas (1948, cited in Wasserman and Faust, 1994) and is very relevant to the study of project organisations. To the three measures of centrality originally identified by Freeman in 1978 (ibid.) we should add eigenvector centrality. Eigenvector centrality is a measure of influence, similar to betweenness, and weights the centrality of nodes in relation to the centrality of the other nodes that a given node is connected to. Whereas, for example, degree centrality quantifies primary connections (those linked to a given node in a single path), eigenvector centrality also quantifies secondary connections – those involving more than one path. The case studies presented in Chapters 11, 12 and 13 (see also Pryke *et al.*, 2015a, 2015b; Soundararaj *et al.* 2015) use degree, betweenness and eigenvector centrality measures – these provided analysis for connectivity, brokerage and influence respectively. We should acknowledge that in fact the distinction between brokerage and influence is sometimes unclear, particularly in complex projects.

Other Issues Relating to the Relevance of Centrality as a Measure

It is clear that a lot of attention has been focused by social network analysts on the subject of centrality in networks (Pryke, 2012). Centrality, as a concept, is fundamental to the interpretation of social network data and originated in the work of Bavelas (1948) and Leavitt (1951) at the Massachusetts Institute of Technology (MIT). The implication of centrality within a communication network has progressed through a number of phases of interpretative thought. Until the end of the 1970s the terms 'centrality' and 'power' were regarded as synonymous by many observers.

Brass and Burkhardt (1992) observed that most analysts would feel quite justified in declaring the actor with the highest centrality (and this is often clearly evident from even a cursory glance at the relevant network diagram) to be the actor with the most power in the network. But these interpretations of the relationship between centrality and power were based upon the study of small groups of people in problem-solving environments (see Mizruchi and Potts, 1998). I argue that this interpretative context serves our purposes reasonably well. Much of the activity within the project environment involves groups of actors solving problems, or reacting to problems of one sort or another. Networks in complex project environments probably need less emphasis on power, which (non-network) management theorists might equate, in part, with leadership.

Networks execute complex activities and function well when prominent actors facilitate and enable, for example, flows of timely and accurate information. We return to this theme throughout the book.

Defining the Population for the Study

As mentioned above, defining the boundary for an SNA study is important. Even a cursory consideration of the mathematics of network density and actor centrality will reveal the importance of making an accurate and appropriate assessment of which actors to include in the network population. It also follows that sampling is not an appropriate approach, unless a very clearly defined subgroup is identifiable (see footnote 2). In one sense, however, all social networks are huge, transitory and potentially infinite. In practice, therefore, we frequently have some difficulty in establishing the boundary of the network for study. Laumann, Marsden and Prensky (1989) identify two possible approaches:

Realist approach to boundary specification – the actors define the boundary of the network themselves. For example, if we start to interview project coalition actors, they will identify other actors with whom they need to interact to achieve the project objectives. If there is no published multi-organisational list of actors, this is frequently the only option available.

Nominalist approach to boundary specification – here the network boundary is defined by the researcher. Wasserman and Faust (1994) give an example of the study of computer messages among researchers in a given scientific activity. The list is constructed by the researcher, perhaps based on published academic papers in the relevant scientific area and the list is not prepared with any reference to the views of those on the list, particularly in relation to others who might also be on the list. It is probably not a realistic option for most project studies.

For the purposes of project research, we should consider the nature of the network before deciding on whether to adopt a realist or nominalist approach. If the researcher wishes to investigate contractual relationships or information exchange relationships, a nominalist approach would be helpful; contractual conditions tend to be dyadic and the parties to the contract are formally identified in documents. With information exchange, outgoing and incoming information ought to be considered and if a project coalition member was not identified by either senders or receivers of information, then the actor concerned does not form part of the network. If a nominalist approach is adopted in project research, there is a tendency toward higher levels of isolates and very often the existence of these isolates is instructive.

What is a Network?

A network is a system of nodes and their linkages. The nodes are the positions where an actor is located and the actor has characteristics, both qualitative characteristics (for example, a civil engineer with 25 years' post-qualification experience) and characteristics as a network actor – a centrality value expressing their prominence within a network (in simple terms the number of connections between the actor in question and all other actors in the network). For the network to be a 'social' network the actors have to be able to influence the relationship that they have with other actors. The actors are all connected by linkages and it might help if we think of those linkages as a pipe or perhaps a pair of pipes where flows occur simultaneously in both directions. The material in the pipe has quality or other measures of strength and the pipe has a diameter which reflects the volume of material travelling through the pipe. The material in the pipe(s) also has direction of travel – in and out flow. The next section considers actor characteristics which relate to the analysis of network data, particularly when attempting to interpret network visualisations.

Actor Characteristics

It has been established that actors' characteristics are related to the network configuration within which they have links and their position within that network. The individual actor's role is partly defined by network topography and partly by the behaviour of other actors. It follows from the discussion above about the nature of networks that it is common for actors to hold differing roles within a range of networks that all relate to one project or supply chain. Next I discuss some common network actor roles. These are distinct from *project* roles.

Prominent Disseminators

These individuals are often surprised by their own prominence or centrality within an information exchange network. They contribute generously and regularly to the network; their contribution is highly valued and they respond regardless of the prominence of other actors. These actors provide personal support to others who are perhaps less knowledgeable. They also connect other actors in useful and fruitful ways and have a relatively high level of knowledge in their own subject area, as well as in other areas. They would generally provide more to the network than a basic minimum. They make a major contribution and sometimes get disheartened at the lack of effort and contribution offered by others. Figure 4.2 illustrates this role.

Prominent disseminators (PD) are valuable network actors. They need to be rewarded and finding an appropriate means of doing this in the network context needs careful thought. There is risk to the network associated with the absence of this type of actor for any reason. The network would need to find a replacement or make a large number of adjustments to its connections to function properly following removal or resignation of a PD. It would be necessary to establish that the cause of the large number of very active connections does not relate to a failure to respond properly to requests for information on the part of the PD and/or the production of incomplete information which requires high levels of iteration to resolve. This can only be established by interviewing relevant actors. Case Study 2, Chapter 12, relates to the issue of 'dysfunctional prominence'. This leads neatly onto another type of highly prominent actor behaviour.

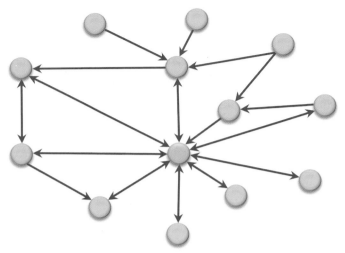

Commentary on Figure 4.2: Prominent disseminators
Look for: centrality – lots of connections to other actors; more connections
to this actor than any other; many of the connections are two-way.

Figure 4.2 Prominent disseminators (information exchange network).

Gatekeeper Hoarders

Gatekeepers hoarders (see Figure 4.3) are generally less welcome in our networks than prominent disseminators. As mentioned already, PDs are always quite surprised at how central and prominent their positions are in the networks. Their centrality has evolved naively and very often almost against the will of the PD. The gatekeeper hoarder (GH), however, is an individual who can see the power that can be harnessed through their position in a network coupled with a role that enables them to filter, or control or manage in some way, the outputs of other individuals. This might apply to long-term projects or very simple day-to-day communications. The gatekeeper hoarder seeks centrality and the power which they associate with it. The GH places themselves in or creates a network environment where many other actors need approval from them, for example. The ability to insert themselves into an existing path and act as a filter or gatekeeper is always attractive to the personality of the GH. So what do we do about the GHs? Certainly, part of their role, which is mostly self-created, does not help the efficient operation of the network. Some of the less desirable aspects of GH behaviour include:

- Some of the gate-keeping may be unnecessary. This simply adds delay to information exchange and communication.
- Some of the filtering may involve bias, uncertainty and loss of clarity, which is unhelpful.
- Most GHs are engaged in *path-lengthening* activity – in order to create a role for themselves they insert themselves as a node within an existing path, adding unnecessary length to a path. Longer paths mean slower communications and more opportunity for ambiguity and dispute.

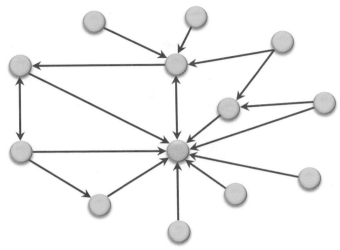

Commentary on Figure 4.3: Gatekeeper hoarders
Look for: centrality–lots of connections to other actors; more connections to this actor than any other; most of the connections are *one-way*, with information flowing into the gatekeeper hoarder. Note the similarity between gatekeeper hoarders and prominent disseminators. It is only the arrow directions that indicate the quite different role and personal motives involved.

Figure 4.3 Gatekeeper hoarders.

- The role of the GH may imply resistance to using more appropriate methods of communication.
- Some gate-keeping activity may involve vested interests on their part.

Gatekeeper hoarders very often evolve their own roles in organisations where a lot of the actors do not seek prominence for its own sake. They often exist in organisations that have grown quickly or that have grown too large. Perhaps they have some specialist knowledge that they feel protective about. The 'knowledge is power' approach does not operate well in networks, where homogeneity provides a better basis for openness and sharing of information and knowledge.

Some networks may be willing to tolerate gatekeeper hoarders, for example, if these actors are willing to deal with relatively dull administrative tasks and attend the meetings that other more creative types do not want to attend. If the network does need to reduce the influence and prominence of a GH how might this be brought about? The role is a function of the connections, their number and direction and the content of the linkage. It therefore follows that we would need to go about dismantling or re-engineering the linkages that lead to the prominence. Typically we might reassign non-core workload and use perhaps an intranet to disseminate information around the GH actor. We create a 'structural hole' (Burt, 2004) around the offending gatekeeper.

Isolates

Isolates (Figure 4.4) are actors not connected to other actors in a given network. We might deduce, therefore, that they are not actors within the network and if this is

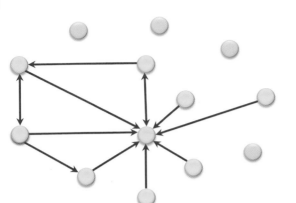

Figure 4.4 Isolates.

Commentary on Figure 4.4: Isolates
Look for: actors not connected to any other actor. There is a
need to understand why any particular actor is an isolate.

the case, why do they appear in the figure illustrating the network? To answer this question we need to return to one of the basic principles of networks; networks exist at a number of levels in organisations. There is a network (or a number of networks) for each system and any project organisation needs to run a range of systems concurrently to function. We might classify an information exchange network relating to financial management for example, or a network that relates to contractual relationships or financial incentives; these may involve the same network population yet when we look at an individual network some of the actors which feature and indeed may be prominent within one network are perhaps isolates in another. Thus the junior in the architectural practice is quite prominent in the dissemination of design information to other design team members but is an isolate in the network that communicates with the client, for example. We show the actors that do not form part of the main network partly to recognise that they are within the project population, even if they are an isolate in one particular project network.

So why are we interested in isolates? When, for example, a manager or project manager looks at a network relating to their area of responsibility there are a number of issues relating to the existence of isolates. The manager would need to consider:

- Why is a particular actor an isolate? Given the actor's allocated (as against adopted) role, is it logical that the actor is disconnected from the remainder of the network?
- Is the actor isolated out of choice or as a result of other actors' inclination to exclude them?
- Do we know anything about the process of the actor becoming isolated? Is this a temporary and/or regular situation and only evident in our single cross-sectional analysis?
- Is the existence of some isolates necessary and perhaps even desirable?

Some isolates in any given network are inevitable given the multi-functional, multi-layered, systems-orientated nature of networks in organisations. We need to ask why the actor is isolated and whether this is desirable given the function of the network under consideration. If the isolation is undesirable for the effectiveness of the network it may be necessary to take action to restore some connections, or perhaps to change the individual role-holding actor. Those with very high levels of expertise and knowledge and who do not need others to contribute to their input to the network have a choice as to whether to engage with others to a greater or lesser extent in their working day. Some may choose to locate themselves remotely, avoid the use of modern communication methods and use the isolation to concentrate more fully on the complex tasks that they very often find themselves dealing with. Authors, academics and composers are among those who might seek or wish to maintain isolated positions in networks. Those with family or carer commitments might seek to provide input to the network but minimise their connection to the network. Sometimes the only connection to the network is through an actor in the role of *bridge* (see below). Isolates are not an undesirable feature of a network even though their very existence must reduce density in communication networks, for example. But good networks are not necessarily dense per se. The quantity of links for a given network or actor needs to be related to the quality and direction of those links. This is discussed further, along with the process of evolution, in Case Study 3 in Chapter 13.

Isolated Dyads and Triads

Isolated dyads and triads (Figure 4.5) are clusters of actors connected strongly to a small number of other actors but with no connection to the main network. They are effective in the sense that their dyad or triad is not cluttered by other, perhaps unnecessary, connections; they are not subject to the throughput of other actors or clusters. They are focused and isolated. In order to understand the desirability of these clusters we need to

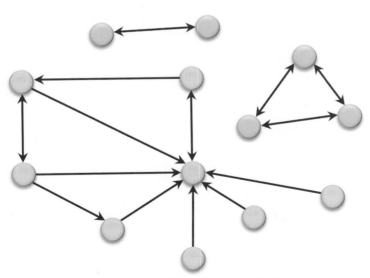

Commentary on Figure 4.5: Isolated dyads and triads
Look for: actors connected to one or two other actors only where the dyad or triad is not connected to the main network in any way.

Figure 4.5 Isolated dyads and triads.

ask about the classification (or role) of the network and the roles of the actors within the clusters. What brings these small groups together and at the same time enables or requires their lack of connectivity to the main networks?

There are a number of possible reasons for the existence of isolated dyads or triads. These might include:

- The dyad or triad is a highly specialised group which shares a common sub-goal for the network and which needs to focus, without the distraction of other throughput from the network.
- The cluster might be engaged in an activity that is highly sensitive commercially, or where for some other reason (perhaps national security) a very high level of confidentiality is necessary.
- Some organisations need to demonstrate 'ring-fencing' of certain information flows to prevent possible conflicts of interest or corruption of processes.
- The isolated dyads or triads might only be isolated temporarily. An example might be a project at bid stage where ring-fencing is necessary but once the project is awarded, the ring-fencing is no longer necessary. At this point the actors forming the isolated triads reconnect to other actors in the main network.

On occasions, isolated subgroups need help to become re-connected to the main group. Those connected with a small number of others actors in isolated dyads or triads are not necessarily likely to connect easily with others. In these circumstances we might need to find some form of broker or boundary spanner.

Boundary Spanners

Sometimes in networks we can observe isolated subgroups that are larger than dyads or triads (Figure 4.6). It is possible that the subgroups are substantial in terms of the total number of actors in the network. Where these subgroups are connected by actors who provide an essential link between two or more subgroups, we refer to the connecting actors as boundary spanners (Wasserman and Faust, 1994). These subgroups are defined, typically, by hierarchical authority levels, functional affiliation, physical location,

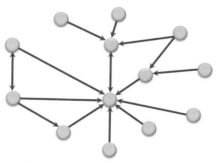

Commentary on Figure 4.6: Boundary spanners
Look for: one actor through whom all communication or other resources flow and without which the two (in this case) distinct subgroups would not be connected. This figure represents the role of the boundary spanner *once they have fulfilled their boundary spanning role.*

Figure 4.6 Boundary spanners.

qualifications or language. The actor whose role it is to reconnect this group, possibly with its own identity, to the main group faces a challenge.

The boundary spanner role (BS) is a tough role. Depending on the reason for the two or more otherwise disconnected subgroups, this actor must *bridge a gap* arising from, for example, hierarchy, knowledge, culture or language. Some would argue that knowledge flows easily across 'boundaries' (Dittrich *et al.*, 2007) partly because it is human nature to share and partly because the possession of knowledge is a source of status and power in human relations. Yet this ignores competitiveness, opportunism and the pressures created by restricted fee budgets and profit margins, all of which impose pressures on project actors in the construction and engineering fields. The boundary spanner role is one that is frequently not identified in construction networks. It is not a role that fits into existing contractually orientated functions, nor does it lend itself to classification in terms of the existing construction professions. It is, therefore, quite difficult to see how this role would be sponsored – that is, who would pay for this role to be carried out?

Being a BS is difficult because many would lack the breadth of knowledge and social skills needed to appeal to a very diverse range of actors, separated into two or more dominant subgroups. There are a number of potential benefits associated with boundary spanning activity:

- The BS creates a link between two or more groups that was previously absent, improving information and knowledge flows.
- There is the possibility of integrating two or more systems; construction in particular with its complex, iterative and transitory systems has a need for integration – integration between projects and programmes and integration between functions such as design, production and maintenance.
- Innovation frequently arises through the connection of diverse, sometimes even antagonistic, groups and allowing subgroups to understand issues that are predominantly the domain of the other group or groups. As Burt (2004) observed, boundary spanning actors, including *firms* that provide a boundary spanning role, have the opportunity to identify and develop creativity and innovative opportunities.

Some contend that in the case of very disparate subgroups, or where the boundaries involve technological interfaces, a pair of boundary spanners are needed – one based initially in each of the two areas of the network to be spanned.

Bridges

Bridges (Figure 4.7) link two actors that are not connected to each other, apart from through the bridge. The bridge provides the shortest link (Figure 4.8) between two actors, aside from a direct linkage.

The bridge as a network role relates to information exchange networks in the context of construction, although the bridge might broker meetings with potential business partners, or owners of expertise or knowledge. Boundary spanners and bridges have similarities. The former tend to be relatively few and to connect large, otherwise disconnected, subgroups; bridges tend to be more numerous throughout the network and to link individual actors rather than dominant subgroups. Promoting the activity of the bridge enables a network to have higher levels of density and in the case of information

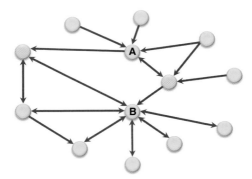

Commentary on Figure 4.7: Bridges
Look for: one or more actors who provide a link between two other actors who would not
otherwise be linked. In this figure actors A and B would not be connected without the two bridges.

Figure 4.7 Bridges.

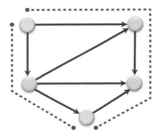

Commentary on Figure 4.8: Path lengths and bridges
Figure 4.8 shows two different paths and path lengths between a pair of nodes.
The path on the left of the figure involves one bridge, possibly a gatekeeper type of
actor positioned between the pair of other actors. The path connecting the pair of
nodes shown on the right of the figure is longer and involves two nodes representing
actors fulfilling the gatekeeper function.

Figure 4.8 Path lengths and bridges.

exchange, might provide better dissemination of material throughout the network. If we are studying a network looking for improvements in effectiveness, we might identify the bridges, draw these to the attention of those who might benefit and perhaps consider some training to enhance and recognise the importance of the role within the network. The identification of prominent disseminators, gatekeeper hoarders, isolates, isolated dyads and triads, boundary spanners and bridges, together with the consideration of their 'network role' in the context of the objectives and function of the network, is important. As projects become more complex technically and organisationally, the possibility of any individual knowing enough about each of the specialist elements to integrate those elements successfully into the project is decreasing (Thayer and Yourdon, 1997; Pryke and Smyth, 2006). An understanding of the network role types is important in our pursuit of successful project outcomes.

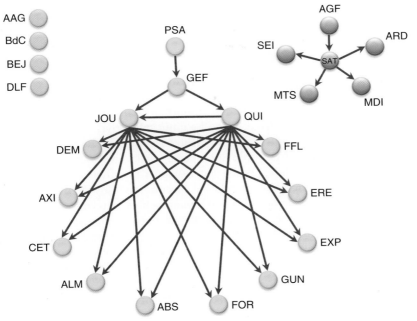

Key: Isolates, density, isolated subgroup

Figure 4.9 Isolates, density and isolated subgroup.

Network Characteristics

Figure 4.9 illustrates several characteristics of networks. Top left actors AAG, BdC, BEJ and DLF are isolates. Although this is referred to above as an actor characteristic, in another sense it is a characteristic of the network too. A network comprising isolates is not a network at all because it lacks an essential ingredient of the network – the linkages between individual actors. The main central diagram within Figure 4.9 illustrates the issue of network density. Network density is valued at between 0 and 1. Zero represents a 'network' of isolates – none of the nodes are connected to any of the other nodes and as mentioned above, this is not a network because it lacks connections. A network with a density value of 1 reflects a network where each of the nodes is connected to all the other nodes. The main diagram in the centre has a value between 0 and 1[3]; JOU and QUI are connected to all other nodes but the majority of the other nodes are relatively sparsely connected.

Finally, the diagram comprising five nodes around actor SAT is an isolated subgroup in relation to the main diagram. This small 'hub and spoke' network has a prominent central actor (SAT) but is relatively sparsely connected overall. It has no links to the main network, which is why as a network it is classified as 'isolated'.

---

3 Density is calculated as follows: $\Delta = l/n(n-1)$, where Δ represents network density, l represents the number of links present and n is the number of nodes. So, for the larger part of Figure 4.9 the density is: $24/14(14-1) = 0.132$.

In addition to classifying the type of linkage between actors, we can also weight the linkage, giving a measure of 'tie strength'; this is discussed in the next section.

Tie Strength, Valued and Directed Graphs

Tie strength is a mathematical representation of the strength of a tie between two actors. The strength of the tie would be given a numeric value (hence the reference to 'valued graphs' where tie strength data is gathered). The important issue is how the numeric value attributed to a given tie is calculated. It can be quite subjective. There are those who recommend simply classifying tie strength on the basis of the type of tie – marriage ties have higher strength than friendship ties for example (Suitor *et al.*, 1997; Keim *et al.*, 2013). This may be a valuable approach but I suspect the divorcees among us would challenge this level of generalisation relating to emotional involvement based upon the legal status of a relationship between two human beings. In terms of analysing organisations, it is argued that the tie strength should relate to the perceptions of the actors at each end of the tie and that there should be some formula for approximating this. Tie strength may well be directional. For example, the extent to which two actors value their linkage in terms of trust should be regarded as directional – to do otherwise would be overly simplistic. Previous research into large, complex project organisations in construction (Pryke, 2012; Pryke *et al.*, 2015a, 2015b) weighted linkages using the following formula:

$$\mathbf{TS}^{A-B} = \mathbf{f}^{A-B} \times \mathbf{i}^{A-B}$$

Where: **TS** is tie strength between nodes A and B, in the direction of A toward B; **f** is the frequency of communication or other 'transaction' between actors A and B, typically based upon a Likert scale of 1–9, 1 being less than once a year and 9 being once an hour, for example; **i** is the importance as perceived by the receiver of the information, instruction or other inflow to the node. Once again a Likert scale of 1–9 might be adopted. It is argued that this provides a reasonable proxy for tie strength in a project environment. A refinement of this formula might include other factors, including accuracy, timeliness, clarity, relevance and trust, for example.

Some may feel that it is legitimate to average tie strengths, taking the average of both directions as the strength of the tie between the two actors. In some situations this may be an oversimplification that risks losing relevant and important aspects of the data analysis. Figure 4.10 illustrates this point. By not averaging tie strengths, we inevitably double the volume of analysis generated in relation to a particular data set.

Some Final Thoughts

Social network analysis exists at two quite distinct levels of abstraction. There are the social network theorists who identify social networks as an interesting social construct and explore, theoretically, the implications for society of such networks. Conversely, there is a group of academics wishing to understand the mathematical structure of networks that are evident in organisations and projects.

SNA has a great deal to offer those interested in studying projects. The large number of possible variables associated with unique buildings in unique geographical and social

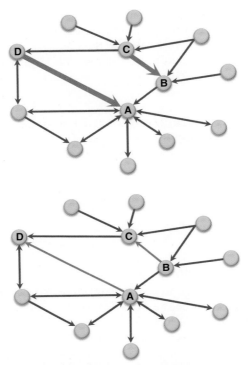

Commentary on Figure 4.10: Tie strength and directed graphs: directionally weighted
Look for: the four nodes with strong ties in Figure 4.9 have been redrawn to show the scenario where the more central nodes (A and B) have higher tie strengths going towards them compared to the strength of the ties between the more central actors and the less central actors (C and D). This might reflect a situation where advice is being given or management information is being provided for reporting purposes.

Figure 4.10 Tie strength and directed graphs: directionally weighted.

settings means that description and classification of the context for projects being compared is important methodologically. An understanding of the project details and the profiles of the actors will provide richness to the SNA data analysis, the absence of which would reduce the value of the analysis. SNA provides us with useful data and significant findings provided that:

- The context for each network study (typically, the project) is classified accurately and the number of possible variations minimised.
- The nodes are described in some detail – the characteristics and their classifications are important and influential for the behaviour of the network.

Software for the Analysis of Networks

Wasserman and Faust (1994) provide mathematical formulae for all SNA measures and examination of these formulae is instructive. Indeed for calculations of network density and actor centrality in networks with fewer than perhaps 50 nodes, the use of a simple calculator is possible and perhaps desirable. Some time spent exploring, analysing and perhaps 'playing' with some simple network data will provide a better understanding of the nature of network data and the value of the basic analytical measures. More experienced analysts and those dealing with large data sets will want to identify appropriate software packages. Many of these packages have the very important benefit of providing a simple means of generating network graphics, as well as the usual matrices and values.

The studies reported in Pryke (2012) used UCINET software (a trial copy of which can be downloaded free at http://www.analytictech.com/ucinet/trial.htm). More recently the CONA team at UCL carrying out network analysis on project organisations has employed Gephi visualisation software (see gephi.github.io), which is free to download. Pryke (2012) listed a selection of software available for the analysis of organisational networks. A step-by-step 'getting started' section was also provided.

Conclusion

This book is intended as a sequel to *Social Network Analysis in Construction* (Pryke, 2012), which gave detailed information on carrying out SNA-based research. The 2012 book focused upon construction because the case studies within that text were construction projects. But the principles within the book are applicable to all project environments and so this most recent offering has widened the discussion to *all* projects. The earlier book gave some background to the origins of social network analysis and its institutional foundations.

The rationalisation of the choice of SNA as a theoretical basis as well as a method is discussed in this chapter, along with some of the problems associated with SNA as applied to project organisations. There is a summary of the main terminology, and those who have already read the previous book (Pryke, 2012) must forgive me for some repetition here. The current book needed to be 'freestanding' and to make sense for the reader who had not read the earlier book.

Network densities and the evolution of thought about which measures of centrality are most appropriate are discussed and I refer to some research by the Centre for Organisational Network Analysis at UCL (http://www.ucl.ac.uk/cona) which was ongoing as this book was drafted.

Finally, there was recognition of the fact that individuals will want to use SNA at varying degrees of abstraction. Some will want to carry out mathematical analysis of network data. Others will want to use network theory as a conceptual framework for the representation and management of projects. Either way, in a world where ever more projects are envisaged, an understanding of context is fundamentally important.

This chapter has hopefully demystified a range of terminology and a method of research which has huge potential for application within the field of project research. Social network analysis enables the researcher to deal with a wide variety of variables using one common method, offering the possibility of more effective comparative study than was previously possible in a field where it could be argued that each project is unique.

SNA provides the project researcher with a rigorous analytical method to deal with a number of the issues confronting an increasingly complex industry associated with increasingly complex projects. Whether we are exploring information flows, knowledge management structures, the operation of risk transfer or contractual hierarchies, SNA as a method provides analysis to a level of accuracy not available to researchers studying project organisations previously. SNA involves no assumptions about hierarchy, which is important and informative when trying to understand how things *really* work in organisations (in our case temporary organisations). The infrequent and relatively recent adoption of the SNA approach in project environments is attributable in part to the complexity of the method. In the past this complexity has acted as a 'barrier to entry' for the average research practitioner or reflective practitioner and may have discouraged many from committing to a study based on SNA. Increasing levels of information are now available to both student and practitioner, enabling wider use of this important analytical approach.

Before embarking upon SNA-based research it is recommended that thought be given to the issues listed above under the heading 'Why choose Social Network Analysis?' A decision should be made at an early stage whether to study networks of *individuals* or networks of *firms*. If in doubt, gather data relating to individuals; the data can always be aggregated manually to produce data relating to firms after data gathering is complete. Disaggregating data relating to firms to produce interpersonal relationships is generally not possible and requires a fresh start in data gathering, which could well result in a loss of goodwill established with the industrial collaborator – a disservice to all those researchers trying to convince firms to collaborate in research projects!

It is hoped that this chapter will encourage more individuals to invest the time in making a start with SNA as a method – the study of actors and their relationships coupled with a very precise means of classification of actor and network attributes and functions provides huge potential for research into project organisations. It is also useful if it helps others to explain and classify phenomena which they observe in a more quantitative sense, using a little of the terminology from the field of network science.

5

Self-Organising Networks in Projects

Introduction

The purpose of this chapter is to explore some 'dangerous assumptions' about the operation of the 'contracting system' and the role of projects and their management within this. I want to make a link between systems failures in the contracting system used to outsource projects (Collet *et al.*, 2005; Winch, 1996) and the formation of networks of relationships between role-holding actors engaged in project organisations. I argue that the uncertainty associated with a number of unrealistic assumptions embedded within the contracting system, particularly where lump-sum contracts are concerned, leads to the formation of networks to manage the uncertainty perceived by each role-holding actor. I further argue, therefore, that we should regard projects as networks of role-holding actors, and by analysing these networks, move toward better management of projects. Toward the end of the chapter some case study material is provided which illustrates the connection between uncertainty and project function-related network configurations.

The establishment of project roles has been identified as an important aspect of successful project management from Tavistock (1966), through Cleland and King's (1975) early work on task responsibility matrices, and more recently the work of Morris (2013), who identified the importance of chains of command, relationships and systems. Authority relationships and routines are important in establishing a successful vehicle for project delivery (Giddens, 1984; Morris, 2013). I will argue that outsourcing, or 'contracting', is not effective in establishing or accurately defining project *network roles*, particularly in the face of high levels of uncertainty associated with the incompleteness embedded in our contracting systems.

Although the choice of procurement is frequently cited as a problem where projects fail during the delivery phase, in fact the 'maturity of project definition' is more important (Morris, 2013). Walker and Pryke (2008, 2009, 2011) investigated the effect that incompleteness (failure to define the project fully in contract documents) had upon financial settlements for completed projects – the incidences of contractual claims and their causes. This extensive piece of research reviewed data associated with contractual disputes in 121 construction projects worldwide, involving a very wide range of contracting arrangements. Each of the sample was selected because of a contractual dispute arising out of uncertainty and a failure to compensate fully. A 'contracting approach' to project procurement and delivery relies on the completion of project design, followed by the definition of project specifications which are then incorporated into contractual documents, followed by delivery within time, cost and specification constraints.

In complex projects, project definition is frequently evolving throughout both pre-contract and post-contract phases (Lewis and Roehrich, 2010). There is a fundamental problem in delivering projects through a contracting system where project definition is not complete at contract bid stage, simply because the contract is based upon incomplete information. Later I argue that an emerging project definition is inevitable in all but the simplest of projects and as project definitions emerge, post-contract, the project actors need to continually review roles and responsibilities, and their interdependencies, as the project is delivered. The open systems that evolve post-contract react to their environments to survive (Burns and Stalker, 2006; Morris, 2013). Morris (2013) contends that size, speed and complexity are important factors in shaping the organisational structures of projects – each factor having an impact on the interdependencies between project actors. Interdependencies are transient and are poorly defined in contract documents (Pryke, 2012) and this is explored in this chapter through reference to research in construction coalitions using social network analysis to study project roles and relationships. Procurement effectively comprises the establishment of a network of *contractual* relationships between *firms*, but project delivery is best observed through the relationships of *individuals* forming transient networks of interdependent relationships during project design and delivery phases (Pryke, 2012).

The aim of this chapter is to explore, among other issues, the relationship between uncertainty and associated incompleteness in the contracting system and suggest that a more useful way to define roles and relationships in projects is by reference to *network roles*.

Many have noted that temporary organisational forms are becoming increasingly prevalent (for example, Pauget and Wald, 2013; Geraldi *et al.*, 2011; Manning, 2005). Indeed the fields of film, software, consulting and construction deal almost entirely with projects (Manning and Sydow, 2011). However, there are clearly differing characteristics between projects in these sectors. Film-making starts with a written story and must deliver a production through a highly creative process. Actors are employed and intensively managed to produce a dramatic spectacle. In contrast to this, some might regard construction as 'routine-based' (Shenhar, 2001; Manning and Sydow, 2011) but this ignores the major challenges associated with moving from project definition (expressed in two-dimensional computer-aided-design files, text files and, more recently, three-dimensional building information modelling) to project delivery in an environment which is unpredictable in terms of working conditions and methods of execution. In complex industrial products and systems, those with responsibility for systems integration tend to collaborate repeatedly with specialised component suppliers (Hobday, 2000). Increasing technical complexity, regardless of project sector, increases the need to access specialist skills and knowledge located at some distance, in terms of network linkages, from the client (Pryke and Badi, 2013). Projects, by their very nature, have a finite period for delivery (for contractual purposes at least) and they are frequently, though not essentially, unique and involve a wide range of project actor types (heterogeneity). Hansich and Wald note that projects frequently lack organisational routines and therefore pose challenges to (project) managers (Hanisch and Wald, 2011). This lack of routines, coupled with complexity arising out of both structure and task, places pressure on what are referred to in this book as 'self-organising' project function-related networks to deal with increased demands for information and coordination (Pauget and Wald, 2013). Role-holding actors[1] in complex projects organise themselves into project function-related networks in response to task complexity, pressures of time and a lack of process definition associated with a role allocated through contractual conditions. Sydow and Staber (2002), in their analysis of German TV-production organisational networks, noted that the network organisational form is a product of 'legally autonomous firms' evolving systems for project delivery – a reminder of the early work by the Tavistock Institute (1966) 'Interdependence and Uncertainty', which identified the contradiction between the *independence* of firms under contract to deliver particular elements of a project and the high levels of *interdependence* that carrying out these activities involves particularly where there is some level of complexity in terms of systems integration. The systems that evolve do so in a regulatory context, almost regardless of the type of project, and are a reflection of past experiences and future expectations in terms of projects (Sydow and Staber, 2002). Networks evolve at different speeds depending on project environment, past experiences with the client and other project actors on previous projects, and reflect firms' experiences during procurement.

As client demands, stakeholder aspirations and technical sophistication increase over time, the transition from procurement of resources through dyadic (two-party) contractual conditions to governance through non-dyadic (multi-party) project delivery networks becomes increasingly difficult to visualise, establish and manage. Using temporary project organisations to deliver large discrete packages of work is increasingly important for many organisations including those that might not traditionally be regarded as project-based. Flexible, project function-orientated networks enable those charged with project delivery (the project manager, or equivalent role title for a particular industry) to accommodate the changing needs of clients and stakeholders, post-contract (Windeler and Sydow, 2001). However, relatively little is known about how the (post-contract design and delivery) networks which function in complex projects are actually established and coordinated (Bechky, 2006).

What Do Project Clients Want?

It is argued that project clients want and seek what Coase referred to as 'completeness' (Coase, 1993; *cf.* Todorova, 2007), even if they do not necessarily identify and articulate such need. Indeed this is implicit in the contracting system, whereby a lump-sum contract is entered into based upon a complete design at tender stage. Some have also argued that those same clients seek, and some would say deserve, flexibility 'post-contract' to make changes to the scope of the works (Windeler and Sydow, 2001), leading to project definitions that are emergent, even post-contract. Clients want completeness pre-contract and an 'open system' (Walker, 2015) approach post-contract. They want the financial certainty that accurate definition of their needs provides and the facility for the project to respond to the changing business, technological and legislative environment in which their organisations operate. It has been argued that clients often suffer from

---

1 A role-holding actor might be an individual or a firm. The point here is that the role is allocated by the contract through which the project is procured. The role-holding actors have to evolve networks through which to exchange information, solve problems, and disseminate knowledge and information to other role-holding actors.

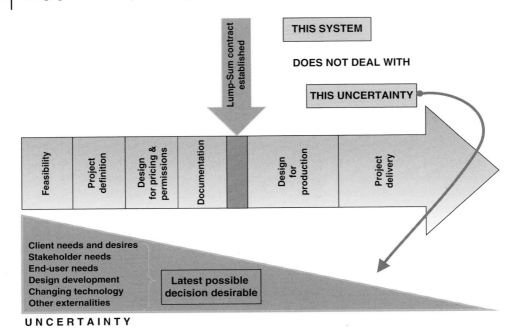

Figure 5.1 Uncertainty in lump-sum contracts. Source: Original, but influenced by Winch (2010).

incompleteness pre-contract, and that they may be unaware of the extent of this incompleteness (see Walker and Pryke, 2009, 2011), leading later to 'claims' for compensation under the terms of the contract, or for breach of contract. This is accompanied by an environment post-contract that clients might regard as a 'closed system' or what some refer to as involving 'premature lock-in' (Rivkin and Siggelkow, 2006; Morris, 2013). At the same time project management research has frequently focused upon the planning and structuring of projects and process-driven approaches to managing projects (Winter *et al.*, 2006; Zwikael and Unger-Aviram, 2010). If we accept that changes to the scope of the project are inevitable post-contract, given the evolving environment in which projects are delivered, then we need to consider the viability of the system that is commonly employed to deliver projects. Figure 5.1 shows a schematic of the stages involved in delivering a project. The client, arguably armed with limited stakeholder awareness, attempts to define the project, using professional advisers to do so.

Project definition is carried out in the knowledge that the project may be completed, for all but the smallest projects, several years in the future. Partial project definition is achieved through a process of 'design for pricing and permissions' (DfPP) and this is just sufficient in detail to achieve the following objectives (Pryke, 2012), explicit or tacit:

- To initiate an iterative design negotiation with an as yet incomplete group of design stakeholders (depending on contract form, many or most of the specialist Tier 2 suppliers and component manufacturers will be yet to be identified)
- To enable calculations of project delivery costs – either by an independent professional services provider directly for the client, or on behalf of an organisation working on a 'with design' basis

- To seek approval related to the regulatory framework applying to that project, sector and geographical location
- To achieve a particular design milestone and in the process to allow professional service providers to claim a proportion of the fee for the project.

Once we have reached a stage where DfPP halts, documents are prepared which reflect the specification and/or performance requirements (depending on procurement route) of the finished project. These documents may be produced under pressure of time and are not always completely accurate (Walker and Pryke, 2009, 2011). Those preparing the documents also have to make judgements about design information that is missing or inaccurate. The final bid document provides a veneer of certainty and completeness that is not always underpinned by the accuracy of those documents (Walker and Pryke, 2009, 2011). The successful bidder takes the risk on the prices but not necessarily the accuracy of the calculations within bid documents sent by the client or their agent, unless a 'with design' approach is adopted. Typically, even where long-term collaborative relationships exist between client and Tier 1 suppliers, a bidding process will occur and a single supplier will be appointed. A lump-sum contract is established based upon a very long list of item prices which reflect the project design at bid stage.

Variations on this theme will depend on the sector in which the project falls and the nature of the project. The point of this overview of the components of this 'contracting system' is that in principle an attempt has been made to define the project and this has been represented graphically and then quantified. We then use this information to appoint an organisation based upon a lump-sum contract. We started with a brief and ended up with a lump-sum contract. But essentially the system of procurement has not procured the finished project as specified – it has procured the *resources to achieve the complete project*. One of the key points that this chapter seeks to make is that the manner in which the resources are organised in the attempt to deliver the project is effectively *invisible* to the client and their professional service providers. The systems, and the networks which constitute these systems, are not identified at bid stage and are not fully understood post-contract. These networks are not, therefore, explicitly managed.

Clients want certainty at tender stage (Potts and Ankrah, 2014; Altshuler and Luberoff, 2003; Jørgensen and Moløkken-Østvold, 2006) and the contract sum is an important 'artefact' in all that follows relating to the project. However, I argue that the process that has led to the formulation of the lump-sum contract is fundamentally flawed. In petrochemical projects, something much closer to 'cost reimbursement' is typically used, and a cost plan showing a provisional quantity of labour drives the financial management of the projects (Merrow, 2011). This avoids the need to try to establish a lump-sum contract, under pressure of time, with insufficiently complete design information.

What clients want post-contract is the ability for their design team to respond to 'context' (Littau *et al.*, 2010; DeFillippi and Arthur, 1998), whether it be physical, economic, social, technical, etc., without the client being disproportionately penalised financially. Although clients may not explicitly request it (although some clients *do* recognise the importance of procuring collaborative relationships with their supply chain), they desire the benefits arising from relationships that continue beyond individual projects between themselves as clients and their Tier 1 service provider, and between their Tier 1 contract winner and the Tier 2 service providers (see also Manning and Sydow, 2007).

In addition, the process of 'recursive constitution' (Windeler and Sydow, 2001) suggests that the project draws upon (inter) organisational practices – sets of rules and resources procured and reproduced by 'knowledgeable agents' – moving from project to project; these lie alongside industry practices based upon industry-specific sets of rules and resources reproduced by knowledgeable agents within a particular industry (Windeler and Sydow, 2001; Spender, 1989). Project networks might be regarded as 'temporary systems' but research in a number of industries has shown that these temporary systems are replicable on subsequent projects through the social networks that constitute the project function delivery systems – see for example, Blair's work on the feature film industry (Blair, 2001), Sieber's work on IT software (Sieber, 1998) and some early work by Stinchcombe and Eccles on construction (Stinchcombe, 1959; Eccles, 1981). Pryke (2012) and Pryke and Smyth (2006) acknowledge the importance of frequency of collaboration on the sustainability of effective project relationships. Social capital can be aggregated between projects if the client avoids adopting procurement approaches that disrupt the process through spot market tendering – that is choosing project coalitions based upon a tendering process with cost as the main selection criteria. What Tier 1 service providers want is to be selected again in the future – 'repeat business', and part of the value that they offer the client is the social capital provided by prior collaborative relationships between client, Tier 1 and Tier 2 (and beyond). Arguably, two important factors influencing the ability of projects to succeed are the continual interruption of project relationships, particularly where clients procure using price-based, competitive tendering, and the 'partial uniqueness and novelty' (Lundin and Söderholm, 1995; Manning and Sydow, 2011) that are inherent in projects.

Dangerous Assumptions

In this section I want to challenge the assumptions that are implicit in the contracting system – where a project is outsourced to a Tier 1 contractor or supplier, through a competitive bidding process – as the project moves from project definition and contract award stage, to project delivery.

Much of the ritualistic behaviour (see for example Spender, 1989) that we see in human behaviour in projects is associated with the achievement of the so-called 'iron triangle' (Barnes, 1988) – the reduction of the definition of satisfactory project delivery to the achievement of specified cost, time and quality. But clients want a little more than they asked for and this is achieved by the project team understanding more about the client and their needs than the client does themselves. This is how 'customer delight' is achieved (Latham, 1994). Implicit in clients' desire for 'customer delight' and, potentially, the failure of project management to deliver this, are the following assumptions:

1) *It is possible to accurately define clients' needs at an early stage, before any visualisation is produced of those needs and desires.*[2] Implicit in the contracting system (where design is frequently not carried out by the Tier 1 contractor) is the

---

2 Please refer to a major piece of research analysing disputes arising out of documentary incompleteness in 121 construction projects associated with failure to define the project accurately pre-tender, as a source for contractual incompleteness. See Walker and Pryke, 2008, 2009, 2011.

assumption that the client can accurately predict their future needs, in the face of environmental uncertainty, and that it is possible to accurately represent this in written and graphical form. In fact, it is quite difficult to understand fully the exact impact of design decisions on the end-user experience, compounding this difficulty. This is a source of uncertainty for clients, project actors and stakeholders. Computer-generated models and 'mock-ups' help, but there is still a source of uncertainty here (see Cherns and Bryant, 1984; Winch, 2010).

2) ***It is possible to very accurately interpret clients' wishes, without any corruption of intention through 'agency' (Aoki et al., 1990), and to represent the physical manifestation of those wishes and desires accurately and unambiguously using CAD (computer-aided design) files and text documents.*** Walker and Pryke (2011) evidenced this incompleteness in construction projects. Each of the individuals in a project coalition can be regarded as being located in a matrix. They are employed by a contractual 'role-holding' firm and are subject to the governance imposed by those formal relationships. Their daily, personal role is derived from a 'project actor' role, as an individual with a function to perform within a network of individuals that contributes to the delivery of the project cited in the document relating to the 'contractual role'. All of the governance in our projects relates to the Y axis of the matrix, and is largely ineffective in influencing the activities of the individual in carrying out their project actor role (see Figure 5.2). So there is 'double jeopardy' in agency terms here (Coase, 1993; Winch, 1989). The individual may or may not be based within the contractual role-holding firm. Their conditions of employment and appraisal may not necessarily relate to project outcomes – requirements and desires articulated in the project contract – and will almost certainly not relate to the individual's *network role*. This individual is then located for part or all of his/her working life, over a fixed period of time (related to the project), in a self-organising network within which s/he must deliver their project actor role. There is very little governance in place for this

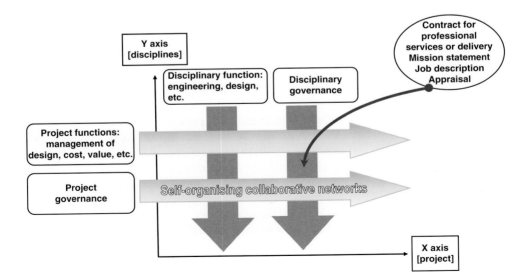

Figure 5.2 Matrix governance.

X-axis matrix role (see Figure 5.2). In fact some of the time the individual will need to carry out network actor roles that do not relate to a project function at all. For example, they may be required to broker relationships between other individuals in the network for the purpose of decision-making.

In summary, a firm employs an individual, a project employs the firm and the project places the individual in a network environment. I argue that governance is light in the project environment and the potential for opportunism and sub-optimal network topography are high. Perhaps there is an argument that building information modelling (BIM) might deal with this lack of governance. The relationship between networks and BIM is explored in Chapter 9.

3) ***Change in project definition is undesirable.*** This assertion is made on the basis that changes in project definition involve bureaucratic procedures and frequently disproportionately high costs because of the nature of the dependent relationship that the client has with the Tier 1 supplier, post-contract. Also, very substantial changes to the project definition post-contract may 'frustrate'[3] the contract entirely (see, for example, 'The radical change in the obligation test', *Davis Contractors v Fareham UDC* [1956] AC 696).

There are mechanisms in the project contract for making changes to the *details* of the work but not fundamental changes to the *nature* of the project. It is argued that, for a client and stakeholders, changes are an inevitable part of a project (other than very short-term, simple projects). Changes, particularly those occurring relatively late in the project delivery programme, are desirable for clients and stakeholders so that:

- End-user needs can be accommodated up to the point of completion of the project (Pryke, 2001, 2014). But the governance imposed by contract documents is at odds with the needs of clients and end-users in this respect.
- The completed project incorporates the latest technological innovations: the programme for appraisal, design, procurement and delivery, typically several years, is at odds with the rapid rate of change in technology, particularly in IT and electrical services.
- Contrary to the idea of the 'iron triangle' (discussed previously), quality is subjective and essentially personal, and its definition evolves over time. Membership of the stakeholder group is also transient.

Davies and Brady (2000) note that projects contain 'routine elements' but are not repeatable as a whole. In fact each project is unique to the extent that most projects do not have the same actors delivering an identical project at the same location and time as a previous project. Human relationships are not repeatable in a literal sense. Yet systems are repeatable within the limitations of the predictability of human behaviour. If projects are to be regarded as successful by clients and stakeholders, they need to operate repeatable project function-related systems, reflected in project network relationships that are replicable between projects. These networks also need to have the flexibility to respond to variation in input from their external project environment, which might include changes in project scope.

---

3 A legal term meaning that the contract has been made impossible to execute, effectively bringing the contract and its obligations to an end.

4) ***It is possible to allocate project actor roles to individuals, through contracts executed by the client with the project actors' employers, that will create temporary communication and information exchange networks that will function to deliver the project effectively without intervention.*** The Tavistock Institute (1966) found that construction projects suffered from poor definition and allocation of roles. Long-term collaboration tends to increase collaborative capabilities, norms and routines (Larson, 1992) and to increase interdependencies between project actors (Manning and Sydow, 2011). Building collaborative capabilities over time is positive in terms of problem-solving abilities and leads to an increased likelihood of reselection for a given collaborative partner. This reinforces the need to manage those relationships to ensure that routines and non-competitive partner selection procedures do not result in complacency and rising costs over time (Pryke, 2012). Sorensen and Waguespack (2006) have observed that film projects with long-term relationships often perform *worse* than those projects using new partners. This contrasts with construction where long-term relationships, provided they are well managed, result in more efficient use of project resources (Pryke, 2012). This difference may be associated with creativity and risk variations between the two sectors.

5) ***There is an assumption that the interdependent project actor roles will be constant over time.*** This occurs because there is no mechanism in contracts for changing these roles. There are mechanisms for dealing with variations under the terms of the contract, in other words changes to specification and scope, but no mechanism for changing actor roles and compensation associated with such changes. Essentially, procurement and the governance associated with these formal contracts within the contractual role-holding firms have to achieve a pattern of human behaviour that will deliver a successful project. These networks are self-defining (although client/contractor contracts and employment contracts have influence, they are not necessarily aligned and may conflict) and self-governing. The project networks function like neural networks – responding to stimuli within the project environment. It is argued that little is known about how these networks evolve and decay (with the possible exception of construction projects, see Pryke, 2008, 2012, 2014) and very little has been done by industry so far[4] to identify and manage these networks.

Implications if these Assumptions are Incorrect

The lack of knowledge about how project function-related networks evolve and decay is, arguably, problematic for successful project delivery. The contracting system (Collet *et al.*, 2005; Winch, 2000) and indeed the various codes of practice (APM (Morris and Pinto, 2004) and PMBok (PMI, 2008), for example) envisage a linear process of client brief, design, measurement and quantification followed by a price-based bid and contract award. From this point onwards the assumption is made that procurement has defined the roles of the project actors in a way that will be sufficient and that will endure to completion of the project. Iterative scope development is preferable to 'design lock-in' in terms of delivering customer delight and this is possible through a move from

---

4 Case Studies 1, 2 and 3 are, however, an example where a UK infrastructure client *has* recognised the value in understanding the networks that deliver the systems that execute projects.

transactional to relational procurement and project management (Womack and Jones, 1996; Salem and Zimmer, 2005). But whereas lean principles may flourish in a volume-manufacturing environment (Hines *et al.*, 2004), large complex projects procured using lump-sum contractual arrangements (where a lump sum is bid for a specified project) rather than cost-reimbursement approaches (where the project is not defined before a basis for payment is agreed) are far more problematic. Clients are loath to enter financially 'open-ended' arrangements, preferring the perceived certainty of the lump-sum contract. And yet this certainty is often illusory in reality, for reasons discussed above.

The project is delivered by a network of individuals with reference to the contract documents, but independently in many senses; the systems for project delivery comprise iterative information exchange relationships in transient network environments; the systems do not relate to linear processes; the networks and associated relationships are transient for the duration of the project. The networks supporting these systems need to be flexible and adaptive.

Networks and Uncertainty

I started with the hypothesis that clients want completeness and the associated certainty at tender stage, with the flexibility of an open system to manage the project post-contract, which I refer to here as (C + O). It was suggested that the client may in fact experience the opposite state of affairs – incompleteness at contract award and a closed system in project delivery, with what Morris (2013) calls 'premature lock-in'. Incompleteness at contract stage followed by a closed-system approach post-contract might be referred to as 'I + C'. The 'contracting system', regardless of sector, is imbued with information asymmetries and to some extent the enterprises involved with contracting *function through those asymmetries*. I argue here that managing projects by monitoring outputs and their timeliness and capital cost, along with a possibly subjective measure of quality, is insufficient. Given this, I also argue that the design and post-contract activities of the project coalition comprise a self-organised, asymmetry-resolving network of role-holding actors seeking to reduce transaction costs within the parameters imposed by contractual conditions linking contractual role-holding firms. Networks of project actors evolve as a response to the need to process information in an efficient manner, in a rather uncertain and poorly structured environment.

Does it Matter How We Conceptualise the Project?

The way in which we conceptualise the project is important because it will influence the way in which we attempt to manage the project. Project management has evolved from traditional tools and techniques (see, for example, Koskela, 1992, 2000; Turner, 1999; Turner and Müller, 2003; Pryke and Smyth, 2006); these approaches tend to have a production orientation arising out of a scientific management ethos. Functional management arguably includes Morris's work with Pinto (2004, for example) on strategic front-end and programme strategies and those strategies based upon long-term collaborative relationships and supply chain management (Green *et al.*, 2005). Winch's information processing model (Winch, 2010) resonates with many practitioners and is a theme underpinning some of the discussion in this chapter. These more recent approaches have evolved toward a greater consideration of the importance of the behavioural dimensions of projects. The dynamics of these relationships were recognised in Pryke and Smyth's 'relationship approach' to project management (Pryke and Smyth, 2006). Pryke and Smyth stressed the importance of achieving an understanding of relationships between people in projects and the relationships that those people have within their employing organisations. But an analytical method is needed for projects that deals with actor interdependence and such a method provides a level of detail beyond traditional analytical methods, enabling study of the 'non-linear, complex, iterative and interactive process' that projects constitute (Pryke, 2004a). Social network analysis enables evolving procurement and project management approaches to be evaluated and compared quantitatively in a qualitative context. In particular, SNA can be used to study a range of project management relationships comparatively. Pryke (2004a, 2012) suggests that a greater understanding of procurement and project delivery and the relationships between them is afforded through comparative study using SNA of contractual relationships, financial incentives and information exchange.

Procurement Through Markets and Hierarchies; Project Design and Delivery Through Networks

We acquire the resources to design and deliver a project – along with the expectation that an appropriate set of systems will be established – through a mixture of market and hierarchy, depending upon the extent of long-term collaborative relationships that the client, their professional service providers and contractors have established. There is an expectation that the governance structure will deal with uncertainty arising out of bounded rationality (Williamson, 1975). The governance associated with the Y axis of the matrix (Figure 5.2) is, however, *remedy* driven rather than *solution* driven. By this I mean that contracts do not commonly deal with relationships and systems – project contracts tend to set out contractual remedies relating to failure rather than methods by which successful projects might be delivered. Powell (1990) has asserted that opportunism is mitigated by 'authority relations' and the stronger identification of project actors through the existence of a common cause. But in a project environment the common cause is associated with project management (X axis of the matrix); it is not associated with procurement (Y axis). In a project environment the 'emotional co-location' for project actors is, or should be, with the *project*, which I argue has quite weak authority relations. Industry best practice comprises a programme of routine meeting cycles, with designated membership and reporting destinations (see, for example, London 2013 Olympic Park protocols cited in Brady and Davies, 2014: Figure 4, p. 32). So this approach delivers resources to a specification, but constitutes relatively weak governance for integrating and managing those resources effectively to deliver the project. Therefore, bounded rationality and opportunism need to be dealt with by the project networks. It is an interesting point that 'complementariness' (the extent to which project role-holding actors complement each other's skills, knowledge and likely behaviours) and the potential for reciprocity (willingness and desire to create and respond to indebtedness in a network) are both very important to networks (Powell, 1990), yet we do not seek or select against these criteria in procurement or indeed in staff recruitment within firms which service projects. We need to create 'balanced networks' (Easley and Kleinberg, 2010) – those in which there is a tendency for all actors to engage in reciprocal exchange of some sort. In many projects this exchange is information-based.

Powell and Giannella (2010) argue that networks are created by individuals in an organisational environment to, inter alia:

- Minimise transaction costs
- Guarantee access to critical resources (in the case of complex projects this might be information, for example)
- Guarantee access to critical skills.

It is argued here that the uncertainty arising out of incompleteness in all but the simplest of projects creates a need for individual role-holding actors (RHAs) to form networks as a means of designing and/or delivering projects. RHAs need to exchange information in an environment where the contract under which they are employed inaccurately defines the project and under circumstances where the activities involved in designing and delivering the project are not adequately described. The RHAs are essentially trying to reduce their transaction costs, where resources can be expensive to acquire. Powell and Giannella (2010) also look at the conditions that enable networks to form:

- 'Know-how' – Powell and Giannella argue that networks are more likely to form where there is diversity and intensity in knowledge-based activity and exchange of distinctive competencies.
- 'Demand for speed' – all projects are time constrained by a statement of contract period. In some cases there is competition at bid stage on project completion times.
- 'Trust' – Powell and Giannella argue that networks are more likely to occur where individual actors trust each other and that (actor) homogeneity is a factor here.

Project procurement deals with the acquisition of resources and the allocations of roles and responsibilities within a specified cost and programme framework. Yet the detail of how the project actors will deal with the high levels of interdependence and the demands of an evolving project definition within that framework is not, typically, well specified in procurement documents. The project actors need to acquire, process and disseminate information themselves within the context of uncertainty and an emergent project definition. Under these circumstances project actors will self-organise information exchange networks in order to deliver their project function with a minimum of iterations. Pressure of time coupled with the need to carry out a role in an uncertain environment precipitates these networks – the greater the time pressure and the higher the level of uncertainty the denser the networks.

There is a pressing need for self-organising networks to establish what Thompson (2003) refers to as a 'mutual orientation'. It is suggested that mutual orientation – the focusing of a group of individuals on common, project-orientated goals – is established through complementarity and accommodation (reciprocity in exchanges and a desire to help others) and this is of fundamental importance to the ability of any project team to deliver 'customer delight'. I argue here that this mutual orientation is currently not managed in any way and its failure to establish may have a detrimental effect on the ability of the project coalition to successfully design and deliver a project.

Summary and Conclusions

It is suggested that research has shown a lack of completeness in contractual documents (Walker and Pryke, 2008, 2009, 2011) and that this incompleteness is an inevitable outcome given the erroneous assumptions that we make in implementing a contracting system to outsource project procurement and delivery. More successful projects might be delivered if there is a focus upon the networks of relationships that role-holding actors establish in response to the uncertainty associated with incompleteness in projects.

A barrier to the provision of 'customer delight' arises out of the uncertainty associated with the transition from the procurement of resources to project delivery and employment of those resources in multi-functional, multi-disciplinary environments where there are low levels of project definition. The five 'dangerous assumptions' question whether we take sufficient account of the difficulty in defining future needs and accurately expressing and evaluating them for the purposes of forming a lump-sum contract; it was posited that scope change post-contract was good and *not* bad, but that it was problematic and that role allocation expressed in functional terms but delivered in a multi-disciplinary network environment is a challenge for the project coalition.

In this context of erroneous assumptions and pressure of time on project actors to connect and collaborate, particularly for information gathering, processing and dissemination, I suggest that self-organising project delivery networks form. I argue that the formation of these networks is inevitable and the analysis of these networks will help to overcome some of the effects of the erroneous assumptions that are made in project procurement and delivery. The matrix provides a reference point for procurement comprising contractual, function-related governance in the vertical or Y axis and project management in the form of self-organising project delivery networks in the horizontal or X axis (see Figure 5.2).

Project definition (front-end), procurement, management of post-contract implementation and 'people' are all undoubtedly important in successful projects. Project definition is difficult and the assumption implicit within the contracting system is that it is achievable prior to bid stage and can, and possibly should, remain fixed or as static as possible. Yet this is problematic in delivering real 'delight' to project clients. Complex temporary organisational networks of relationships constitute a form of governance acting as a substitute for more formal organisational governance. Understanding the formation of these network relationships and the roles that actors acquire through these networks is important for the delivery of project-related functions. High levels of uncertainty in the project context precipitate dense information exchange networks as the project actors attempt to manage uncertainty and carry out the roles imposed by the project networks (Pryke, 2012) as well as those roles outlined in the contract documents. The transition between procurement through dyadic contractual relationships and delivery through network-based systems is important. Managing post-contract implementation is also important without doubt and yet I argue that we know relatively little about how a large group of heterogeneous people 'implement' our projects. The networks that they create in order to implement the project are subject to very little design, monitoring or control by the client or their professional advisers. It is argued that these largely invisible networks hold the key to reducing uncertainty and improving completeness in our projects.

Clients find it difficult to predict exactly how their completed projects will be used several years hence and desire the flexibility to make changes late in the implementation phase; late changes have the potential to add disproportionately large additional value (benefit to client and end-users) to the project but our project role-holding actors must try to accommodate uncertainty created by the client and others, and make a profit from providing a service. Accurate role allocation is difficult and the uncertainty in task definition for each role-holding actor, in the context of an ambiguous project definition, leads the project coalition members, as individuals, to form themselves into networks and clusters within networks to deliver the project functions that are necessary for project design and delivery.

This chapter has discussed the proposition that routinely in our projects we procure resources and that the individuals that comprise those human resources sit within a matrix that is governed hierarchically (Figure 5.2) – Y-axis governance is formalised through mission statements, job descriptions, appraisals and dyadic contractual arrangements between the contractual role-holding firms and the client. Yet X-axis governance is less formalised; *outputs* are defined in contract documents but the *processes* needed to achieve the outputs are designed, established and maintained by the actors themselves within the networks that are formed. These post-contract delivery networks are 'self-organising'.

Powell's (1990) work helps us to make the link between hierarchies and networks and Nohria and Eccles (1992) reinforce the rationale behind choosing networks as a means of conceptualising the activity of the role-holding actors – the individuals who hold roles related to the delivery of design and project management functions. It is argued that RHAs form networks to minimise the transaction costs of fulfilling their role in an environment of uncertainty and ambiguity. They also form networks (after Powell, 1990) to guarantee access to critical resources, which in the case of projects is information – they form networks to gain access to the information that they need to deliver their roles in a manner that is timely and that provides a profit to their employer. Finally, the network enables a very diverse group of RHAs to engage with a wide group of others in order to gain access to critical skills, in a highly interdependent environment. The desire for 'know-how' and the pressure of time enables or compels the formation of networks and yet the lack of homogeneity among our RHAs means that trust is more elusive than it might otherwise be and the network intuitively seeks mutual orientation through reciprocity and the discouragement of opportunism.

There is limited research on the examination and analysis of these self-organising project networks. This chapter (and to a lesser extent, the previous chapter) sought to make the following points specifically in relation to self-organising project networks:

- Self-organising project networks form at the beginning of the project delivery phase in response to uncertainty about sources of information and roles and responsibilities. Clusters form which reflect the uncertainty perceived by the role-holding actors – these clusters or communities have no contractual status but are fundamentally important to the delivery of the project – problem-solving is an important self-organising project function.
- Density of networks is a function of the levels of uncertainty prevailing and the condition is transient. Dense networks form to deal with high levels of uncertainty, for example, where the project is not defined adequately at delivery stage.

- Where previous collaborative relationships do not exist, the achievement of high levels of network density may need to be facilitated by the client or their project manager.
- Some actors create prominent roles for themselves within their networks which are dysfunctional and not helpful for project delivery. Case Study 2, Chapter 12, deals with this in more detail. The identification and management of these actors is essential for effective project organisations.
- Despite the presumptions supporting lump-sum contracting procedures, some projects are incomplete contractually, requiring dense information networks to compensate.
- Experienced clients deal with risk by dealing directly with specialist Tier 2 suppliers. They manage Tier 2 risk effectively and these direct connections enable knowledge transfer between client and Tier 2.
- The transformation from dyadic contractual relationship to complex information exchange networks is self-organising. Facilitating the formation and evolution of these networks would be beneficial to our projects.
- It is suggested that in future it would be valuable to consider personality traits relating to network roles when recruiting project-based staff. At present this does not appear to be a consideration. Chapter 7 returns to this topic in more detail.

Research and practice needs to move forward to provide a much better understanding of the self-organising networks that evolve and decay and through which the role-holding actors organise and facilitate the design and delivery of projects. The hard tools and techniques of project management respond to basic cost, time and quality requirements – but delivering 'delight' to project clients may increasingly focus upon understanding and managing the self-organising, largely invisible, transient, interactive networks that solve problems, allocate and modify transient network roles, disseminate information and ultimately deliver the project. At present we do not design these networks; we do not even facilitate their formation and evolution; we do not employ project actors whose profiles and behaviour relate to their network roles rather than their functional roles. The shift from a focus on project-based firms to project-based relationships and their management (Manning, 2005) is overdue. Having the means to visualise, analyse and communicate the nature of, and value embedded within, these relationships is important to the way in which we must manage our projects in the future.

Finally, I suggest that project organisations will not so much change to *network organisations* but rather that *the way in which organisations are conceptualised by those whose responsibility it is to manage needs to change*. If those charged with managing projects understand their behaviour and role in the context of the networks in which they are involved, if they recognise that procurement is the beginning of a relationship between firms and individuals and that the value created for clients is derived from the human capital within those relationships – then we have the opportunity to observe, analyse and move toward a situation where contracts reflect networks of relationships rather than dyadic relationships, and project actors are assigned *network* functions rather than solely *project* functions. In this way we shall be able to more easily replicate effective project team configurations and actor behaviour and design interventions for managing networks delivering projects in a way that has not been possible to date.

In later chapters I will look at the findings of some research carried out with a major infrastructure project management organisation in London by the Centre for Organisational Network Analysis at University College London (CONA@UCL). This research studies the formation, structure and classification of self-organising networks in the context of a major engineering project (see Chapters 10–13).

6

Game Theory and Networks

Introduction

Project actors are formally allocated roles through the governance mechanisms associated with their employment with a firm within the project coalition and the contracts to which those firms are party – these are referred to here as 'Y-axis roles', as per the matrix diagram in Chapter 5 (see Figure 5.2). Project actors also acquire considerably more roles relating to their *network* functions – the behaviours that they need to adopt in order to successfully operate within a network environment and to play their part in delivering a project – these are referred to here as 'X-axis roles'. On this latter point, the actors will need, for example, to make connections and repair 'structural holes' in the network to enable effective communication. Individuals and project actors hold complementary and contradictory roles and hold a transient nodal position in relation to all other actors in the network. One of the themes which is recurrent throughout this book is the relative permanence assumed in the contractual allocation of roles – the Y-axis roles are allocated through contract and those contract conditions place emphasis on outputs and remedies for non-compliance – but those documents place less emphasis on processes and systems, the 'how' of delivering excellent projects. So when the individuals as actors transition from procured resources to project function deliverers – through the networks that start to evolve as transition occurs – they need to start making decisions about how they behave as *network actors*, alongside their project roles.

In simple terms, project actors need to make decisions as to how, for example, they see their prominence in the communication networks. Is there an ambition to develop prominence, perhaps to pursue individual personal objectives? Conversely, is there an ambition to reduce prominence in some networks? To become less well connected and become part of an isolated subgroup or cluster? Or indeed to become completely isolated (an isolate)? Individuals will also have to make decisions about who to connect to and who deliberately not to connect to. They will also have to make decisions about speed of response to others and the quality of the ties that they establish. These decisions relate to our own views about other actors and the strategies that they adopt as network actors. An understanding of game theory is useful at this point. Essentially, we are all 'gaming' on a minute-by-minute basis as part of our network actor roles and as an integral part of our decision-making. The construction project provides an environment where a relentless high-volume stream of decisions are made, as an

Managing Networks in Project-Based Organisations, First Edition. Stephen Pryke.
© 2017 John Wiley & Sons Ltd. Published 2017 by John Wiley & Sons Ltd.

integral part of project design or delivery. When I turn to the case study material in later chapters (10–13), I will discuss how these problem-solving activities are prominent features of our projects and yet are not prominent in the terms and conditions of contract under which we engage project resources (contractors and consultants). One of the challenges of decision-making in projects is that the information required to enable good decision-making is frequently incomplete. Chapter 5 explores some of the reasons for this incompleteness. Walker and Pryke (2008, 2009, 2011) have presented findings relating to the impact of incompleteness upon construction projects. Construction has survived thus far on a mixture of optimistic and simplified deterministic decision-making, combined with typically high levels of industry/sector-specific experience. Catastrophes may be avoided but optimisation is accidental rather than a strategic goal.

Game theory is rooted in economics and comes complete with quantitative metrics. Some may find the quantitative aspects rather subjective – perhaps finding the assumptions about complete knowledge and the focus on dyadic or small cluster games unrealistic. The principles of game theory are, however, important in understanding individuals' behaviour and effectiveness in networks, and how some networks function well while others are slow or dysfunctional in some way.

To Begin: Some History

The first recorded discussion about game theory occurred in 1713 (Peldschus *et al.*, 2010). It was referred to in a letter written by James Waldegrave which alluded to the idea that a competitive, two-person game (in this case a game of cards) featured best strategies for each player, based upon complete information on both sides about the intentions and preferences of each party. In the two hundred years that followed, some refinement of these basic concepts evolved. Borel (1921), von Neumann (1928) and Luce and Raiffa (1957) focused upon the conflicting preferences of the players and the implications for the game of these conflicting preferences. Von Neumann and Morgenstern (cited in Leonard, 1995) looked into the implications for the game of one player's imperfect knowledge in relation to the other parties' intentions. There are assumptions about consistency of behaviour and rationality that some might find surprising. Early theory development focused upon two-player scenarios but as game theory developed, attention turned to larger groups of players. Luce and Raiffa's (1957) work dealt with games comprising an infinite number of players and perhaps this is analogous with the project scenario – particularly the very large project. This piece of work also established the idea of the 'zero-sum' game, where an individual player can only benefit at the expense of another player or players.

By the 1970s game theorists had turned their attention to the development of logarithmic normalisation[1] methods (see, for example, Zavadskas and Turskis, 2008;

---

1 Decisions made in complex environments often lack 'reach'. Decisions are made on a conveniently small sample of data and this is particularly relevant to construction and engineering projects. Normalisation of criteria is used in complex decisions to take account of the range of different units related to various relevant data.

Meszek, 2007). Peldschus *et al.* (2010), unusually, looked at the construction project and focused upon 'equilibrium' in games – a situation where each player understands accurately the way in which others behave in a game and no player can benefit by changing strategies while the strategies of others remain constant. See also the work of Annamdas and Rao (2009) and Aumann *et al.* (2011). A number of game theorists have concentrated on the construction project,[2] a sample of which is shown in Table 6.1.

What is a Game?

The relevance of game theory to this discussion of projects and their management is that game theory looks at decision-making in the context of the decisions of others. Much of what we refer to in project management theory ignores the important interdependency of decision-making. This is surprising since we have been talking about interdependency in projects since the early work of the Tavistock Institute (Higgin and Jessop, 1965; Tavistock Institute, 1966). The intention is to look at game theory in the context of interpersonal relationships initially but to apply it to coalition members as firms later in the chapter. There is some mathematics associated with game theory, and this can be quite subjective (context-dependent), but let this not detract from the importance and relevance of the *principles* of game theory to network management and in particular the relevance to the discussion about projects as networks of relationships.

An example will illustrate the principles of game theory. We start with an example relating to two students making decisions about their strategies toward course assessment. Looking at Box 6.1, we can see that each student has to decide upon a strategy at the outset. They do this in the absence of information about the behaviour of the other student. Each needs to decide whether to prepare for the exam or the team presentation. It is important to take a view about the actions of the other individual because greater marks are delivered where there is collaboration. But if one decides to work on the presentation, providing a higher mark for both students on the presentation (because the mark is a shared mark), then the non-collaborator gets a higher average mark than the collaborator. Box 6.1 describes a very simple two-party – or perhaps we might call it *dyadic* – game.

The essential elements of a 'game' are:

- There is more than one participant or 'player' interacting in a social environment
- Each player has a choice of behaviours or 'strategies'
- There is a compensation to each player for the strategy chosen and these are normally expressed arithmetically
- The compensation or 'payoff' is dependent on the strategy chosen by an individual, in the context of the strategies chosen by other players. This interdependency is fundamental to the operation and outcome of the game.

---

2 Excluding road building and property research. I have also excluded those articles not published in English (solely because this book is published in English) and articles more than ten years old at the time of writing.

Table 6.1 Game theory applied to construction projects.

Author(s)	Date of publication	Title
Antucheviciene, J. and Zavadskas, E.K.	2008	Modelling multidimensional redevelopment of derelict buildings. *International Journal of Environment and Pollution*, 35 (2–4), 331–344.
Banaitiene, N., Banaitis, A., Kaklauskas, A. and Zavadskas, E.K.	2008	Evaluating the life cycle of a building: A multivariant and multiple criteria approach. *Omega-International Journal of Management Science*, 36 (3), 429–441.
Brauers, W.K.M., Zavadskas, E.K., Turskis, Z. and Vilutienė, T.	2008	Multi-objective contractor's ranking by applying the MOORA method. *Journal of Business Economics and Management*, 9 (4), 245–255.
Gajzler, M.	2008	Hybrid advisory systems and the possibilities of its usage in the process of industrial flooring repairs. *Proceedings of the 25th International Symposium on Automation and Robotics in Construction ISARC – 2008 (Vilnius 26–29 June)*, E.K. Zavadskas, A. Kaklauskas, M.J. Skibniewski (eds), 459–464.
Ginevičius, R., Podvezko, V. and Raslanas, S.	2008	Evaluating the alternative solutions of wall insulation by multi-criteria methods. *Journal of Civil Engineering and Management*, 14 (4), 217–226.
Hajdasz, M.	2008	Modelling and simulation of monolithic construction processes. *Technological and Economic Development of Economy*, 14 (4), 478–491.
Janusz, L. and Kapliński, O.	2006	The application of multi-factor modelling LITCAC in the organisation of assembly work of flexible corrugated steel structures. *Technological and Economic Development of Economy*, 12 (3), 195–199.
Kapliński, O.	2008	Usefulness and credibility of scoring methods in construction industry. *Journal of Civil Engineering and Management*, 14 (1), 21–28.
Karłowski, A. and Pasławski, J.	2008	Monitoring of construction processes in the variable environment. *Technological and Economic Development of Economy*, 14 (4), 503–517.
Mickaityte, A., Zavadskas, E.K., Kaklauskas, A. and Tupenaite, L.	2008	The concept model of sustainable buildings refurbishment. *International Journal of Strategic Property Management*, 12 (1), 53–68.
Pasławski, J.	2008	Flexibility approach in construction process engineering. *Technological and Economic Development of Economy*, 14 (4), 518–530.
Peldschus, F.	2008	Experience of the game theory application in construction management. *Technological and Economic Development of Economy*, 14 (4), 531–545.
Peldschus, F.	2008	Multi-attribute decisions in construction. *Transformation in Business and Economics*, 7 (2), 163–165.

Table 6.1 (Continued)

Author(s)	Date of publication	Title
Peldschus, F.	2008	Experience of game theory application in construction management. *Technological and Economic Development of Economy*, 14(4): 531–545.
Peldschus, F., Zavadskas, E.K., Turkis, Z. and Tamosaiteiene, J.	2010	Sustainable assessment of construction sites by applying game theory. *Inzinerine Ekonomika – Engineering Economics*, 21 (3), 223–236.
Peldschus, F. and Zavadskas, E.K.	2005	Fuzzy matrix games multi-criteria model for decision-making in engineering. *Informatica*, 16 (1), 107–120.
Reichelt, B. and Peldschus, F.	2005	The application of multi-criteria decision analysis (MCDA) in risk management of civil engineering and environmental engineering projects. *Foundations of Civil and Environmental Engineering*, 6, 159–163.
Sarka, V., Zavadskas, E.K., Ustinovičius, E.S. and Ignatavičius, C.	2008	System of project multi-criteria decision synthesis in construction. *Technological and Economic Development of Economy*, 14 (4), 546–565.
Thiel, T.	2008	Decision aiding related to maintenance of buildings: Technical, economic and environmental aspects. *International Journal of Environment and Pollution*, 34 (2/3/4), 158–170.
Turskis, Z., Zavadskas, E.K. and Peldschus, F.	2009	Multi-criteria optimisation system for decision-making in construction design and management. *Inzinerine Ekonomika – Engineering Economics*, 1, 7–17.
Ustinovichius, L., Zavadskas, E.K., Migilinskas, D., Malewska, A., Nowak, P. and Minasowicz, A.	2006	Verbal analysis of risk elements in construction contracts. *Lecture Notes in Computer Science*, 4101, 295–302.
Zavadskas, E.K., Peldschus, F., Ustinovičius, L. and Turkis, Z.	2004	*Game Theory in Building Technology and Management.* Technika, Vilnius (published in Lithuanian).
Zavadskas, E.K.	2008	History and evolving trends of construction colloquia. *Technological and Economics Development of Economy*, 14 (4), 578–592.
Zavadskas, E.K. and Antucheviciene, J.	2007	Multiple criteria evaluation of rural building's regeneration alternatives. *Building and Environment*, 42, 436–451.
Zavadskas, E. and Kaklauskas, A.	1991	Automated multivariant design of buildings, multi-purpose comprehensive evaluation and selection of the most efficient versions. Aalborg University, Aalborg Universitetscenter, Aalborg.
Zavadskas, E.K. and Kaklauskas, A.	2008	The model for Lithuanian construction industry development. *Transformations in Business and Economics*, 7 (1), 152–168.

Box 6.1 Game theory example: Study decisions. Adapted from Easley and Kleinberg, 2010: 140.

A student has two pieces of assessment to deal with: an examination and a team presentation. They are both due on the same day (tomorrow). It is not possible to deal with both the presentation and the examination in the time available, so the student must choose one task over the other. We also have to assume, for the purposes of the illustration of game theory, that there are accurate predictions for the marks that would be achieved by the student in each task. Given that students submit a number of pieces of work during their programmes this is not an unreasonable assumption. The presentation will be undertaken with another student. Here are the predicted marks for three scenarios:

Scenario 1: Students A and B study for exam but not presentation

	Presentation	Exam	Average mark per student
Student A	84	92	88
Student B	84	92	88

In the case of the exam, if Student A studies s/he will achieve 92; if s/he does not study, 80 is predicted. The same marks are predicted for Student B. In the case of the presentation two students are involved. If both students study a mark of 100 will be achieved. If one student studies but the other does not, 92 will be achieved. If neither student works for the presentation a mark of 84 will be awarded to both students.

Scenario 2: Student A studies for the exam; B studies for presentation

	Presentation	Exam	Average mark per student
Student A	92	92	92
Student B	92	80	86

Scenario 3: Students A and B study for the presentation only

	Presentation	Exam	Average mark per student
Student A	100	80	90
Student B	100	80	90

Each student has to decide whether to put their efforts into the exam or presentation without consulting the other student beforehand. Once they make their respective decisions Scenario 1 achieves 176 marks in total, 2 delivers 178 and 3 delivers 180. So collaboration is better overall, but concentrating on the exam is better if an individual student suspects that the other student will not collaborate on the presentation. The student who concentrates on the exam whilst their partner works on the presentation scores the highest mark, but the yield over the pair is not maximised. If both students concentrate on the exam because they believe that their partners will not work on the presentation the total yield of marks is at the minimum.

Many of the examples described in the game theory literature relate to games with two players. This is for simplicity of explanation and accessibility for the novice. Some examples of more complex games are:

- Tennis players deciding whether to serve to the left or right side of the court
- The only bakery in town offering a discounted price on pastries just before it closes
- Employees deciding how hard to work when the boss is away
- An artisan rug seller deciding how quickly to lower his price when haggling with a tourist
- Rival drug firms investing in a race to successfully apply for a patent on a new drug
- An e-commerce auction company learning which features to add to its website by trial and error
- Property developers guessing when a given area or neighbourhood will commence the process of gentrification, resulting in price rises ahead of the markets in surrounding areas
- Rail commuters deciding which route to work will be quickest when there are signal failures on a given rail route
- Airline workers hustling to get a plane away from the gate on time
- MBAs deciding what their degree will signal to prospective employers (and whether quitting after the first year of their two-year programme to join a dot-com startup signals courage or stupidity)
- People bidding for goods on eBay.

Adapted from Camerer, 2003

The majority of games that are played out in the project environment involve more than two players and consequently are also potentially complicated. Table 6.1. (as distinct from Box 6.1) provides some indication of the complexity of the application of game theory in the construction environment.

Key Assumptions

What assumptions need to be made when considering how players decide on their own strategy? Consider the following (based upon Myerson, 1991, and Easley and Kleinberg, 2010):

1) The calculation of the so called 'payoff' for each player must accurately reflect the interests of the player. The assumption tends to be made in discussions about game theory that each player is solely self-interested. But for our discussion of self-interest in the context of game theory we hope for more than this from the players. Project actors are paid to perform a range of project functions. This financial incentive sits alongside the payoff from multiple project-focused games.
2) We assume that each player has complete and accurate knowledge about the game and the environment in which it is being played. Each player does not, however, know in advance about the behavioural decisions that others will make.

3) We assume that the players know in advance who the other players are. In the project environment, some protocols (competitive tendering for example) require that players do *not* know who the other players are. In construction, players go to great lengths to discover the identity of the other players.[3]

4) Game theory in environments where there exist low levels of knowledge about structure and payoff for other players is developing into a separate field in its own right – see the work of John Harsanyi for example (Harsanyi, 2004, cited in Easley and Klienberg, 2010).

5) We assume that each player chooses strategies that maximise their payoff, in relation to the beliefs that they have about the behaviour of other players. The game theorists regard any other sort of behaviour as irrational.

6) Finally, we assume that each player is successful in selecting the strategy that they prefer – they are not prevented from selecting their preferred strategy.

(Myerson, 1991; Easley and Kleinberg, 2010)

Point 5 above is important in the context of managing projects. How do individuals engage with a large and diverse network of actors? For networks to be effective in delivering a range of project functions, individuals' behaviour must exhibit more than consideration of maximising their own payoff. Elsewhere I also discuss the destructive effect of competitiveness in networks. Myerson (1991) and Owen (1995) refer to *competitive* game theory and *non-competitive* or *collaborative* game theory.

Non-cooperative game theory deals with the strategic choices made by players when in a network of competing players. The Nash equilibrium (Basar and Olsder, 1999), to which I return later, helps to explain how these non-cooperative games are resolved. Cooperative game theory, however, studies the behaviour of rational players when they collaborate routinely. Myerson (1991) refers to the formation of 'cooperative coalitions'.

Most leading game theory research (Myerson, 1991; Basar and Olsder, 1999; Owen, 1995, for example) focuses upon non-cooperative or competitive games. Cooperative or collaborative game theory provides a theoretical framework and some tools for the analysis of networks of actors (or 'players' in the context of the game theory literature) when those rational players cooperate. Cooperative games involve the formation of coalitions (Myerson, 1991) that can strengthen a player's position in a game but also, perhaps more importantly in this discussion about projects, focuses on outcomes that optimise information dissemination, decision-making and problem-solving. Cooperation therefore is an important attribute of network behaviour and can have a dramatic effect in improving the performance of those networks (La and Anantharam, 2003; Han and Liu, 2008; Mathur *et al.*, 2008) and the performance of the projects based upon those networks. But establishing consistent cooperative behaviour in large complex networks has to be done with consideration of efficiency (Saad *et al.*, 2009) and fairness. The framework of collaborative game theory potentially provides a structure

---

3 This ranges from subscribing to agencies that collect and disseminate information about tender lists to all bidders included on a given tender list, to simply contacting local suppliers for items specified in the bid documents to see which other organisations in the area have also expressed an interest in those items. Both practices in themselves fall short of price rigging. But the information provides the potential for unethical bidding behaviour. Unfortunately those organising bidding on behalf of clients sometimes fail to promptly communicate the information that bidders need to run their businesses effectively. As a result the bidders resort to these information-seeking activities.

for designing communication networks that are fair and sustainable over the period of a large project. One of the important themes for this book on managing networks is the transience of project relationships. Projects move through various phases and within those phases need to deal with changing tempos and priorities, on a day-by-day or perhaps hourly basis. So flexibility and adaptability are important in the sustainability of appropriate and effective network relationships over the duration of the project.

Benefits of Applying Game Theory to Project Networks

- Adopting a game theory framework enables investigation of the adaptations needed in a network as it moves toward some form of steady state. In fact projects move quickly between tasks and phases and adaptation is almost constant. But the pursuit of some form of stability is desirable, in the interest of maintaining an environment to enable accurate and consistent decision-making.
- Decisions made by individual project actors may reflect future or past decisions by other actors – either anticipatory decisions or retaliatory decisions. The perhaps anticipatory enabling and facilitating decisions potentially promote collaborative behaviour. Retaliatory decisions are always undesirable and destructive. Game theory might help us to identify and deal with this second category of strategy.
- Incentive mechanisms (Srivastava *et al.*, 2005), known as 'mechanism design' in game theory circles, and their design are important. Leading independent, self-interested human beings toward behaviours that maximise the benefits for a given network is an important function in network enabling. Game theory helps to design these incentives through developing an understanding of likely behaviours – discouraging likely behaviour that is detrimental to the network and encouraging other less likely behaviours that are beneficial to the network.

Game theory, in common with network theory, exists at a number of levels of abstraction. There are those who seek to employ the quantitative aspects of the theory. There are others who wish to understand the principles and let those principles influence them when designing and managing systems. Yet others may be content building theory around existing published ideas and principles.

Other Considerations in Applying Game Theory to Project Networks

There are challenges associated with using game theory to analyse performance and anticipate collective behaviour in project networks:

- Complexity – projects deal with a massive number of complex and interdependent tasks; the achievement of these tasks contributes to the delivery of specific project functions (Pryke, 2012) and ultimately the successful integration of systems and delivery of a project that inspires 'customer delight'. The networks are dynamic because the complexity of the project places a demand for flexibility on the actors and the networks. Imperfect information is endemic due to a range of assumptions made about the procurement and management of projects that have become unrealistic as project types and processes have evolved over time (see Chapter 5 – 'Dangerous Assumptions').

- Rationality – game theory is based upon the assumption that players act rationally, in a context where each player perceives that they have a role to play within constraints imposed by a range of internal and external influences. Procurement and project-delivery systems and the fact that they are in a temporary coalition make truly 'rational' decisions difficult to classify and quantify objectively. There is clearly a conflict between individual, rational decision-making which has the objective of maximising the payoff for the individual actor, and network behaviour leading to optimal project and indeed social outcomes. Christin *et al.* (2004) proposed the concept of 'near rationality', particularly where 'inceptive' systems are absent and the network is essentially self-organising.
- Utility – a view has to be taken about how an individual actor will value the utility of various interdependent and conflicting functions. Trade-offs have to be made and each actor has their own metrics for weighting utility.

Choices About Actions and Co-Players

No discussion about game theory would be complete without a description of 'The Prisoner's Dilemma' (see Box 6.2). The 'study decisions' game presented in Box 6.1 above is also an example of a type of game known as 'The Prisoner's Dilemma'.

Actors choose their own actions and may choose their co-players. If we consider games involving more than two players (which are complicated enough) we add considerable complexity for the game. The choice of action and the choice of co-player selection is made based upon local information (Biely *et al.*, 2005). The project comprises a finite number of actors at a given point in time, although actors enter and leave the project network population depending on the phase of the project. The network is predominantly designers pre-contract but becomes dominated by constructors in the post-contract phase. Within the context of the project, individual actors have transitory membership of project function networks (Pryke, 2012). Hence when the financial managers form networks for the purpose of enacting the financial management function, they invite non-financial management actors and find that their networks are subject to entry from other non-invited actors. So in any given communication network, particularly where the network is taking decisions, there is a choice for each individual actor about their personal behaviour and there is a context where, although the membership of the network is known, the choice is not made by the individual actor in relation to membership of other actors. So if we continue the game theory analogy, individual actors or players in the game sense need to make decisions about their own personal behaviour without knowing which other actors might enter the network or withdraw from the network or be invited to enter or withdraw by other actors.

To be set against this environment of uncertainty about the final membership of a network once decision-making or information-sharing activity is under way is the adaptability of the network topology. To return to network terminology in this discussion of

---

Box 6.2 Game theory example: The Prisoner's Dilemma. Kreps *et al.*, 1982, 1–11; Easley and Kleinberg, 2010, 144–145.

Two suspects have been caught by the authorities and have been taken for questioning. The police suspect that both detainees were involved in a criminal offence – a robbery. They do not, unfortunately, have enough evidence against the two men to convict either of them of the robbery. However, they both resisted arrest and both could be charged with this lesser offence which would involve a one-year custodial sentence.

The two suspects are kept in separate rooms during the interrogations and have no way of communicating with anyone, including each other. The following scenario is presented to each suspect individually: if you confess to the robbery and your partner does not, then you will be released and your partner will be charged with the robbery. Your confession will provide sufficient evidence to convict your colleague and he will go to prison for ten years as a result of the robbery. If you both confess to the robbery you will both be charged and would receive a prison sentence of four years, based upon pleading guilty; you would not have to testify against your partner in crime. Finally, if neither of you confess to the robbery, we cannot convict either of you of the robbery and would convict you both of the lesser crime of resisting arrest. Your partner has been offered the same deal. Would you like to confess to the robbery?

Here is the mathematical representation of the payoff:

		Suspect 2	
		Non-Confession	Confession
Suspect 1	Non-Confession	$-1, -1$	$-10, 0$
	Confession	$0, -10$	$-4, -4$

The payoffs are expressed in years of detention in prison. In summary, if Suspect 2 confesses, Suspect 1 receives a payoff of -4 if they confess themselves and a payoff of -10 if they do not confess. So a rational Suspect 1 should confess to the robbery in this instance. If Suspect 2 does not confess, then Suspect 1 would have a payoff of 0 by confessing themselves and a payoff of -1 by not confessing to the robbery. So in this case also, Suspect 1 should confess. Note that there are no good outcomes for the two suspects; it is a matter of choosing the least worst outcomes.

So we might say that confession is the 'strictly dominant' strategy – the best overall position for both prisoners. But neither can rely on the actions of the other prisoner and there is no way to achieve this outcome reliably under rational play conditions. So they both make choices which are worse for both of them to avoid a much worse outcome based upon their non-confession and the confession by their partner.

---

game theory, structural holes may appear in information-sharing communication networks. These structural holes may have been caused by actors choosing to exclude themselves, or actors being excluded by the actions or omissions of others. But the network provides the opportunity to respond to this problem of an emerging structural hole by either finding a different path for the communication, or by replacing the missing actor with a structural-hole-fixing broker. The possibilities and opportunities both theo-retically and in terms of practice in a project environment for combining game theory and network theory are therefore important.

Game theory is related to the measurement and evaluation of other players' reac-tions in a given game. In addition to being static or dynamic (and the case has been made that projects are almost inevitably as dynamic as games, as well as being dynamic from a structural point of view), games are also classified as 'zero-sum' or 'non-zero-sum'. Zero-sum games involve a situation where no wealth is created or destroyed overall. So, in a two-player, zero-sum game, whatever is gained by one player will be matched by a loss to the other player. Zero-sum games are relatively simplistic, since an optimal solution can always be found. Most real-life games are non-zero-sum; most construction project environments would involve non-zero-sum games (Barough *et al.*, 2012).

Nash Equilibrium

If neither player in a two-player game can find a strictly dominant strategy (see Box 6.2), then it is necessary to find another way to predict likely strategies of the players. Although we would hope that our projects operate in a collaborative environment, the reality frequently is that actors are competitive with each other for a variety of reasons. So an understanding of the Nash equilibrium is useful at this point. The underlying principle is that where there are no dominant strategies, we can still expect players to adopt strategies that constitute the best possible response to each other, assuming rationality and complete awareness of the conditions under which the decisions are being made. If two players both adopt strategies that represent the best response to each other in the circumstances, this is a Nash equilibrium. In fact this idea is not rooted solely in rationality – it is essentially an equilibrium concept (Nash, 1950, 1951). In a sense the Nash equilibrium is an *equilibrium of beliefs* (Easley and Kleinberg, 2010). If one player believes that the other player will adopt a strategy that is part of a Nash equilibrium, then that player has an incentive to contribute to the equilibrium. Where multiple equlibria exist it becomes more difficult to predict behaviour and a coordina-tion game provides a good example of this. As an example, let us assume that the mechanical services design engineer needs to start designing a scheme immediately and has to decide which software package to use for that design. He needs to coordinate with the electrical service engineer, who is unavailable. The implication of getting this game right is that both engineers choose the same software package, which is quick and convenient with no risk of file corruption, to exchange design files and to share design information as work proceeds. The problem with finding out that the other engineer has chosen a different software package for design is that file sharing and coordination of design is less convenient, with some risk of lack of compatibility and file corruption. This is called a 'coordination game' because both players need to coordinate using the same strategy – it is not necessarily important *which* strategy is chosen, the important point is that both or all parties make the same choice. This type of coordination is important in projects, particularly complex projects. Increasing the numbers of players in a coordination game disproportionately reduces the probability of coordination being achieved.

Anti-Coordination Behaviour: 'Hawk–Dove' and 'Chicken' Games

The Hawk–Dove game is based on the scenario that two animals are engaged in the same area to find food (McAdams and Nadler, 2005). Each animal can decide whether to adopt the strategy of a Hawk or a Dove. The Hawk is an aggressive strategy and the Dove is passive. If they both behave passively they divide food evenly between them. If one behaves aggressively while the other behaves passively, then the aggressive party gets the food. If both parties behave aggressively they destroy the food and risk injury; neither gets fed. This is a game with two Nash equilibria. The Hawk–Dove game has been applied in number of contexts (McAdams and Nadler (2005) looked at the focal point of legal compliance and the effects of third-party expressions of interest).

The focal point refers to the situation where there are environmental reasons that tend to make the players focus particularly on one of the possible multiple equilibria. An example of this is illustrated by a game referred to as 'Chicken'. Two drivers race toward each other in their cars. The 'chicken' (a disparaging term used to describe a coward) is the driver to swerve out of the way first. So both drivers hold their line as long as possible, hoping that the other driver will swerve first. The order in which the drivers swerve is important to both drivers. But possibly of more importance is the direction of the swerve; if they both swerve toward to the same point of the road then they both face death or injury following the inevitable collision. If they both turn the wheel in the same direction (from the drivers' viewpoint), moving their vehicles to opposite sides of the road, then they both survive and pass each other safely. The probability is that if the game of 'Chicken' is played between two English drivers in England, the drivers will intuitively turn their steering wheels left at the crucial moment, a reference to the convention of driving on the left-hand side on English roads. Hence a social convention provides a focal point for the decision-making in this game with multiple equilibria.

Game Theory and Information Exchange Network Formation

Each individual actor's behaviour is a function of the network with which they engage, or with which they are associated, even temporarily. The individual is influenced and affected by their own network prominence and the access that they have to the other actors in the network. Each linkage is like a pipe or conduit carrying information (in the case of an information-sharing network, specifically). Information can move at varying speeds and through conduits of various sizes (continuous diameter between nodes, but varying diameters for various links in a network). So our project actors are embedded within those networks and have the benefit of, or are limited in their activities by, the linkages and actors around them. Similarly and conversely, actors are able to influence the networks with which they become associated. As an actor we can try to build prominence by increasing the numbers of links that we connect to personally, or by placing ourselves strategically in a gate-keeping location, or filling a structural hole left by others – and so on. An understanding of network structure is crucial in determining the outcome of many important social and economic relationships (Jackson, 2008). It is hoped that in this book we will move to a position, through discussion of theory and case study material, where we can begin to consider how to design project networks for predictable and desirable behaviours and to satisfy certain project performance metrics.

Game theory has the potential to provide an understanding of how information exchange networks function and evolve over time. Essentially we are all 'gaming' on a minute-by-minute basis as to the outcome of a multitude of small transaction sets (Pryke, 2012). The view that we take individually is important and can change frequently over time, and the view that clusters take, affecting the whole network, is informed by a range of environmental factors and will change over time, perhaps rapidly on occasions. As project actors we are gaming in relation to our own personal transactions with the individuals around us; we are also gaming in our role as representatives of our employer – we may be engaging in games with other firms within the project coalition. These gaming environments change over time and this is a factor in achieving a transition between the two main stages of a project: pre- and post-contract. The 'five dangerous assumptions' (from Chapter 5) are used as a vehicle for the discussion here.

Game Theory and the Five Dangerous Assumptions in Projects

What are projects all about? Some will say they are about providing a service to a client and perhaps the end-users and other stakeholders. Some might say they are about innovation – the project is a vehicle for innovation. Most fundamentally, if projects are to be regarded as successful, they need to build value for 'customers' through the relationships that can legitimately form between actors within the project. But networks sit within a shifting environment and this is important for the ability of project actors to behave in ways that lead to successful projects. Game theory works at the level of games between pairs and groups of individuals and increasingly many regard relationships between firms as a legitimate forum for the discussion of game theory. So the plan here is to think about the evolving game environment as our projects move from phase to phase of design and delivery. The environment in which construction projects are designed and delivered present some problems, which were referred to in Chapter 5:

Dangerous assumption 1: It is possible to accurately define the client's needs at an early stage, before any visualisation of those needs and desires is produced.

So, what is the gaming environment? How are the games constructed and played? And what are the implications for the project? The gaming environment is characterised by a high level of uncertainty for all project actors including the client. The games are constructed based upon the needs of each individual firm within the bid coalition. The client wishes to move as quickly as possible to lump-sum-contract stage, with a group of designers and a contractor who will deliver a successful project. The inability of the client to accurately define their needs prompts consultants to carry out some design work speculatively in the expectation that more commitment will be shown by the client where a designer has given free design services. The client has to make a judgement between competitive tendering and negotiation within a partnering arrangement.

Financial modelling tends to be optimistic at this stage of the project and the bias is beneficial in getting the project committed but is negative in terms of overall financial management between this very earliest of project stages and the final outturn cost reconciliation. The implications of this gaming environment are partly dependent on the market for both consultants and constructors.

As noted previously, implicit in the contracting system (where design is carried out independently) is the assumption that the client can accurately predict their future needs in the face of environmental uncertainty, and that it is possible to accurately represent this in written and graphical form. In fact, it is quite difficult to understand fully the exact implications of design decisions on the end-user experience, compounding this difficulty.

Dangerous assumption 2: It is possible to very accurately interpret clients' wishes, without any corruption of intention through 'agency' (Aoki** et al, 1990), **and to represent the physical manifestation of those wishes and desires accurately and unambiguously using CAD (computer-aided design) files and text documents.

The protocols embedded in the contracting system used in construction and engineering projects require that the design for the project is documented and that this documentation is passed to other parties and used as a basis for the calculation of their bid price. But if dangerous assumption 1 (DA1) was incorrect and clients commence the process of design and preparation of documentation before they are able to articulate their needs accurately, then a difficult start is made to the next decision-making milestone, which involves taking the clients' requirements and deriving a design that meets those requirements accurately. DA2 adds a further dimension to the games at this point. We start with a lack of clarity over building use and compound the risks through the natural tendencies of individuals that lead to agency problems. The client is effectively delegating the role of designer to a range of consultants and some specialist subcontractors. But each of these actors has vested interests and become players in a number of games associated with the development of design and the representation of those designs for the purposes of bidding by others. We commence with the perceptions that individual designers have about the clients' objectives and the relevance and validity of those objectives. We add the individual designer's perception of the solution in the context of their own vested interests, not least the need to move quickly in order to secure bids and to carry out the design profitably. Those who have to produce tender documents press designers for details of the design; designers need to leave the final detail of the design as late as possible in order to comply with the most current regulations and indeed requirements of the client. The compromise, in the end, is made in information completeness. The interests of the designers are partially reflected in the design prepared for tender stage, and the consultant responsible for preparing the documents used to invite tenders (the quantity surveyor in the English system) is forced to make some assumptions about missing or ambiguous information before finalising the documents and passing them to the bidding actors.

The bidding actors are then involved in a number of games associated with the bidding process. Tendering protocols require opacity in terms of the identity of the primary (main contractor) bidders. But bidders often bid in environments where they are very unlikely to be successful, and seek more complete information about the competition. This is achieved through informal social contacts and agencies that exist to notify bidders of the existence of competing parties and their identities, once the bids have been submitted. There is a question as to whether this complexity of process results in a truly competitive game being played between genuine bidders.

Once the successful bidder is announced this bidder has to face the reality of delivering the project within a context with a great deal of uncertainty.

Dangerous assumption 3: Change in project definition is undesirable.

The point here is that although the whole premise underpinning the contracting system is that the contract is a *lump-sum* contract (not one based upon the prime cost of the work), once changes are made the benefit of establishing a 'lump sum' is reduced incrementally as changes are introduced. And yet the changes are of fundamental importance in the delivery of a project that most closely meets the client's needs in a complex environment where the client faces continually changing scenarios. But problems, and risk associated with those problems, also accumulate from DA1 and DA2. The client's attempts to articulate their needs are corrupted by agency and vested interests in an environment where there is great pressure of time to achieve tender invitation. The incomplete contracting model is then subject to changes, particularly in the case of complex projects and/or those that have a long duration. Perhaps, as noted previously, for a client and stakeholders, changes are an inevitable part of a project, other than very short-term and simple projects. Changes, particularly those occurring relatively late in the project-delivery programme, are desirable for clients and stakeholders so that both end-user needs and the most recent technical innovation are accommodated.

The scenario described above must surely comprise a most fertile environment for the application of game theory.

Dangerous assumption 4: It is possible to allocate project actor roles to individuals, through contracts executed by the client with the project actors' employers, that will create temporary communication and information exchange networks that will function to deliver the project effectively without intervention.

The procured resources transition into the actors who will deliver the project (this transition is discussed in more detail earlier in the book). They establish roles that enable the exchange of resources and information needed to create client value and start to create the networks (through their actions and inactions) which become the networks delivering a range of project functions. The case has been made that the vertical axis of the matrix contains the firms and the contracts that procure those firms, yet the governance of the horizontal (project) axis is relatively weak and the detail of the roles and systems needed to deliver a successful project are left to the project actors to formulate – there is an emphasis on the formation of networks which are effectively self-organised. These self-organising networks also provide a canvas upon which game theory can be illustrated and observed.

Dangerous assumption 5: There is an assumption that interdependent project actor roles will be constant over time.

As noted previously, there are no mechanisms in the contracts for changing these roles. Essentially, procurement and the governance associated with formal contracts within the contractual role-holding firms have to achieve a pattern of human behaviour that will deliver a successful project. These networks are self-organising and, arguably, self-managing. One of the objectives of this book was to set project managers and clients thinking about interventions needed during the process of the design and delivery stages of projects, particularly large and/or complex projects. The assumption that roles are constant between bid stage and completion of the project must clearly be incorrect and this has created a gaming environment. The reality is that the networks absorb the ambiguities, but in the process an environment is created in which game-playing is prevalent.

Summary and Conclusions

The aim of this chapter was to create an agenda around the discussion of game theory and its application to the networks associated with projects, in particular construction and engineering projects.

The chapter started with reference to the matrix structure that is embedded in projects and their procurement and management. The point was made that governance is strong in the vertical axis, with formal contracts linked to each package of work, whether for professional services or some form of production activity. In contrast, the horizontal axis relates to the resources procured in their post-contract state as they transition into project design and/or delivery mode. Although protocols and custom and practice apply here, I argue that the networks that emerge to deal with the information exchange associated with design and production are essentially self-organising – partly because the exact task has not been carried out before, partly because the network needs to absorb ambiguities created by unrealistic assumptions made in the contracting system and partly because the networks need to be more transient than is envisaged or provided for in the contracts procuring the resources.

I discussed the idea that individual project actors need to function within the context in which they are placed (in network terms) and are able individually to have some influence on other actors and their roles and the topography of the network. There followed discussion and description of game theory on the basis that the reader may not have any previous knowledge of this topic. A list of references specifically related to construction projects was given – although it has to be said that the emphasis of those papers was not necessarily project management. Some analysis was made of the relevance of game theory to the project environment and six key assumptions were identified relating to:

- Calculation of payoff and self-interest
- Accuracy of knowledge about the game, the players and the environment
- Identity and behaviour of all other players
- The fact that games played with low levels of knowledge might be regarded as a distinct and separate type of game
- The rationality of players
- The fact that the external environment does not prevent players from selecting a given strategy.

For some the constraints of those assumptions might prove difficult but the principles nevertheless provide fertile discussion and analysis in the context of project networks.

I then moved on to discuss the benefits accruing from the application of game theory to projects. In particular, the point is made that project networks are not 'steady state' as contracts envisage – the multiple layers of networks serving a whole range of project functions are transient and self-organising. Game theory helps us to understand the adaptations that need to take place in a network as it moves toward some form of steady state. I referred to decision strategies made by individual actors and how these decisions sit within the context of collaborative behaviour. Although the aim would be for the games to be collaborative, once the assumptions made about the operation of the contracting system were considered, the intrusion of non-collaborative games was seen as inevitable. On a fundamental level, I looked at the issues associated with placing self-interested individuals in a network with other self-interested individuals and the challenge that arises when this group is faced with the task, jointly, of designing and delivering a complex project. Complexity, rationality and the mechanisms by which we calculate utility were all issues that needed to be considered in the application of game theory to project networks.

Having discussed some of the issues associated with game theory in the project network environment and some of the ambiguities that this application implies, the chapter moved on to look at the ubiquitous 'Prisoner's Dilemma', perhaps because no chapter on game theory would be complete without some discussion of this topic. Nash equilibrium is important in the context of project networks. The relevance links back the point made earlier in this summary – that contracts assume continuity of behaviour and environment but people form networks that are far more transient. These networks need to find stability and Nash is relevant in relation to establishing this stability. Coordination games are important in this discussion because the delivery of a complex project is a very large coordination game in some senses. The discussion in the chapter looked specifically at game theory in relation to information exchange network formation. Individuals are gaming in relation to their transactions with other project actors on a minute-by-minute basis for the duration of the project. Individuals are also gaming in their role as employee of a role-holding coalition member.

Finally, I reflected on the assumptions that we make in adopting the contracting system to deliver projects and how the assumptions, if incorrect, compound the problems associated with subsequent decision-making foci. The interdependence of systems is a recurring theme both for the chapter and indeed the book as a whole.

I have aimed in this chapter to leave the reader with a sense that some simple assumptions are made about process, environment and behaviour of individual actors in our procurement, design and management of projects. The interdependencies in processes and decision-making are not reflected in the procurement of the services that we have decided constitute the project team. I suggested that an understanding of game theory might provide an insight into the way in which networks function and why some networks function efficiently and others do not. The idea that we procure resources but essentially allow these resources to self-define the systems that deliver the project is problematic. Perhaps if our future project managers understand the relevance of game theory for the operation of project networks, they will be able to more accurately design systems that monitor the operation of project networks and to recommend interventions to manage the complex interdependent activities that are carried out by individuals in the context of project networks.

7

Network Roles and Personality Types

This chapter comprises a discussion about the links between personality and the roles that individuals enact within project networks. The discussion here has been stimulated by various SNA-based studies carried out by the Centre for Organisational Network Analysis at UCL, but the intention is not to present and analyse data here. The intention in this chapter is to set an agenda and stimulate thinking about the relationship between personality and network roles in projects.

When the findings of network studies are presented, typically involving large projects in construction and engineering, occasionally someone in the audience will ask in relation to the networks forming the basis of the study, 'Who's in charge?' We have long regarded projects as hierarchical and rational, static and formally governed by contract conditions. Yet our projects are delivered by people operating in quite difficult circumstances and with all the usual human frailties. We recruit resources based upon narrow disciplinary skill sets. We then turn this large group of individuals to face a very complex and daunting task – the project. So I want to stimulate thinking about what type of personality we need to work effectively in a network, and what *mix* of personalities we should seek for effective network evolution. If we accept that project systems are best observed through the lens of interpersonal relationship networks, then we need to understand the characteristics of the actors. In this way we can move to a position where we are able not only to conceptualise organisations as networks of relationships but also to analyse and manage these project and supply chain networks. We might want to formalise the possibly subjective selection criteria related to 'ability to work with others'.

Before further discussing network actor roles and personality traits, some detail about the classification of networks used in network studies will provide context.

For the four case studies dealt with in the sister publication to this one, *Social Network Analysis in Construction* (Pryke, 2012), the following networks were identified and analysed:

- Contractual relationships between (project) employer and contractor, and (project) employer and consultant;
- Performance incentives (any payments beyond the basic contractual 'consideration');
- Information exchange.

Managing Networks in Project-Based Organisations, First Edition. Stephen Pryke.
© 2017 John Wiley & Sons Ltd. Published 2017 by John Wiley & Sons Ltd.

Information exchange in turn was sub-classified by project function, defined for the purposes of the research project as follows:

- Building use – information exchange essentially relating to client requirements
- Specification – exchange relating to the specification of the building
- Progress – relating to progress of the works on site
- Financial management
- Build process – information relating to the process of construction – for example, health and safety, access requirements, etc.

The contractual ties were typically related to the dyadic relationships between the client and a Tier 1 contractor or consultant, and between Tier 1 and other tiers designing or delivering the project. These were, therefore, inter-organisational relationships. All other relationships were essentially interpersonal. The research also gathered data relating to a very specific type of information exchange – the issuing of 'instructions', this being one of the few types of communication referred to in forms of contract for delivering construction or engineering projects. The networks were analysed in relation to comparative density. The roles of individual actors were quantified using normalised point centrality.

The study (which was being carried out while this book was being written), involving a very large central London infrastructure scheme, expanded on the structure used for gathering data outlined above. Some of the findings of this study are presented in Chapters 10, 11, 12 and 13. This was partly in response to a desire to refine the research method on the basis of lessons learnt. It was also partly in response to the perceived needs of the client for the study. We looked at networks of contractual relationship. We then moved on to deal with the following list of project functions as reflected in information exchange network roles, classified as follows:

1) Project management
2) Risk management
3) Commercial management (including contract administration and cost control)
4) Design/engineering management
5) Project controls (including planning and reporting)
6) Mechanical and electrical services design
7) Architectural design
8) Tunnelling design
9) Civil engineering and structures
10) Track and signalling design
11) Building information modelling and computer-aided design
12) Document control
13) Health and safety
14) Quality management
15) Assurance
16) Systems engineering
17) Geotechnics
18) Utilities (water, gas, telecoms, etc.)
19) Project support and administration
20) Environmental issues

21) Operations
22) Maintenance
23) Other.

These classifications were chosen by the client for the research project partly because their system of timesheets for all white-collar workers employed these categories. Against each of these network classifications data was analysed using 'degree centrality' (a measure of direct linkages between actors), 'eigenvector centrality' (a measure of influence where the number of secondary connections held by an actor also provides weight) and 'betweenness centrality' (a measure of 'brokerage' – the extent to which an individual actor is 'between' other actors). We shall return to the detail of this case study later in the book (see Chapters 10–13). As mentioned previously, the purpose of providing this detail here is to provide a context into which a discussion about network actor roles and personality traits might fall.

The purpose of the two outlines of role classifications provided above is to set the scene for a more detailed discussion about roles in networks. So, initially we have identified a list of project function classifications within which we can study actor behaviour. The first group of case studies used a relatively brief list of fairly simple project functions – this served its purpose well in the context of a study comparing two public sector projects with two private sector schemes, while looking at the effects on those projects of collaborative working. The second list of project function classifications was derived from the systems of a single large infrastructure client. This most recent research project looked at two cases studies longitudinally. Because both case studies involved the same client, it was possible to adopt a very context-specific project function classification. The client for the research (a government-funded Knowledge Transfer Partnership between Transport for London and the Centre for Organisational Network Analysis at University College London) also desired to link network behaviour with cost of function, based upon staff time sheets where time was allocated to project function.

So, in looking at projects using SNA we have had the opportunity to focus on specific project functions and to understand the behaviour behind the delivery of these functions. Our analysis looked at two main measures:

Firstly, we looked at density of the project function network and what this means for the effective delivery of that function – it is better to let the detailed analysis using the mathematical values associated with each network inform judgements, but in broad terms high-density networks (where more people are connected to others in the network) tend to indicate better communications and perhaps more democratic communications. Sparsely connected networks tend to point to a relatively small number of relatively powerful actors communicating with their own elite group but not disseminating more widely within the network. There are occasions where this sort of network characteristic is desirable (in matters of security, for example) but in a project scenario, where actors are producing and processing information, higher density is generally desirable. The case studies discussed in Chapters 10–13 indicate that it might be possible to identify an optimum density at a given point in the programme for a project. In addition, to claim that 'higher density is better' is too simplistic – there is clearly an optimum density beyond which communications are not sufficiently selective.

Secondly, we are interested in the actors and their prominence and type of role in the network. Here we use centrality and a range of different measures of centrality depending on the nature of prominence that we seek to identify (see above and further detail in Chapter 4). In Chapter 4, some actor characteristics derived from case studies in construction projects were identified; these were dealt with in some detail in Pryke (2012) but are summarised here in order to provide context.

There follows a discussion of the project actor types discussed originally in Chapter 4 – the purpose here is to explore their network roles and later in the chapter to link these network roles to personality traits.

Network Roles

Prominent Disseminators

This type of project actor is very important in information exchange networks. They have these characteristics:

- They contribute generously to information exchange.
- They behave in a non-hierarchical manner with their network; although these actors may be highly rewarded or have senior status conferred by contract of employment or project contract, they need not necessarily have a high status. The network confers a prominence on this actor through their endeavours in the project.
- They tend to have a high level of expertise in their area.
- Occasionally this actor type gets disheartened by the behaviour of other network actors – those that are perhaps less generous, or who are controlling of information resources in their flow to others.
- Some prominent disseminators will need rewarding to maintain this type of network behaviour. Others will find reward enough in their prominence and the recognition of their prominence. Are prominent disseminators extrovert in character or are they compensating for an introvert character by enjoying prominence in this way?
- There is also a negative side to this prominence – studies have shown (in particular Pryke, 2001, 2012) that prominence in project information exchange networks can also be derived from the dissemination of poor quality information, increasing the

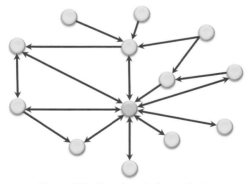

Commentary on Figure 7.1: Prominent disseminators
Look for: centrality – lots of connections to other actors; more connection to this actor than any other; many of the connections are two-way.

Figure 7.1 Prominent disseminators (information exchange network).

iterations needed to resolve ambiguity. I refer to this as 'dysfunctional prominence' and the extrovert can be susceptible to this sort of behaviour, which is undesirable in project networks. Chapter 11 deals with the issue of dysfunctional prominence.

Gatekeeper Hoarders

Whereas prominent disseminators make a positive contribution to the promotion of effective information flows in our projects, gatekeeper hoarders comprise a barrier to effective project information flows. They can be a nuisance and we need to make a conscious decision about recruiting this type of actor. We also need to monitor projects to identify the evolution of this type of network behaviour. So, what sort of characteristics do gatekeeper hoarders have?

- As noted above, Figures 7.1 and 7.2 are actually very similar. The most important difference is the direction of the arrows. Prominent disseminators disseminate generously. Gatekeeper hoarders (GHs) are controlling, for their own satisfaction.
- GHs tend to be slightly obsessive, perhaps insecure; they may lack the expertise of some of those around them, or they may perceive that they lack the expertise of some of the other, perhaps competing, actors in the network.
- These actors seek power for their own satisfaction and comfort. The power is used in a way that does not serve the network or the project functions associated with the network.
- There is a legitimacy associated with gatekeeping where the accuracy of information is paramount, perhaps where information requires checking, or perhaps where coordination is very important. It is clearly very undesirable that a personal bias or loss of clarity be introduced during filtering of information provided by others. It is possible that filtering by gatekeepers codifies information and enables it to be presented to a wider audience, or renders it more readily assimilated in some way.

Figure 7.2 Gatekeeper hoarders.

Commentary on Figure 7.2: Gatekeeper hoarders
Look for: centrality – lots of connections to other actors; more connections to this actor than any other; most of the connections are one-way, with information flowing into the gatekeeper hoarder. Note the similarity between gatekeeper hoarders and prominent disseminators. It is only the arrow directions that indicate the quite different role and personal motives involved.

- Very often the gatekeeper hoarder simply slows down the movement of information within the network; perhaps they enjoy the ability to control the flow of information to others.
- Gatekeeper hoarders very often evolve their own roles in organisations. These actors would have some status conferred by contract or custom and practice. They may flourish in organisational forms that evolve quickly (and most projects transition from procurement of resources to delivery of project very quickly and with little facilitation).
- Gatekeeper hoarders may be tolerated in highly regulated or high-risk environments, where time must be traded off against the achievement of certainty or safety.
- The important point about gatekeeper hoarders is the extent to which their self-created network role is desirable and contributes to the relevant project functions. Observation and intervention is necessary with this type of behaviour to avoid the negative effects of unnecessarily high levels of gatekeeper hoarding.

Isolates

In Figure 7.3 the isolates are the nodes shown with no connection to other actors – four blue nodes. The isolate is not an actor in the network shown but it is often instructive to represent actors who are prominent in other networks that are closely associated with the network under consideration as isolates to show that they might have been connected, but in the context of a given project function are not connected. So a relatively junior designer might be quite prominent in design information dissemination but simultaneously an isolate in the financial management function – his line manager deals with financial reporting and links to those responsible for budgetary reporting to the client. So, why are we interested in isolates?

- Some individuals naturally acquire for themselves an isolate role in networks. The introvert seeks isolation. Those with very high levels of specialist expertise are often seen as isolates – they do not necessarily need linkages to perform their project function especially if others take responsibility for coordination with other designers, for example.

Figure 7.3 Isolates.

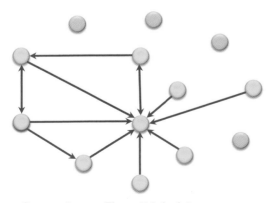

Commentary on Figure 7.3: Isolates
Look for: actors not connected to any other actor.

- Are the actors isolated out of choice or because they have been excluded by others? What do we know about the evolution of the network leading to the isolation?
- Can we see from the nature of the project function that isolation is inevitable or desirable in some way?
- We are interested in a comparison between a range of networks involving the isolated actor. Are they isolated in a large number of functional networks? Or are they isolated for good reason but relatively well connected in other networks? To what extent is the isolation a function of personality and to what extent is it a function of the network environment in which the actor is involved and the role of the individual actor within that network? As noted in Pryke (2012), authors, academics and composers often cast themselves as isolates in the networks with which they engage.

Isolates are not necessarily undesirable. The importance for those wanting to understand and manage networks that deliver the functions that constitute the delivery of a project lies in the *reason* for the isolation.

Isolated Dyads and Triads

Isolated dyads and triads appear for similar reasons to the isolate actor – essentially they reflect perhaps a highly specialised group of actors, perhaps engaging in something where a high level of security is essential. Isolation might be temporary. As with isolates, we need to understand the reasons for the isolated subgroups. If we feel that these isolated subgroups need connecting to the main network or other isolated subgroups we need to enlist the help of the next category of actor – the boundary spanner.

Boundary Spanners

The boundary spanner in Figure 7.5 is the blue node in the centre of the figure. This actor is providing a link between two or more otherwise isolated subgroups. As with all the actor characteristics that we are discussing here, we do not procure these actor roles in our projects. The boundary spanner is one of the more important roles that we do

Figure 7.4 Isolated dyads and triads.

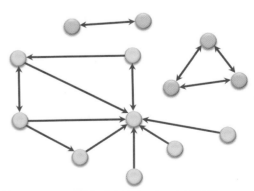

Commentary on Figure 7.4: Isolated dyads and triads
Look for: actors connected to one or two other actors only and where the dyad or triad is not connected to the main network in any way.

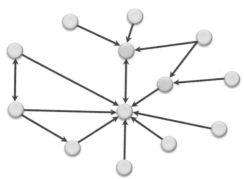

Commentary on Figure 7.5: Boundary spanners
Look for: one actor through whom all communication or other resources flow and without whom the two (in this case) distinct subgroups would not be connected.

Figure 7.5 Boundary spanners.

not procure. So our boundary spanner in Figure 7.5 provides a link between two groups and connects the two halves of the network together. The upper half is one loosely connected subgroup which, but for one connection, could be two isolated triads. The lower subgroup is larger and more densely connected. There is a sense that the upper subgroup is more at risk from remaining isolated from the main group. But we do not really know if this is the case until we understand the context of the network(s) and the function that we are observing. This network would typically be an information exchange network. So we are interested in boundary spanning as an activity because:

- There may be a lack of homogeneity between the two parts of the network and the boundary-spanning actor is an important interface between two otherwise disparate subgroups.
- The single link facilitated by the boundary spanner may make an important connection between technologies and/or enable innovation in some way. Perhaps there is a systems integration function being performed at this point.
- Sometimes competitive and opportunistic behaviour promotes the existence of isolated subgroups. Overcoming the impact of these behaviours might be important to the more effective functioning of the network in performing its project function.
- Both subgroups need to identify with the boundary spanner in some way. Some might argue that the best boundary-spanning links are provided through a pair of boundary spanners – one acting for each of the subgroup linkages.

Boundary spanning is an important function associated with repair and evolution of networks. What about the boundary-spanning actor – what do we know about this actor type? The boundary spanner facilitates important strategic linkages. This actor type would need to:

- Have a good understanding of the characteristics and context factors associated with the two possibly quite different subgroups
- Empathise with both groups, or at least be seen to empathise in some way
- Be motivated in some sense to act as a boundary spanner. In some industries, although the terminology might not reflect this, boundary spanners are employed predominantly to perform that function with key clients and suppliers.

Figure 7.6 Bridges.

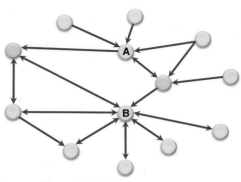

Commentary on Figure 7.6: Bridges
Look for: one or more actors that provide a link between two other actors who would not otherwise be linked. In this figure actors A and B would not be connected without the two bridges (shown in blue).

The boundary spanner may be quite gregarious, perhaps extrovert and almost certainly confident. This actor type provides an important, possibly strategic and enabling, role in projects. We do not procure this role in our projects. Later we will consider in a little more detail what personality types might be attracted to or well suited to this network role.

Bridges

In Figure 7.6 the two blue nodes are 'bridges'. If we remove them nodes A and B cease to be connected. We might say that bridges are similar to boundary spanners. But bridges are really focused on network path lengths. In networks that represent information flow, for example, we might be interested in the route that information takes through a network. We would also be interested in the characteristics of the respective actors in those two separate routes. Very often a bridge makes a link between two actors who are already connected but by a relatively long path. Now it might be that this long path is important in terms of the various actors and their contributions. But it may be that the long path length simply takes more time and introduces the potential for gatekeeper hoarder to intervene and negatively affect flows through linkages.

Like boundary spanners, bridges can be strategically important. From the point of view of those managing networks, or seeking to control them, the bridge must be a collaborator and supporter. The bridge needs to be someone that can be trusted. Later in the book I will look at trust in networks in more detail (Chapter 8). Bridges and boundary spanners may be sponsored by opportunistic parties seeking to influence flow through networks for their own benefit. So it is important to understand whether anybody outside of the legitimate management group has control of the actor.

The purpose of this chapter was to look at network roles and personality types. I started by thinking about network classification because it is not possible to look at a project as a whole. Network science requires, or perhaps enables, us to think about project functions and then to focus in some detail on the operation of those individual project functions. Within the networks associated with the delivery of project functions we have actors (for our purposes, individuals), each of whom adopts a network role, or adapts in some way to assume a network role within the context of a particular project function. Examination of those network roles has identified some characteristics of network actors. Some become very prominent in the network; others work in small clusters, dyads or triads. So a start has been made on thinking about what sort of personality would suit these various network actor roles. In the next part of the chapter I review some of the literature relating to personality types and try to formulate some criteria for personality profiling in relation to particular network actor roles.

Personality Traits

Trait theory, also known as disposition theory, relates to habitual patterns of behaviour, thought and emotion (Kassin, 2003). A list of traits is shown in Table 7.1 below.

Table 7.1 is a review of the literature dealing with personality traits. Later in the chapter I will reflect on these personality traits in the context of project-based organisations. I will suggest that the link to humour, while not immediately obvious, is important.

Humour and Behaviour in Networks

It is said that humour and laughing in humans occur in all cultures, in all individuals throughout the world (Apte, 1985; Lefcourt, 2001). Apes and chimpanzees can also exhibit humorous behaviour, including the facility to appreciate and enjoy humour (Martin, 2007). To produce or construct humour, or humorous situations, individuals need to 'mentally process information' (Martin, 2007: 6). Our actors' roles in project networks also involve processing information. I would argue that the link to humour is not frivolous. The link between networks and humour is the issue of *information processing*. There is also a need to understand project organisations outside of a framework that places emphasis on a historically military view of management associated with 'leaders', 'instructions' and 'directions', with reward and punishment systems to reinforce compliant or non-compliant behaviour.

Long and Graesser (1988) classified humour based upon analysis of television shows and audience reaction to particular phrases and events. These classifications are:

Irony – the use of an opposite meaning to emphasise something: for example, suggesting that someone needs a haircut in response to their presenting themselves with a particularly short haircut.

Satire – aggressive, potentially critical, humour that ridicules (typically) institutions and policy of various types. *Private Eye* (a weekly UK magazine) has become famous for making fun of various prominent institutions and figures under the banner of social justice. The satire is powerful and potentially undermining for those who become targets for 'The Eye'.

Sarcasm – a typically aggressive type of humour. A cutting, often ironic, remark intended to express contempt or ridicule, possibly involving exaggeration for comedic effect.

Overstatement and understatement – deliberate exaggeration to emphasise a point.

Table 7.1 Personality traits.

Trait classification	Observable characteristics/manifestations
Openness to experience	Openness to experience and intellect. Look for: wide interests; imaginative; insightful behaviour; DeYoung *et al.* (2005)
Conscientiousness	Scrupulous; meticulous; principled; need to be conformant, including to individual's own conscience; Heaven *et al.* (2001)
Extroversion	Gregarious; outgoing; sociable; opposite of introversion; Lou *et al.* (2010)
Agreeableness	Compliant; trusting; empathetic; sympathetic; friendly; cooperative; Graziano *et al.* (1993)
Neuroticism	Tendency to become emotional; sometimes linked to negative life experiences; Jeronimus *et al.* (2014)
Self-esteem	Favourable or unfavourable attitude toward self; valuing, approving, appreciating, prizing or liking oneself; Button *et al.,* (1997)
Harm avoidance	Associated with shyness; fearfulness; uncertain outlook; worrying; Paulus *et al.* (2003)
Novelty-seeking	Impulsive; exploratory; fickle; excitable; bad-tempered; extravagant; Gardini *et al.* (2009)
Perfectionism	Might be 'socially prescribed' in the sense of belief that others will only value you if you are perfect; or exhibit 'self-orientated' perfectionism related to a desire to be perfect for one's own sake; associated with obsessional behaviour; Halmi *et al.* (2005)
Alexithymia	Inability to express emotions; sometimes linked to post-traumatic stress disorder; Frewen *et al.* (2006)
Rigidity	Inflexibility; resistant to change; Peskine *et al.* (2004)
Impulsivity	Risk taking; aversion to planning; lack of consideration in decision-making; oblivious to impact of decisions; lack of focus on the future; Eysenck and Eysenck (1977b)
Disinhibition	Inability to constrain impulses; Young *et al.* (2000)
Psychoticism	Typified by aggressiveness; interpersonal hostility; tendency toward schizophrenia; Eysenck and Eysenck (1977a)
Obsessionality	Persistent, unwelcome, disturbing ideas, thoughts and images or emotions; Salkovskis *et al.* (1998)

Self-deprecation – placing oneself as the object of the humour. Useful to demonstrate modesty, to put other parties present at their ease and to ingratiate oneself with listeners.

Teasing – humorous remarks directed at an individual and related to appearance or behaviour. Lighthearted and not intended to be destructive (unlike sarcasm, for example). Frequently used between friends to emphasise the informality and strength of their relationship.

Replies to rhetorical questions – a rhetorical question like 'Now where am I going?' is not intended to elicit an answer, so an answer like 'I have no idea – I don't even know where I am going!' can seem amusing.

Clever replies to incongruous statements – an answer following a serious question that ignores the original question in favour of another question altogether.

Double entendres – a deliberate misconstruing of the question so as to evoke a dual meaning, frequently sexual in nature.

Transformation of frozen expressions – transforming familiar sayings into humorous statements by modifying slightly. As in 'Who cares who wins', a corruption of 'Who Dares Wins', which was originally attributed to the SAS (an elite military group in the UK).

Puns – humour associated with dual meaning for a given word or phrase. Try: 'I used to be a banker, but I have recently lost interest.'

Irony, satire and sarcasm might well find their way into organisations but their effect would be negative and likely to be destructive for the formation, evolution and maintenance of communication networks. Overstatement and self-deprecation, among other forms of humour, might prove useful in creating positive relationships between actors. When people experience positive emotions, they exhibit improvements in a variety of cognitive abilities (cognitive abilities are brain-based skills we need in order to carry out tasks). We also see improving social behaviours – better problem-solving, for example (Isen, 2003). These cognitive abilities and social behaviours benefit our organisations by providing cognitive flexibility, which can help with creative problem-solving, better use of memory, better planning and judgement and more socially-orientated behaviour (helpfulness and generosity). Positive emotions also have an impact upon physical well-being, creating a tendency in individuals to have less sickness and a lower propensity to be depressed. Perhaps humour can therefore make a contribution to mental as well as physical health (Frederickson *et al.*, 2000; Frederickson and Branigan, 2005).

How Might Humour Help in Project-Based Organisations?

Martin (2007) speculates that as the human race evolved from small groups of hunter–gatherers, humans might have used humour to enhance group identity. Alexander (1986) observes that humour is used in more modern organisations to enforce social norms and exclude members of other groups from entering. Relief of tension and the ability to cope more easily with adversity was found by Lefcourt (2001) and Lefcourt and Martin (2012) to flow from the use of humour in the workplace, reducing anxiety, depression and anger. Work by Janus (1975) and Janus *et al.* (1978) looked into the personality traits of professional comedians and found that they tended to be intelligent, angry, suspicious and depressed, and that typically their early lives had involved suffering, isolation and deprivation. Humour enabled these individuals to establish a defence against anxiety.

Is Work Really Meant to Be the Antithesis of Play?

Why do we tend to associate humour with leisure, and non-amusing activities and boring behaviour with work? There is certainly an issue of credibility and confidence for those on the receiving end of other people's humour, particularly in the case of initial meetings with clients and customers. Dentists and financial advisers with a great sense of humour might need to rein back a little, at least initially, until both parties allow humour to form part of their interactions. Project managers and other professionals might need to avoid humour, certainly initially, to establish confidence prior to introducing a slightly less formal atmosphere. Martin (2007) found that humour in the workplace tended to invoke higher levels of happiness, better health, less stress and better productivity. It also engendered better social interactions, creative thinking and problem-solving. One of the case studies presented later in this book (see Chapter 11) demonstrated the importance of problem-solving in the temporary project organisation. This is a function that we do not expressly procure pre-contract. There is very little research into the use or effects of humour specifically in relation to the construction project environment – the psychologists, sociologists and anthropologists have been busy elsewhere. Here is a selection of studies carried out involving the use of humour in the workplace:

- Psychiatric hospitals (Coser, 1960)
- Childcare centre (Meyer, 1997)
- Hotel kitchen (Brown and Keegan, 1999)
- Factory (Collinson, 1988; Ullian, 1976)
- Petroleum exploration (Traylor, 1973)
- IT manufacturing (Hatch and Ehrlich, 1993)
- A zoo (Martin, 2007)
- Various private sector companies (Grugulis, 2002)

These may or may not be project environments, depending on your view of what constitutes a project – but many of these examples refer to service sector activities. In the context of construction projects Kelly *et al.* (2014) and Green (2006) briefly refer to humour, but these are not studies into the use of humour in projects. Clearly there is more work to be done in relation to the use of humour in managing projects in the construction and engineering sector. The focus here is to consider the use of humour in the context of managing project networks.

Humour and Socialisation

Humour has a social, or perhaps more accurately, 'socialisation' function. The idea of humour as 'play' which can release tension and provide a style of communication has a role in our networks because the effectiveness of communication is one of the criteria that we need to apply when considering how effective a given network is in relation to a particular project function. Our workplace is characterised by ambiguity and uncertainty (Martin, 2007). Complex project networks involving very large sums of money are particularly ambiguous and uncertain environments. There is uncertainty where hierarchies are less prominent – and we are pursuing the principle in this book that projects are not delivered by hierarchies at all. I propose that the day-to-day business of the project is dealt with by largely self-organising networks of human beings. So we might consider humour as a means of improving 'cohesiveness' (and cohesiveness as a term has its roots in network science). Cohesiveness is the propensity to connect with others, frequently relating to empathy and trust. Martin (2007) argues that we can build cohesiveness through humour. In particular, he argues that we might use humour to:

- Socialise new employees into the culture of the organisation, network or cluster within the network.
- Create a more pleasant work environment, with the benefits of staff retention, improved productivity, reduced friction and improved communications.

- Lessen status differentials – networks are essentially non-hierarchical, so creating a collaborative, democratic and enabling environment might usefully be fostered through humour.
- Improve cooperative behaviour.
- Create a form of non-confrontational and legitimate coercion – charm, rather than superiority, reinforced by incentives and sanctions.

Consalvo (1989) refers to 'transition points' in task-orientated environments. Chapter 5 refers to the transition that projects make from the procurement of human resources through typically formal dyadic contracts between client and service provider to the integrated team that has as its task delivery of the project. The output is specified in some detail, but the process is frequently not articulated by client or service provider at the same level of detail. We rely on routines and custom and practice, and on consultants and other service providers appointed to manage project actors with whom these managers do not have contractual relations. All of this in an industry where profit margins are typically slim. The uncertainty of business environment and the uncertainty of role combine to create potentially tense relationships between the actors comprising our self-organising networks. It is not difficult to see how humour might play a role here. We can convey an open, accepting, mutually supportive attitude – we can use humour to signal a willingness to work together (Consalvo, 1989).

Humour can be subversive – used to express disagreement and create division. It might be used to undermine the power or status of individuals or groups of individuals or to challenge values, attitudes or goals (Holmes and Marra, 2002). But perhaps there is an argument that using humour to express disagreement is more constructive and useful than the suppression of feelings of disagreement, which can lead to resentment and frustration. Dwyer (1991) noted that humour is used in organisations to deal with the inadequacies of managers, to highlight poor working conditions and to air frustration about contentious rules and procedures. Managers might use humour to mask the authoritarian nature of a message, weaken the collective power of subordinates or to support norms and expectations. Dwyer also observed that the relative power of an individual influences:

- Who tells the joke (or perhaps is given the opportunity to do so)
- Who (or what) is the target of the joke
- Who laughs.

Humour: Summary

Humour is a behaviour, or perhaps even a competence (and associated with emotional intelligence) (Yip and Martin, 2006), that operates within the context of the work environment and relates to personality traits. We might use humour to reduce tension between individuals in a network. Humour might help improve cohesiveness and improve the flow of information within our networks. It is a means of communicating and reinforcing norms and the associated behaviours. It is a means of dealing with some of the issues that can create friction between human beings – disagreements for example. It can also be used negatively to exclude individuals and groups of individuals and to reduce cohesion by emphasising the lack of homogeneity between groups, subgroups and networks. The use of humour to indicate empathy with other actors and a willingness to collaborate is important.

Profiling an Ideal Project Network Actor

When we either procure an individual as part of the service provision of a consultant or contractor or employ an individual to work within our own organisation, we tend to place an emphasis on their competencies within the context of their professional role. Some organisations will consider personality traits when employing staff directly, but most project procurement would not list individuals, their roles and the personality traits desirable in each case. In this next section, the traits that might be considered desirable for all project actors (aside from their professional experience and knowledge) are reviewed. Desirable and undesirable personality traits for network actors are considered. Finally, we make a link between network actor types and personality traits. I suggest that, to work well in a network environment, individuals need to exhibit the following behaviours:

- Generosity rather than meanness with communications containing information and knowledge relevant to the project. Those who are tardy with responses to queries from others slow the activities of the network down to the speed of the slowest actor.
- Discreet behaviour. Openness brings risks and all network actors need to avoid behaving in a way that abuses the privilege of being a member of a network.
- Ability to apply good judgement, perhaps based on experience and supported by training. Those exhibiting poor judgement tend to slow network activity. Those applying good judgement become prominent through the confidence that other actors show in their ability.
- Willingness to see that the objectives of the group and network as a whole must prevail over selfish interest.
- Ability to accurately assess the personality traits and abilities of others. This affects role allocations and reliability of communications.
- Conscientiousness. Because networks are not led or directed – they are *enabled* and *facilitated* – network actors are not necessarily under constant scrutiny from a line manager. We work in a matrix type of environment with conflicting demands from a relatively large group and frequently little support in deciding on how to prioritise time and other resources.
- Willingness to identify relationships that need to be established, to maintain these relationships over time and to intervene when relationships are not working well.
- Ability and confidence to work independently and make decisions independently of others within the employing organisation.[1] To do this an actor needs to have authority from his employment organisation to respond to individuals in project networks.

Specific Personality Traits

I now return to the specific personality traits listed in Table 7.1 to consider their relevance to network actors and their network-related roles.

Openness to experience – evidenced by a wide range of interests, imagination and insightful behaviour. This trait is important to all network actors and should become a metric in recruitment for those working in networks. Openness enables actors to assess network environments and adapt their own behaviour appropriately.

---

1 'Employing organisation' refers to the organisation that pays an individual's salary in the first instance.

Conscientiousness – evidenced by scrupulous, meticulous and principled behaviour; this trait involves a need to be conformant and focuses upon an individual's own conscience. This trait is desirable in moderation, particularly where actors are involved in complex and important activities involving interdependent and high-risk decisions. Meticulous and principled behaviour is what is needed where individuals are not closely managed – they are self-organising and to some extent self-managing. A problem can develop where this trait become excessive – an overly conscientious person, one who places an excessive emphasis on compliance with their own conscience, could lead an actor to become a gatekeeper hoarder (see Chapter 4) in the belief that they need to act to prevent the unscrupulous and unprincipled behaviours of others. Individuals with this trait in excess might also tend toward dysfunctional prominence (Chapter 12) – seeking to put themselves in a central position so that they can prevent the frailties of others manifesting themselves. Look for evidence of conscientiousness (through the type of work activity in which the individual excels), but watch out for those who are overly conscientious – see Heaven *et al.* (2001).

Extroversion – an extrovert relishes the opportunity of engaging with a group of people whom they have never met before; the introvert is horrified at the thought. So an extrovert might be an ideal network actor. But there is a degree of extroversion that is desirable, beyond which it is not desirable. We need actors who are extrovert enough to be willing to seek relationships with others and to maintain those relationships. One of the reasons that extroverts enjoy the company of others is that it provides a vehicle for them to express themselves and be heard. Extroverts do not necessarily listen very well and this might be a disadvantage in our project network environment. Extroverts like the authority and status that a hierarchy confers upon them; they may be less enthusiastic about winning a prominent position in a 'flat', non-hierarchical, network environment. This may cause excessively dominant behaviour. Extroverts make good boundary spanners and fill structural holes quickly because that is very much how they live their social lives – making connections to meet more people. Extroverts need to think about the needs of the introverts and to remember that the introvert is not motivated to be heard in the way that the extrovert is. The introvert may be aware of important information relevant to the network, but not feel the pressing need to make everyone else aware. Introverts are found in projects because those with very highly specialised skills might well be introverts – look for those who cast themselves in the role of isolate or as a member of a small isolated subgroup. Introverts need more extrovert boundary spanners to make connections when the communication within a subgroup needs dissemination, perhaps for coordination or integration purposes, with a larger part of the network population.

Agreeableness – this trait brings compliance, trust, empathy, sympathy, friendliness and cooperative behaviour. This is an important trait for all network actors. I argue that the single most important trait needed for successful collaborative behaviour is empathy. We work so much more effectively in networks if we understand the needs and perceptions of others.

Neuroticism – evidenced by emotional behaviour. Unemotional individuals might tend to be less empathetic or sympathetic. Minor, occasional displays of emotion can be endearing to other humans with frailties and perhaps might help to create an environment where trust develops. Much of what has been written about management and project management ignores human frailties and assumes that 'human resources' will behave consistently and with rationality, under instruction from others. It would be foolish to reject emotional behaviour or evidence of it in the workplace. We want more empathy, sympathy and cooperation and a move away from dictatorial behaviour and the display of leadership, which presumes the existence of a passive group of people who desire, or are willing, to be led. It is argued that in a project environment we will deal with a very diverse group of individuals and they do not need dictatorial leadership; they need support and enabling behaviour.

Self-esteem – actually the trait really should refer to high or low self-esteem. Excess on both ends of the spectrum should be avoided. Excessively high self-esteem might be regarded as arrogant and would tend to inhibit the formation of collaborative relationships. Those with excessively high self-esteem might seek prominence in networks as a way of illustrating their value to the network, with lots of connections and lots of material flowing through these connections. Dysfunctional prominence (see also case study in Chapter 12) in networks arises where an individual casts themselves in a very prominent role but where their prominence is associated with repeatedly delaying information flowing from others or the dissemination of information of low quality, resulting in highly iterative and relatively long exchanges. Those with low self-esteem might be eager to please others and may therefore make good network actors, responding promptly to requests for information from others, despite the perceived status of the individual requiring information.

Harm avoidance – individuals with this trait tend to be shy and fearful, possibly uncertain; they tend to worry. They are trying to avoid harm falling upon them, typically in the form of humiliation before colleagues. Those with high levels of harm avoidance do not make good prominent disseminators, boundary spanners or bridges (Chapter 4 refers) but in all other respects the desire to avoid harm motivates the actor to play an active and conscientious role in the activities of the network.

Novelty-seeking – this trait manifests itself in impulsive, experimental, fickle, extravagant and sometimes bad-tempered behaviour. Those with this trait lack consistency. While it might be desirable in computer game design or roles that rely on continual innovation, the lack of consistency and unpredictability would lead to poor risk management and a lack of reliability in a network representing an engineering or construction project. We would need to look in more detail at the project function being delivered by a particular network to understand where a novelty-seeking personality might fit. In subgroups dealing with highly specialised design and problem-solving, novelty seekers might well find a prominent role.

Perfectionism – this trait can indicate an obsessive personality; perfectionism might be useful in the sense of ensuring compliance in a technically complex, or high-risk environment, but Halmi *et al.* (2005) observed that perfectionism can be self-orientated. This is the pursuit of perfection for its own sake rather than in response to a need expressed by others. It may involve the pursuit of perfection that delivers no value to other project actors or the client/stakeholders for the project. This sort of obsessional behaviour can be disruptive to other actors who have to compromise to fulfil their roles within the network and to respond to the actors around them. Perfectionists might be found isolated or in small subgroups, partly because their behaviour disrupts others, but also perhaps because they find working with non-perfectionists quite difficult.

Alexithymia – an inability to express emotions, frequently linked with other traits and resulting from difficulties in early life. As a personality trait it might be regarded as not relevant in the work environment. But empathy and sympathy rely on the ability to engage emotionally with others and this may be difficult for those with alexithymia. Collaborative working in a network might also be difficult. This personality trait might manifest itself in introverted behaviour and a lack of understanding of the problems associated with others' perceptions.

Rigidity – resistance to change is a barrier to the effective operation of networks. If we accept that projects are delivered by networks of self-organising actors within the context of, in some cases, a relatively poorly articulated project delivery system, then we need flexibility. Rigidity works well if we still regard projects as delivered by static systems embedded in, and derived from, contractual conditions. Chapter 5 looks at the problems associated with unrealistic assumptions about projects, their procurement and delivery. Rigidity is one of the problems that we have to deal with in projects and the networks that deliver them. Complex projects involve flexibility during the whole procurement and delivery cycle. Those with rigidity as a personality trait might be uncomfortable and find it difficult to survive.

Impulsivity – the impulsive personality is risk taking and irrational. This personality tends to ignore the impact of their behaviour to be comfortable with themselves. They tend not to consider the future sufficiently. This trait is certainly not desirable in the context of projects. In relation to a network role, impulsivity would reduce the empathetic and sympathetic response to those around the impulsive actor, which would inhibit network formation and maintenance.

Disinhibition – inability to constrain impulses. It is difficult to see how this could be anything but negative for network actors. An undesirable trait in any network actor.

Psychoticism – the aggressive and hostile aspects of this trait would be most destructive to the formation and maintenance of network relationships. We need to avoid those with psychotic tendencies.

Obsessionality – many would argue that a tendency toward obsession is undesirable (see for example Salovskis, 1998). Unwelcome and disturbing ideas, thoughts and images would certainly be difficult for network actors to deal with. Yet there is a place for obsession if it is linked to a project function where perfection, for example, is important. Any activity where high risk is involved or where accuracy of a large number of small calculations is vital would benefit from the input of someone with an obsessional aspect to their personality. Those with high levels of obsessionality might be found in small subgroups, or as isolates, partly because the individuals find it difficult to relate to others who do not share their obsessive focus, and partly because others find it difficult to work with an obsessive personality.

If we accept that the best way to conceptualise the project is as a network of inter-organisational and interpersonal relationships providing a range of project functions, then we want to manage those networks and move forward to designing interpersonal networks for effective project delivery. Having considered some of the traits that are desirable for effective network actors in general, it might be useful to return to the particular network roles related to projects identified earlier in the book (see Chapter 4).

Network Roles and Personality Traits

Prominent Disseminators and Personality Traits

In prominent disseminators, we would look for the imaginative and insightful behaviour attributed to openness to experience. Disseminators are not necessarily designers or originators of information and we tend to assume that designers or information originators of some form or another are not necessarily the best disseminators. So, although we might think of the prominent disseminator as an extrovert, our projects might be better served by regarding the disseminator as a conscientious introvert, one who is slightly obsessive about detail, a perfectionist perhaps. In this way we might avoid some of the highly iterative behaviours associated with the sociable, agreeable extrovert, who is less than perfectly accurate and complete in regard to the detail that is so important to the many other actors reliant on the accuracy and timeliness of information. We need to consider the separation of problem-solving from design and from dissemination. If we think of these as three separate roles within the project function network, we will allocate roles to personality types more effectively.

Gatekeeper Hoarders and Personality Traits

These actor types may be an undesirable feature of our project networks through the self-defining nature of actor roles in complex project organisations. Alternatively the nature of the project may lead to the deliberate positioning of a gatekeeper in the network. Let's look at the first of these two scenarios.

Self-defining gatekeeper hoarders – these actors may design a gatekeeper hoarding role for themselves to address a low level of self-esteem. They may be perfectionists of the socially prescribed type – their mission being to create a world where others comply with their definition of perfection. In an environment with high levels of technical complexity the perfectionist may become obsessive.

Project function-enhancing gatekeeper hoarders – these actors are planted in the network. They exploit the natural tendencies of the actor to control information flows through the project network. The beneficial aspect of the gatekeeper hoarder is the performance of a filtering, controlling function. Hence in a situation where high levels of design coordination are needed, or critical design metrics need continual monitoring and control as information moves throughout the network, we might actively seek out an individual to fulfil the gatekeeper hoarder role. In this case, an actor with a mix of conscientiousness, perfectionism, rigidity and an allowable element of obsessionality would be sought. If they were also introverted and/or not entirely high in agreeableness, we would probably accept these undesirable traits as part of a human personality encompassing useful traits for fulfilling the controlling and detailed focus required of the gatekeeper hoarder.

Isolates and Personality Traits

Individuals with personality traits that closely match the network role that they have adopted or that the network has imposed will be happy. Those with traits that match less well to the network role will be uncomfortable. This principle is nowhere more evident than with the isolate actor type. Isolates are not connected to any other actors within the context of a particular prescribed project function. This does not mean that they are never connected to any other actor. Isolates who are introverted and/or conscientious, possibly a little rigid and obsessional, might be quite happy as isolates. Indeed to place this actor in a highly connected environment might be stressful and uncomfortable for them, leading to anxiety and perhaps aggressive or psychotic behaviour. It follows that the extrovert, novelty-seeking, impulsive personality type might find an isolated network position quite difficult, leading to *connective behaviour* – the desire to link to others, regardless of purpose. Isolated dyads and triads are small clusters of two or three individuals who are comfortable being disconnected from the remainder of a relatively large network. It follows that these small clusters are the evolution of individual isolates connected perhaps by a need to share risk or information in some way. Personality traits are not absolute; they are a matter of degree. Some individuals might be happier in a dyad or triad with some connectivity as opposed to the total isolation of the isolate. Appropriate personality types for dyads and triads will be similar to those for the isolate type.

Boundary Spanners – the Best Fit for Personality Traits

If we accept the hypothesis that human beings engaged in projects operate within essentially self-organising networks (Chapter 5) within possibly poorly defined boundaries set by various contracts and protocols, then we have to accept that boundary spanners are a function of the needs of the actors. I suggest in Chapter 5 that actors make connections to other actors as a result of their need to gather and share information. In this chapter I add the dimension that actors may design network roles that respond to emotional needs – their desire to communicate with others or be prominent in a social group, or alternatively to be isolated from others. Perhaps the happy boundary spanner is a combination of both factors: an actor anxious to gather information in order to carry out their highly interdependent role in the project, and an actor whose personality lends itself to the establishment and maintenance of positive and enjoyable working relationships with others. So, boundary spanners are self-defined rather than placed within the project network.

To operate and be happy as a boundary spanner an actor might arguably have a mix of the following personality traits:

- Openness to experience – imaginative and insightful
- Extroversion
- Agreeableness – including being friendly and cooperative by nature
- High levels of self-esteem, providing confidence
- Perhaps a 'novelty seeking' aspect, including a tendency toward exploratory, fickle, excitable, bad-tempered and extravagant traits.

And it follows that a successful and happy boundary spanner would be less likely to be introverted; to have low self-esteem; to be shy, fearful or worrisome; to be a self-orientated perfectionist, rigid or overly obsessional.

It is clear that the problem-solver, disseminator and boundary spanner roles are suited to somewhat different personality types. This is important because in our projects we expect that problem-solving dissemination and boundary spanning will be carried out by very similar actors appointed for their abilities and knowledge in, for example, the area of structural design.

Bridges and Personality Traits

We make the distinction between boundary spanners and bridges because the former links groups that would otherwise be isolated or weakly connected while the latter focuses on the path lengths associated with the removal of a particular actor in a network. They come into play where two or more groups would still be connected without the bridging link, but where individual actors have to use longer paths once a bridge is removed. Boundary spanners may be responding either to the motivation to gather or disseminate information in order to earn a living within a given network, or responding to a personal need to make contact with other human beings, perhaps to be heard. The bridge does not have these characteristics. The bridge is less likely to be self-defined by an actor and more likely to be placed or removed by those in network roles who influence the flows between the connections in a network. Bridges are of strategic importance and may be removed or inserted for strategic reasons. The bridge is therefore a compliant individual with a high level of cooperative tendencies. They may have some incentive to please another actor who might benefit from the bridge and path-shortening associated with the insertion of the bridge.

Summary

At the beginning of the chapter the link was made between the personality traits of individual actors in a project environment and the characteristics of the networks that ensued. The impact that personality might have on the establishment, evolution and maintenance of networks responding to project functions was also explored. Chapter 4 considered the transition from procurement of resources to the establishment of the networks that deliver the project functions. This self-organising aspect of projects and the implication for governance are important.

The discussion was provided with context by restating the project functions that were used for the primary research reported in Pryke (2012). This previous research project classified the activity of construction projects, post-contract, into five key functions. These functions provided the classification for the networks derived from the data gathered from those four comparative project case studies. The major infrastructure case study in Chapters 10–13 of this book employed a larger group of project function classifications, providing more detail in relation to the operation of these networks. The point of reviewing both lists of classifications was to understand the project environments in which analyses of construction projects are carried out.

In exploring the environment for our project function-related networks, I revisited the actor characteristics for the four construction projects reported in Pryke (2012). These were essentially *network roles* rather than *project function-related roles*. The distinction between these two role types is important in moving forward in the way in which we manage projects – towards a greater emphasis on understanding and managing the networks underpinning and responding to the project function-related roles.

At this point the discussion moved on to a review of generic personality trait classifications. I discussed the possibility of a network actor personality profile – characteristics that are beneficial in all actors in networks. I then linked personality traits with the main classifications of network roles derived from the primary research in Pryke (2012).

What sort of personality do we need for prominent disseminators? What sort of personality traits can we expect to find in isolates or those operating in isolated subgroups? It was acknowledged that a range of personality traits might feasibly be involved in particular network roles – but the issue of whether the actor is comfortable with their network environment is a factor for consideration.

The topic of humour was introduced and I discussed the relevance of humour in social networks. If we accept that humour has a role to play in our social lives, that humans approach work in a very similar way to play, and that there is no reason for work to be regarded as the antithesis of play – then we start to see the importance of humour as a contributor to the establishment of effective project delivery networks and their evolution and maintenance over time. Whether we want to regard humour as a personality trait or an emotional competence is a matter for further discussion.

The link between this chapter and the book as a contribution to the future analysis and management of projects and their supply chains is this: as discussed in Chapter 5, we procure resources for our projects, and these human beings, typically motivated by a desire to deliver their project role and make a return in the process, form networks that are not prescribed in any of the documents providing and underpinning the governance of the project. If we analyse these networks we can find ways to understand the detail of how projects are delivered and so manage the networks that we identify. Personality is a factor not commonly considered by social network analysts, there being a tendency to focus on the characteristics of the linkages rather than the characteristics of the nodes. I hope that this chapter will help to establish an agenda for further discussion of the value of considering nodal characteristics and personality traits, and their relevance to project function-related networks. If we understand the effects of various personality types on network roles, then we might move toward designing and maintaining more effective project networks.

8

Network Enabling

What Do We Mean by Network Enabling?

Some have argued (Oliver and Liebeskind, 1998, for example) that there are three kinds of network present in organisations:

- Intra-organisational, interpersonal
- Inter-organisational, interpersonal
- Inter-organisational.

The relationships for the latter category are frequently formal, dyadic relationships of a contractual nature (Pryke, 2012). Increasingly we see a tendency to reduce the emphasis on the adversarial and remedial aspects of contracts and their management, towards a more collaborative position where the emphasis moves towards relational agreements, sometimes in parallel with formal dyadic contracts. There is some value in the comparison between the contractual relationships – perhaps with some 'governance modifying' (Pryke, 2012) collaborative, relational arrangements – and the day-to-day behaviour of the individuals subject to these arrangements, that is, the first two of the network categories above. We can compare formal and relational agreements with actual practice; the study of intra-organisational interpersonal relationships and inter-organisational interpersonal relationships provides very rich data for this purpose. Typically we would study intra- and inter-organisational interpersonal relationships concurrently and code the respective nodes (perhaps by colour or shape) to facilitate the interpretation and analysis of this network data.

As with any type of structural analysis in organisations, we need to understand the context. The context impacts upon behaviour and vice versa. In our study of project organisations we might like to consider:

- External threats – external to the project and external to the firms forming the project coalition.
- The extent, strength and nature of interdependencies existing between project actors – these interdependencies will be durable in some cases but transient in other cases.
- Reputational context of the project, previous similar projects; is there a history of failure in this type of project or for this type of coalition, or for this coalition specifically in the past? This will affect the expectations and aspirations of individuals.
- Nature of the technical environment for the project – highly innovative, experimental or traditional and shaped by an emphasis on safety, for example.

Managing Networks in Project-Based Organisations, First Edition. Stephen Pryke.
© 2017 John Wiley & Sons Ltd. Published 2017 by John Wiley & Sons Ltd.

- Pressure of time
  - At the front end during the project definition phase
  - Lead time, during the startup and mobilisation phase
  - Post-contract delivery.
- Risk context – lack of certainty about scope; levels of risk transferred legitimately and non-legitimately; reputation among the network actors for fair risk compensation behaviour.
- Certainty about the scope of individual tasks, as well as the scope of the project and the programme within which it might sit.

Within these contexts, to which I will return in later chapters, there are 'network enabling factors' that affect the configuration and other characteristics of the network. These 'network enabling factors' will have an impact on the density of the networks, the distribution of prominence among the actors, the existence or otherwise of isolates and isolated clusters, the strength of ties between the actors and the existence of structural holes,[1] for example. These network enabling factors will affect the speed and accuracy of communications and the ability of the network collectively to solve problems, resolve disputes and provide integration (Holti *et al.*, 2000). These factors are important to our understanding of projects and their effectiveness. This chapter will review these factors and provide a framework for their application. The factors are as follows:

- Trust – the existence and maintenance of trust; how trust is derived, established and consolidated over the life of the project.
- Empathy – objectives and needs are misconstrued, disputes arise and in some cases networks fail, because of a lack of empathy. Empathy is the ability of an individual to put themselves in the position of others and to relate to that position and the constraints and anxieties associated with that position.
- Reciprocity – the extent to which an individual is willing or able to reciprocate in network terms. If an actor freely shares ideas with another, the other actor might be inclined to freely share ideas also.
- Favours – one of the transaction currencies of network is the 'favour'.
- Generosity – linked to the two factors above.

Set against these network enabling factors, we have a range of actor behaviours that disenable network formation and development and tend to lead to decline and redundancy in previously successfully established networks. The disenablers are:

- Competitiveness and opportunism
- Narcissism
- Egotism.

These three factors are destructive to networks and tend to create lower levels of density in information exchange networks and to lead to structural holes and inappropriate levels of prominence (temporarily) in some actors.

The remainder of this chapter will explore network enabling factors and network disenablers.

---

1 Structural holes are disconnections in an otherwise connected network. These might involve, for example, a lack of connections between two interdependent parts of a project organisation. Ron Burt (see for example, Burt, 2004, 2009) is widely recognised as the most prominent writer on this subject.

Trust

We start with the question of whether trust is a product of the relationships within a network, or a *prerequisite* for the formation of relationships and the evolution of the associated networks. Jensen *et al.* (2006) contend that trust emerges from long-lasting relations among individuals (actors) who have good reputations within the network. Others have noted that trust is context dependent and relates to the perceptions of individual actors (Kadefors, 2004; Wong and Cheung, 2004). Very few studies have attempted to link trust to project performance (but see Diallo and Thuillier, 2005, for an exception).

> Trust is a psychological state comprising the intention to accept vulnerability based upon positive expectation of the intentions or behaviours of another
> *Rousseau et al. (1998: 395)*

It is suggested that trust is a characteristic and function of *interpersonal interactions* and can only exist between *organisations* to the extent that individuals within those organisations maintain a degree of trust between them. Jeffries and Reed (2000, cited in Pinto *et al.*, 2009) contend that the way in which trust develops and the perceptions about the level of trust existing are related to the differing expectations of clients, Tier 1 and Tier 2 organisations. So behaviours that might engender trust with clients or employers would not necessarily work with professional service providers or contractors and subcontractors.

The problem with engendering and maintaining trust is that the project has a finite duration and this may be a relatively short period of time (Hartman, 2002). In terms of facilitating interpersonal relationships, fixing problems and moving on to reap the benefits, the construction project of perhaps 18 months to 3 years does not provide an ideal environment. The effect of this is compounded by the fact that most organisations do not enter the procurement phases of their projects with network evolution and maintenance as a focus, primary or otherwise. Many have attempted to classify trust and the behaviour associated with trust (see Mayer *et al.*, 1995; Romahn and Hartman, 1999; Rousseau *et al.*, 1998). Mayer *et al.* (1995) emphasised benevolence, ability and integrity; Chowdhury (2005) and Webber and Klimoski (2004), among others, opted for a simple classification citing 'affective'[2] and 'cognitive'[3] trust.

If we use the rationale of the transaction cost economists (Williamson (1996) being one of the most prominent) we come to the conclusion that an individual actor's behaviour, particularly in relation to opportunism (which is a destructive force in relation to trust), will relate to their view about the likelihood of further work within the current context and from the same client organisation. In network terms, opportunism has an inverse relationship with the desire to maintain current connections in a network – we modify our behaviour in network transactions based upon future anticipated transactions with a given actor (Pinto *et al.*, 2009) – see also the section on reciprocity, favours and psychological contracts below.

---

2 Affective trust is based upon mutual concern for others and/or some sort of emotional link between actors.
3 Cognitive trust is based upon the personal belief that an individual actor has in the competence and ability of another actor in relation to a particular task.

Some (House *et al.*, 1995) suggest that trust is a 'meso'-level concept, integrating micro-level psychological processes and group dynamics with 'macro-level' institutional arrangements. This links to a point made earlier about whether trust can exist between organisations or whether it is a product of interpersonal relationships spanning organisations within a project coalition.

Social psychologists often see trust as 'existing or not' (Rousseau *et al.*, 1998), yet the social network analyst would 'value' those linkages in terms of degree of trust and perhaps consider trust in terms of different aspects of a relationship – for example: 'I trust you to come up with an innovative design but not to act solely in my interest in terms of financial management.' But we must also consider the value or weighting of trust over time. Trust is transient and partly a function of the experiences of the individual within a given network environment. So trust cannot be a single value over time, it is transient, like so many of the other factors that influence the effectiveness of relationship networks.

Implications of Trust for Networks

Trust must be a factor when project actors 'filter' the information that they process as part of daily life. Perhaps they are trying to reach information or knowledge that is remote in network terms (long path lengths from one actor to another). If the role allocated, either contractually or acquired from the network, requires an actor to filter, process or disseminate information from other actors, then trust will influence the extent to which filtering, processing or dissemination takes place, and the time at and extent to which these might be abandoned due to pressure of time. Low levels of trust in a project network would manifest themselves in low levels of density within communication networks. But the network environment would be a factor. Networks become denser as actors become more desperate for information. So the effects of pressure of time would need to be isolated from the effects of levels of trust. In addition to network density for information exchange networks, we need to focus on the prominence (centrality) of a given actor and the distinction between in-degree and out-degree centrality values. So it follows that an actor with a low trust value might feel confident to disseminate widely (high out-degree centrality) but other actors might seek to reduce their own in-degree centralities to deal with this low-trust-value information. We might also consider using a broker (perhaps one with high levels of relevant knowledge or experience) to provide a connection to a low trust isolate or isolated subgroup.

I am considering the design of networks that foster the establishment and maintenance of high levels of trust – we should seek to establish networks with an absence of extreme levels of prominence. Diversity in levels of prominence may tend to undermine the establishment of trust. We seek a 'democratic network' rather than an 'autocratic network'. This means that we want to see low levels of standard deviation in point centrality, eigenvector and betweenness centrality for project actors. We want to avoid a small number of very prominent actors with a wide variation between in-degree and out-degree centrality.

Empathy

The ability to understand and relate to the feelings and perceptions of others is a human attribute that is overlooked in the world of complex projects. Empathy has relevance to projects and their management in two senses. Firstly, project managers need to understand how they conceptualise the project, and there is a range of ideas here. Pryke and Smyth (2006) identified four main groups of conceptual approaches:

Traditional project management approaches – based upon a range of tools and techniques. There are, for example, critical path analysis (Higgin and Jessop, 1965), flow charts (Franks, 1998) and linear responsibility analysis (Walker, 2015), among other techniques for managing projects.

Functional management approach – strategic management of projects focusing on 'front-end' supply chain management and what might be referred to as 'task-driven' agendas. Morris (1994, 2013) has emphasised the importance of a strategic view applied to project definition and the importance of building systems to deliver the project.

Information processing – Winch (2000) has conceptualised the project as an information processing system. The case study material presented in Chapters 10–13 very much emphasises this as a useful conceptual position.

Relationship approach to managing projects – Those who focus upon techniques and systems in project management frequently forget to mention people. Projects are initiated, designed, managed, constructed, maintained and serviced by networks of people (Pryke and Smyth, 2006: 23). Relationships exist within a context and affect that context as well as being affected by that context. Projects are delivered through relationships between firms, organisations and individuals (perhaps as employees) and interpersonal relationships, both inter-organisational and intra-organisational.

So, there is an issue relating to how we choose to conceptualise the project and this conceptualisation very much defines the terminology and approach in managing the project. There is also an issue at a personal level. Each role-holding actor, as an individual, has a perception of their role in the project, as a project in itself. We individually try to understand our own roles and the delivery of the services which those roles comprise. This perception is influenced by how we perceive the definition of the project and the definition of our own role. It is also influenced by the agency problem – the idea that we have our own agendas and as agents we do not necessarily execute our role with the same focus on the client's objectives as the principal or client might do themselves. What we enact is a function of our understanding of the objectives of the project as a whole and the compromises that we overlay in pursuit of self-interest. Dave Taylor's now classic cartoon sequence, summarises that agency problem and its manifestation in our projects wonderfully (see Figure 8.1).

Defining Empathy

Empathy allows us to 'tune in' to how someone else is feeling, or what they might be thinking. Empathy allows us to understand the intentions of others, predict their behaviour and experience an emotion triggered by their emotion (Baron-Cohen and Wheelwright, 2004: 163). Empathy is related to sympathy but *empathy* is of more interest to us in a project environment. Sympathy is a special case of the 'affective'[4] component of empathy. Empathy is the ability to understand how someone is feeling. Sympathy is the need to respond to that feeling in some way. Sympathy occurs when the observer response to the distress of another leads to the desire to take action to alleviate the other

---

4 'Affective' relates to emotions.

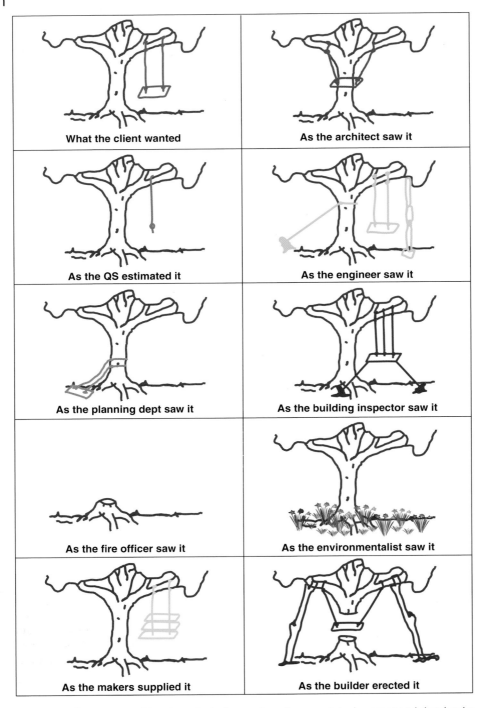

Figure 8.1 The agency problem in projects. Source: based on an original concept and sketches by Dave Taylor, c. 1965 (exact origin obscure).

person's suffering (Davis, 1994). Empathy can be classified as affective – the emotional response to someone else's situation (see Eisenberg and Miller, 1987, for example), or cognitive – understanding how someone else's feelings are derived (see the classic work of Kohler (1929) and Mead (1934), for example),

A person walking past a homeless person sleeping rough on the street in winter who felt pity would be classed as empathetic; a person walking past who felt pity and then stopped to respond by giving money or a warm coat would be sympathetic; the person who walks past thinking that they feel fortunate not to be sleeping rough themselves would be neither empathetic or sympathetic (Baron-Cohen and Wheelwright, 2004).

So, in our complex and highly interdependent projects, we should value the ability to understand and relate to the feelings and perceptions of others without the desire to intervene and change their situation.

Implications of Empathy for Networks

It is not clear at present whether the degree of empathy held by individual project actors would have a structural effect on project networks. Empathy does, however, undoubtedly have an effect on the *value* of the links in a network. More specifically, empathy has the effect of reducing the iterations necessary to complete a process or task. Complex tasks are rarely achieved in a single outgoing action by an actor.[5] The design of a particular aspect of a building is issued to others, for the purpose of coordination and integration, and this gives rise to a response relating to problems with the initial proposal in the attempt to integrate it with other project elements. This process may comprise multiple iterations and rarely leads to a totally 'complete' solution. Empathy would help in reducing the number of iterations. And the value of the linkage, expressed in the frequency of communications, would be lessened. The difficulty we face is in disaggregating the effects of efficiency and urgency in project communications from the effects of empathy.

Reciprocity, Favours and Psychological Contracts

There has been lot of discussion about the psychological contracts that exist between organisational employers and their employees. Yet a very similar situation exists between individual role-holding actors in projects and the other role-holding actors. Project actors need to manage relationships in order to coordinate activities and share information. Legal documentation, particularly where the task and the relationships are complex, rarely deals with these relationships with the flexibility required (Hill *et al.*, 2009; Kingshott and Pecotich, 2007). Documentation is frequently incomplete in terms of dealing with all eventualities over the duration of a large or complex project (Walker and Pryke, 2008, 2009, 2011). The project is a network of role-holding actors exchanging information and providing a range of project management functions in pursuit of project delivery. The relationships between these actors in processing information through multiple iterations over time also involves psychological contracts.

---

5 Although contract conditions commonly presume that an instruction or direction *is* a single outgoing action.

If an individual actor issues information to another actor in the network, the speed and accuracy of the other's response is a function of the psychological contract that exists between those two actors. If at some point in the future an actor knows that they will need to ask for a very quick response to a request for approval, for example, it would be unwise to routinely delay in replying to requests for approvals, for example.

Where an actor does not honour the unwritten rules of network engagement a 'contract violation' (Robinson and Morrison, 2000) occurs. Psychological contract violation can occur in two ways (Hill *et al.*, 2009): an actor might renege by intentionally failing to meet an obligation to one or other actors; an actor might also violate the contract through *incongruence* (Morrison and Robinson, 1997). Incongruence might lead to *perceived* violation of the contract as a result of differing understandings of obligations or commitments, complexity or ambiguity in the relationship(s), or a lack of communication between the parties.

These three aspects of incongruence violation seem to link the offerings of Mr Taylor in Figure 8.1 and the early but still unresolved issues arising out of the work of the Tavistock Institute ('Interdependence and Uncertainty', Tavistock, 1966). Half a century after the seminal work of the Tavistock Institute, we may at last have the opportunity through the study of information exchange networks in projects and the multiple incidences of violation of psychological contracts to begin to understand the nature of the problem with interdependence and uncertainty in our projects – and more importantly the resolution of these issues.

In an enterprise (as against a project organisation) we would expect to deal with psychological contract violation through discussion, managerial intervention, appraisals, peer pressure and ultimately a sanction of some sort or even dismissal. In a project environment, we are in a network with a large group of actors from a range of other coalition member organisations. Long term, those who violate psychological contracts between network actors may find that they may not be invited to bid or negotiate framework agreements (long-term relationships). But this decision is frequently not available to those suffering as a result of the violation in the project context, and their voices might not be heard when the relevant (project and supply chain) decisions are made at a later date. We may also choose to remain silent for the purposes of avoiding reduction of opportunities for further work. So, once the contracts are signed, we are in a network that is *unlikely* to lose actors through violation of their psychological contracts. The contracts that we have all signed typically do not deal with violation of psychological contracts. There is further discussion relevant to this point in Chapter 5.

So there is a sense that the currency of the network embedded in our project is the *favour*. We essentially trade favours with one another. Reciprocity is a matter of ethical behaviour and some actors will not behave ethically, or may be prevented from behaving ethically because of pressures from within the project environment or from their own employers. So we build credit with other project actors and use that credit when we ourselves have need of reciprocity from others.

Implications of Violation of Psychological Contracts

Networks within which there is a culture of reciprocity are more likely to function effectively. Email as a means of communication, which is now predominant in projects, provides transparency in relation to reciprocity. Unintentional violation of the

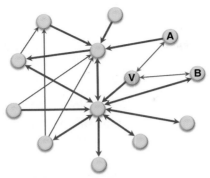

Commentary on Figure 8.2a: Network response to violator
Look for: node reference 'V' is the violator, causing slow reciprocity for nodes A and B and possibly slowing the flow from A and B to the central node. The network responds as per Figure 8.2b.

Figure 8.2a Dealing with psychological contract violators in networks [before].

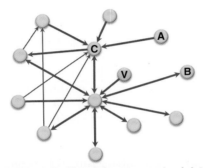

Commentary on Figure 8.2b: Network response to violator
Look for: node reference 'V' is the violator. Node A responds by using an alternative route to the central actor via node C. This provides the same path length through an alternative actor. We assume that node C has similar or substitutable attributes to node V (which might not be the case). Node B already had a direct link to the central actor and, providing that the reciprocity or lack of it with node V is not a barrier, is free to link directly to the central actor. It possibly raises the question as to why node B was connected to node V initially. Node V finds that it has a one-directional link to the central actor, but is no longer fed by nodes A and B. There may be implications for the viability of node V's role in this network reconfiguration.

Figure 8.2b Dealing with psychological contract violators in networks [after].

psychological contract within project information exchange and processing networks will be tolerated in the short term, where it is associated with absence due to illness or peaks of workload. Intentional violation should be regarded as a 'structural hole' (Burt, 2004) by the non-violating actors around and dependent on the violator, and the network should endeavour collectively to find a means of bridging that structural hole. Figures 8.2a and 8.2b illustrate how the psychological contract violator is isolated and alternative paths created.

This simple example of the treatment of a psychological contract violator is an illustration of one of the network issues that can frustrate or disrupt projects. This type of fix is self-organising and decentralised. Awareness might provide better identification of and better choices about interventions, and ultimately the design of network topography that enables better project execution.

Generosity

Generosity is an economic and social phenomenon present to a greater or lesser extent in all forms of social activity (with work activity included in the term 'social' here); see d'Exelle and Riedl (2010). But why is a discussion about generosity appropriate at this point in a book dealing with the management of project networks? In our networks relating to projects we see low levels of network management and governance. In Chapter 5 the self-organising nature of interpersonal project exchanges is discussed. Actors are allocated a role, in part by the contracts in which the services they provide are stated – both employment contracts within their employing firms and contracts for service provision which their employing firms have entered into. In a network environment, because of the nature of communications, which are essentially personal communications rather than inter-organisational communication, there is a degree of freedom of behaviour. Hence, relatively junior individuals will have the authority to address clients and customers directly, protocols such as letter drafting and signature by a senior member of staff having long been abandoned.

So actors each have a role in the network in which they are members to deliver a project. These roles will include originating information, processing information originated by others, commenting on and agreeing the detail of information provided by others and making decisions about the 'completeness' of information destined for other parts of the network. The manner in which and extent to which network actors input and contribute to various collaborative tasks with which the network must deal is partly a result of their tendency or otherwise toward generosity.

Humans are quite remarkable in their exhibition of 'prosocial behaviour' (Haley and Fessler, 2005) in a purely social and recreational environment. Prosocial behaviour is the tendency to cooperate with and show altruism toward others. Where prosocial behaviour occurs, actors behave in a way that reduces opportunistic behaviour and makes 'free-riding' more difficult and expensive. But very little has been written about prosocial behaviour in the project environment, which is essentially a business environment. I argue here that information exchange networks essentially comprise a sequence of interdependent games (see Chapter 6) and the effectiveness and efficiency of these games are dependent upon the generosity of project actors.

It is not common practice for organisations to issue behavioural guidelines to employees relating to network behaviour. When we engage with other networks for the purpose of buying goods we have reputational data that is provided as a condition of engaging with the network (eBay buyer and seller references, for example; seller information on Amazon). But any such feedback in relation to project networks is anecdotal and less methodical in its collection. Project actors have therefore to create a network good-behaviour culture. Although once again the research was not in a business or project environment, Tsvetkova and Macy (2014) argue that generosity in network behaviour can be promoted through social contagion. They argue that we learn to exhibit generous behaviour principally through two mechanisms: firstly, those who

Commentary on Figure 8.3: Generalised reciprocity
Actor B helps actor C because B has been helped and has received a
measure of generosity from A. B helps C out of a sense of wishing to
help another in the same way in which they themselves have been
helped.

Figure 8.3 Contagion of generosity: generalised reciprocity. Source: Adapted from Tsvetkova and
Macy (2014: 2).

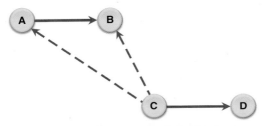

Commentary on Figure 8.4: Third-party influence
Actor C helps actor D because C has observed A helping B. C helps D
through a desire to replicate the actions of A. Solid lines represent help
(generosity) and the dashed lines represent observation.

Figure 8.4 Contagion of generosity: third-party influence. Source: Adapted from Tsvetkova and
Macy (2014: 2).

receive generosity from others are more likely to behave generously themselves.
Secondly, observers of generous behaviour are inclined to emulate such behaviour (see
also reciprocity above). Social contagion of generosity is therefore either a function of
being a beneficiary of generosity and wanting to respond, or observing generosity and
feeling the desire to behave similarly. Figures 8.3 and 8.4 illustrate this point.

Generalised reciprocity differs in the pattern of transmission. In the case of generalised reciprocity, the contagion is spread from one actor to another. In the case of third-
party influence a number of other actors could be influenced by actor A's generosity to
actor B. Third-party influence is therefore potentially much more influential in terms of
the network as a whole.

The effects of third-party influence, shown in Figure 8.4, are essentially a result of
informational influence (Deutsch and Gerard, 1955) in which an actor behaves in a
manner that s/he regards as socially approved. When influence is informational, the
actor is responding to a descriptive rather than a prescriptive norm (Tsvetkova and
Macy, 2014). When the influence is 'normative' an actor is effectively behaving in a
manner that will lead to that actor being liked and accepted by the network (or group).
Normative social influence is also referred to as peer pressure and its effectiveness is
related to individual desire on the part of actors for social approval from others. Pre-
existing social relationships (such as where extra-project collaborative relationships
have been established and maintained perhaps through a framework agreement or
other long-term partnering arrangement) are likely to lead to a stronger desire for an

individual actor to seek peer group approval for their behaviour. Novel or transient relationships (such as where 'spot tendering' in a non-collaborative contracting environment is the norm) tend to rely on cues from network neighbours to influence behaviour, rather than social approval influencing behaviour.

Social distance (the number of links between one individual and another) is a factor in the extent and depth of generosity. Homogeneity (the extent to which actors are similar in their characteristics) is a factor in the density of networks that a given group will establish and maintain. Homogeneity is also, therefore, a factor in generosity within a given network. It is suggested here that part of the homogeneity measure relates to 'expertise distance' as well as social distance. The wider the differences in education and knowledge between actors, the more difficult it is to form dense networks and the less likelihood there is of generosity between actors.

Generosity in the context of project networks has two components. Firstly, there is a tendency to connect to others; for example, the generosity manifests itself in a tendency to copy more individuals into a message, rather than fewer – the generosity is measured by the number of connections an actor makes when disseminating information (a given actor's out-degree centrality). The second aspect is the value of the linkages with other actors expressed in terms of accuracy, frequency and reliability, including timeliness of information exchange. Generosity is an important characteristic of behaviour in project networks. It may be cultivated in a homogeneous environment or one where relationships have pre-existed prior to project commencement, perhaps through a long-term collaborative arrangement; it may also be cultivated through some form of best-practice behaviour where champions exhibit generous network behaviour and social contagion spreads that behaviour to others. We have focused upon actor behaviours that are beneficial to networks and therefore need encouragement and management. Individual actors do not necessarily behave in ways that are beneficial to the network, however. I now look at the destructive network behaviours.

Characteristics of Individuals that are Destructive for Networks

Competitiveness is part of our daily lives, whether in finding a mate, obtaining gainful employment or involvement in the daily commute. Yet the 'need to win' (Franken and Brown, 1996) is a negative influence upon the effectiveness of a diverse network of experts faced with the design and execution of a complex project. Indeed some individuals find competition inviting in almost every aspect of their lives. Some might refer to this as 'hypercompetitiveness' (Mudrack *et al.*, 2012). Not all individuals feel compelled to compete in all contexts, but generally if you are a competitive type you will feel the need to compete almost regardless of context. We are employed by enterprises that compete for work in projects and need to compete with other enterprises in order to win work. Within the employment context of those firms, individuals are expected to compete with each other on an inter-firm basis – this is 'accepted, praised and routinely encouraged' (Pfeffer and Sutton, 2006: 64); indeed it is the basis of promotion within the enterprise and career advancement beyond the enterprise. So there is a dichotomy here. In order to gain employment and succeed in that employment we are mostly expected to behave competitively toward our fellow employees. Those individuals are unlikely then to behave very differently when dealing with personal inter-firm relationships – in the way that individuals do in project networks. Small-group research conducted over extended periods (Glaman *et al.*, 2002; Tjosvold *et al.*, 2006) has shown that competitive behaviour in a group environment produces 'undesirable outcomes'. Conflict-damaged or dysfunctional relationships and poor psychological health have been attributed to competitive behaviour in groups. Furthermore, highly competitive or hypercompetitive individuals rarely make high performers (Bing, 1999; Elliot and McGregor, 2001). Competitive attitudes can lead to unethical behaviour – lies, cheating, espionage and sabotage are no strangers to the highly competitive business environment (Mudrack *et al.*, 2012). So why is individual competitiveness so frequently seen, certainly in so-called 'Western' societies,[6] as desirable and important, particularly when the evidence suggests that competitiveness has a negative impact upon our activities?

Leibbrandt *et al.*'s (2013) work on the comparative competitiveness of fishermen based on the environment in which they have to fish may help here. The authors contend that individuals evolve traits that respond to specific needs associated with their environment at a given time. So we are partly a product of the environments that we have experienced throughout our lives. We effectively expect our project actors to exhibit low competitive network behaviour in project networks in contrast to the sort of behaviour that is acceptable and normal in the enterprise from which they, as project resources, are taken.

Narcissism

Narcissism is an exceptional interest in, or admiration of, oneself. Individuals seek to regulate their self-esteem (deal with the way that they feel about themselves) by employing defences such as denial, rationalisation, 'attributional egotism', sense of entitlement and ego aggrandisement (Brown, 1997). So the need for self-esteem in some measure is located within the individual. Organisations and temporary project organisations in particular are constructed by and exist within the minds of the individuals who have actor roles in networks serving project functions. So individuals behave in a manner that serves their own sense of self-esteem – located within who the individual believes that they are, their status and the value which they attach to themselves. Enterprises have a collective self-esteem, reflected in their promotional publicity material, their mission statement and the symbolic gestures of those charged with management functions. Perhaps the project can also have or acquire a collective sense of self. Narcissism in individuals is accompanied by, and relates to, a sense of anxiety – narcissistic individuals and those around them in their network need to validate the individual's self-esteem (Watson, 1994; Weick, 1995; Zaleznik, 1966). The anxiety of individuals in attempting to fulfil their role in the context of a network of other actors holding project roles is an important subject area. The move toward project function-related networks and away from institutional hierarchies of authority leaves actors with fewer reference

---

6 In Asian economies, certainly in the past, competitiveness between individual employees is less prevalent and acceptable. More emphasis, typically, is placed upon the team and the enterprise, rather than individual competitiveness. Indeed in some Asian environments it may be embarrassing to an individual to be identified as one who is in some way distinguished.

points for behaviour. In a sense, the network of actors defines what constitutes normal and accepted behaviour.

Clearly, narcissistic behaviour is unhelpful in project networks. If individuals seek to affirm their self-esteem through their interactions in the network, inappropriate prominence is likely to occur. One of the manifestations of narcissistic behaviour is 'dysfunctional prominence' (dealt with in Chapter 12). This occurs where an individual actor builds their own prominence to a level where it becomes disruptive to the functioning of the network. An individual who acquires information for the purposes of coordination but then retains that information for an inordinate length of time, creating increasingly iterative interactions, is creating dysfunctional prominence in relation to themselves. Dysfunctional prominence is undesirable in project networks and one of the benefits of the examination of project networks is the early elimination of dysfunctional prominence. I return to this topic in Chapter 12.

Egotism

The extent of egotism in individuals is important where individuals contribute to a cooperative group (Miller, 1992; Schlenker, 1982) or project network. Inevitably, individuals claim more credit personally and privately than perhaps their contribution and involvement really justifies; conversely individuals tend to negatively exaggerate their contribution to failures within their groups, privately at least. Publicly, on the other hand, individuals tend not to emphasise their personal contribution to success as a means of maintaining good relations and trust within their network. Tetlock (1981) showed that an individual's attributions (the extent to which they claimed credit for their positive contributions and denied or accepted some responsibility for their negative contributions) varied considerably with the conditions under which they are reporting and most importantly, varied with the interpersonal images that an individual actor wished to create (Reiss *et al.*, 1981). So individual actors may exaggerate their contribution to the successes achieved by the network. They may also feel that they deserve more credit than other actors in the network. The egotist feels that s/he is superior to other actors, whether in success or failure conditions.

Clearly, if each actor's egotistical perceptions are made known to other actors in the network, this could have a disruptive effect on the operation of the network – speed and quality of information flows, iterativeness and accuracy, for example. Egotistical perceptions might be made known verbally but of more concern is the individual actor casting themselves in the role of gatekeeper – an actor who seeks to route information flows through themselves and attempts to excessively control the outputs of others. In extremis these actors become dysfunctionally prominent and affect the flows of information through a network. This form of unfair distribution of network prominence prompts competition for prominence that serves individuals' egos and not network functions. The egotist wants to grow their prominence and as it grows, almost inevitably (particularly in the short term), the prominence of others reduces. The ultimate network configuration for the egotist is the 'hub and spoke', where other actors have low prominence because they are not connected to other actors and the egotist has short links to all other actors. Ego has control of all information flowing between other actors – see central actor in Figure 8.5.

Figure 8.5 Hub 'n' spoke.

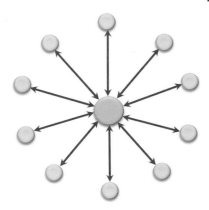

Summary

This chapter set out to look at some of the factors that might enable or, alternatively, inhibit the evolution of networks between individuals in a project environment. I started by identifying three main groups of networks:

- Intra-organisational, interpersonal
- Inter-organisational, interpersonal
- Inter-organisational.

Context was identified as an important factor – context affects the way in which networks evolve and respond to that context. Externalities are important as is the extent to which interdependencies exist – they are a reflection of the complexity of the process and processes involved in our projects. Reputation is important and the technical environment will inevitably impact. Pressure of time and the risk landscape are also important factors. Certainty about the definition of individual tasks within a project will also affect the way in which individual actors position themselves in relation to others in the networks, and the extent to which ties develop.

The following behavioural factors were identified as important:

- trust
- empathy
- reciprocity
- generosity and the granting of favours.

Some behaviours in individuals that are inhibiting and potentially destructive for project networks were also identified:

- competitiveness
- narcissism
- egotism.

Trust affects interpersonal relationships and can be aggregated to represent trust between organisations. Trust is transient and fragile, sometimes difficult to establish, and quickly lost. Procurement contracts and contracts of employment assume a static condition. But networks, self-organising project networks, are not static; these must inevitably evolve over time and then decay. Networks need facilitation and support; they need regular interventions to ensure that appropriate relationships are maintained. Empathy has the potential to reduce iterations in our communications and knowledge exchange networks. Empathy is a factor affecting the value of the linkages in interpersonal networks. Good network behaviour is contagious. We need to pursue behaviour that promotes trust and exhibits empathy, where reciprocity and the granting of favours are generous, and at the same time we need to avoid competitive network behaviour.

Project networks have to operate in an environment where expertise distance is particularly large.[7] We also, typically, use competitive processes to select organisations. Those organisations promote competitive behaviour in their staff – and competitive behaviour is often essential in order to achieve success as an employee. The problem is that these competitive individuals are then placed in project networks that function best if a range of other non-competitive behaviours are employed and where the use of competitive behaviour can have a negative effect.

---

7 A wide diversity in the levels of expertise between project actors.

9

Project Networks and Building Information Modelling

The discussion in this book of the identification and management of project networks would be incomplete without some discussion of the relevance of building information modelling (BIM). A number of ambitious claims have been made about the benefits of implementing BIM (see, for example, the UK Government's paper entitled 'Industrial strategy' (HM Government, 2013)) and yet the literature that deals with the link between BIM and networks is sparse. The purpose of this chapter is to give those interested in networks an overview of the relevance of BIM to the subject of networks and to establish an agenda for further work in this area. It is also intended to provide some indication of the relevance of network theory to those primarily interested in BIM.

Chapter 5 dealt with five 'dangerous assumptions'. Assumption 2 was:

> It is possible to very accurately interpret clients' wishes without any corruption of intent through agency...and to represent the physical manifestation of those wishes and desires accurately and unambiguously using CAD files and text documents.

I rationalised this position by citing the work we have been doing over the last decade looking at construction projects in the UK which have resulted in contractual disputes related to contractual incompleteness (see for example Walker and Pryke, 2011). Once BIM has been used in construction projects over a period of time, sufficient to cover a significant number of complete project cycles, it will be possible to look for evidence of whether it improves the completeness of the contracts made between the various parties, but most notably between client (employer) and Tier 1 contractor. Is there a possibility, perhaps, that BIM will improve coordination of design but reduce contractual completeness?

BIM Origins

Robert Aish is frequently cited as the first person to refer to a 'building model' in his Council for Research and Innovation in Building and Construction (CIB) conference paper of July 1986 (Aish, 1986). The paper was presented at the 1986 CIB conference, when Aish was an employee at GMW Computers; he referred to the use of information modelling for a large project procured by British Airports Authority (BAA) at London Heathrow Airport (van Nederveen and Tolman, 1992). Building information modelling

Managing Networks in Project-Based Organisations, First Edition. Stephen Pryke.
© 2017 John Wiley & Sons Ltd. Published 2017 by John Wiley & Sons Ltd.

as a term was perhaps first documented in van Nederveen and Tolman's article in *Automation in Construction* (van Nederveen and Tolman, 1992). By 2002 Autodesk had released a paper (Autodesk, 2002) using the term 'building information modelling' and the acronym 'BIM'. The terminology was then adopted more widely by software developers such as Graphisoft and Bentley Systems (Laiserin, 2003) although many claim that the term was concurrently engineered and that there was no single source for the terminology.

Building information modelling provides a digital format for information exchange and coordination. Ostensibly, it provides a focus for decision-making in design and the data outputs are intended to provide the basis for the management of the completed facilities throughout the life of those facilities. Traditionally, building design was represented in the form of two-dimensional files (hard-copy drawings and subsequently computer-aided design (CAD)). Those two-dimensional representations used 'sections' to represent the third dimension, but essentially in a two-dimensional format. BIM brought the third dimension into the representation of the design so that all three dimensions were viewable on the screen. Development of the software added a fourth dimension – time – and subsequently cost was added as the fifth dimension. Much of the excitement surrounding the implementation of BIM is associated with the potential for clash detection in the 3D model and the ability to access time and cost implications for design changes in real-time through fourth- and fifth-dimension system features.

Building Information Modelling and Information Management

The need in projects to manage the exchange of information across the supply chains serving projects has, as mentioned above, led to the development of a range of software. This software enables new forms of project management; indeed I argue here that this technology *requires* alternative ways of conceptualising the project and new ways of managing the activity for which the technology provides a vehicle. Levitt (2011) has proposed an alternative approach to project delivery in dynamic and turbulent environments, where the emphasis is moved away from tracking and preventing changes in a base-line model towards an approach allowing more emphasis on monitoring, integrating and analysing information in real-time, using contiguous 'bottom-up' adaptation of systems as the project environment evolves. Schwaber's (2004) agile approach has also been widely adopted in the development of software.

Some of the issues that present in projects when considering information management and modelling are associated with:

- The management of flows of information between project actors, and the timelines and quality of those information flows.
- Establishing ownership of information in an environment where information is created iteratively between a relatively large group of specialist designers. Projects are becoming increasingly complex and while there will always be a role for coordination of aesthetic design, typically by the architect in a construction project, the coordination of the technical interfaces must inevitably migrate to lower tiers of the supply chain as the pursuit of expertise moves ever further into the realms of highly specialised subcontractors and design consultants.

- The management of intellectual property rights becomes more difficult, partly because of the iterative process through which design is created. Walker's discussion on linear responsibility analysis (cited in Pryke, 2012) involves each piece of information being tagged with the responsibility that the receiver has in relation to that item of information, for example, 'check and approve', 'adopt and modify', 'contextual information only', etc.
- The centralisation of information but the decentralisation of decision-making relating to that information. Whyte and Levitt (2011) may be of relevance in understanding this problem more clearly.

Information Management and Organisation Structure

Whyte and Levitt (2011) contend that new forms of information management also imply a renegotiation of 'modes of coordination and control', referring back to the early work of Thompson (2003), where the differentiation and integration of activities formed the focus of analysis and discussion. This may well still be relevant but it is very much more specialised as projects become increasingly complex. Some management researchers (see for example, Hodgson, 2004) have characterised projects as being dominated by comprehensive bureaucratic planning and tight management control. Yet I have argued in this book that the reverse is the case. The planning embedded in procurement and project management systems simply cannot deal with the highly specialised and complex nature of design and the evolution of relationships that facilitate effective information flows between a relatively large group of highly specialised Tier 2 suppliers. More recently Bechky (2006) has argued that coordination (see also Söderlund, 2004b) is increasingly achieved through the promotion of professional norms and social interactions, rather than the use of prescriptive routines.

Information technologies have allowed a restructuring of relationships between firms in the supply chain. The project is a 'construct' that facilitates the management of some rather basic project delivery metrics (cost, time and quality being the most notable). Yet the reality is that projects involve networks of actors (Sinha and Van de Ven, 2005) with concurrent workloads across a number of projects. Projects continue to be plagued by the routinised use of 'fantasy documents' (Clarke, 1999) presenting false assumptions which have an impact upon systems that are put in place to manage information flows. Spender (1989) has one explanation for this phenomenon – an inability to see beyond the protocols and standard documents that form the artefacts around which our behaviours orbit. Organisations operating in environments with high levels of uncertainty and low levels of profitability typically seek standardised solutions to some very complex problems.

BIM as an Artefact

The quality and timeliness of information associated with a construction project are factors that materially affect the success of the project – but there is a need to move beyond cost, time and quality as the metrics that are applied to project success. Clearly, industries outside construction and civil engineering have been transformed by the classification and accurate directing of information. We need only refer to retail and manufacturing (Crotty, 2013) for evidence of the drastic transformations possible in these sectors. Buildings and physical infrastructure are some of most complex things that are created. The creation of these complex things requires the utilisation of some of the most complex human systems. Case study material presented in Chapters 10–13 illustrates those systems and the way in which they are quite different to the systems that are procured as part of the resource acquisition process.

Crotty (2013) cites two separate issues relating to information and projects:

- The quality of the information being generated
- The means by which that information is shared with project team members who become stakeholders in that information.

Quality in the context of building and engineering projects is an interesting concept. We might include accuracy, and timeliness in terms of period of time taken but also timeliness in relation to other important events; quality might also deal with relevance and empathy in relation to other project actors' requirements and interests.

The means by which information is shared with other project actors is associated with the transition from hard-copy drawings and the occasional physical model to files containing information in a form that is accessible to others. The point was made earlier (see Five Dangerous Assumptions, Chapter 5) that drawings, whether hard-copy or digital, are not always a highly effective means of conveying information. The second barrier to sharing is software compatibility – very often, time-consuming transfer of data across interfaces is required, with the inherent risk of data corruption or misinterpretation. So, protocols are needed to manage this transfer of information between systems. Arguably, manufacturing has made more progress than construction and civil engineering in this area.

BIM software operates around the properties of a series of components. These properties and the parameters for operation are held in the form of parametric equations (Crotty, 2013). This partially enables the designer to build a model using intelligent virtual components in a way that is analogous with the 'real' construction environment, using materials and components on site. In a sense, the process might work more effectively if only one designer were carrying out the design using one software system. In fact complex construction and engineering projects use increasingly specialised design and the location of the expertise in this design tends to move further down the supply chain (away from Tier 1). Pryke (2009) deals with the issue of supply chains and their management and the increasingly specialised nature of design and construction in building and civil engineering projects.

Sharing information requires IT protocols to enable a substitute for a common system across an entire project, regardless of location of expertise in the supply chain. The classification of components is dealt with by the International Alliance for Interoperability (IAI). IAI has established industry foundation classes (IFCs) which provide system compatible component specifications (Crotty, 2013). But almost inevitably there are limitations to the completeness of the information that may be exchanged when it is derived from across specialist design systems located in a range of industries serving construction and engineering.

So, BIM, in the guise of a technical system that provides components with design parameters and interfaces between a range of specialist design systems typically encountered in a construction project, has its limitations. There are clearly constraints on the completeness of information being transferred. What is missing is systems that solve problems associated with the compatibility of components – the systems integration function is largely a human response to limitation within the BIM system. In Chapters 10–13 we deal with case study material looking at the way in which project actors self-organise in order to resolve problems at design stage. It may be claimed that BIM can overcome some of the deficiencies of the graphical representation of design information, including providing greater and earlier client certainty, better consistency, easier design coordination, improved completeness of documents presenting the design for bid purposes and improved information enabling constructors and component manufacturers to visualise both the finished project and the processes needed to execute construction. Whether this case is convincingly and reliably proven is not yet clear. In relation to context and technology, the success of the latter so often relies on a really good understanding of the former.

Self-Organising Networks in the Context of Design

So, BIM software packages might be viewed as artefacts around which human project actors evolve networks through which those actors collaborate in order to carry out the roles allocated by contract and acquired through their place in those networks. The implementation of BIM software is claimed to achieve the following benefits to the project (Kaner *et al.*, 2008):

- Improvement in engineering design quality
- Reduction in design errors
- Improvement in productivity on the part of designer.

The challenge is how to capture the configurations of the actors in temporary project coalitions interfacing with BIM. Each time a project comes to an end, a new network of actors has to be established and each actor will bring experience, knowledge and various opinions and prejudices to that forum. Clearly the adoption of BIM will tend to modify the roles that actors regard as normal.

An examination of self-organising project design networks (Pryke *et al.*, 2017) has pointed to the fact that a study of network topography might help us understand the information management process and perhaps contribute to the social aspects of the design phase of projects. The paper looked at information exchange network density, path lengths (the distance between actors in terms of links) and community structure (which is a function within SNA software packages that identifies subgroups with higher levels of density compared to the average for the network as a whole). Projects that are complex both technically and organisationally need to look beyond the governance arising out of standard forms of contract (Pryke, 2012) – these static and non-adaptive relationships are just not flexible enough to support the complexity of the task being undertaken by project actors. Multidisciplinary networks employing highly specialised actors are brought together for a temporary period of intense activity, activity loaded with risk and potential liabilities, both personal and corporate. Networks and their rapid evolution become the vehicle by which project actors seek to discharge their contractual responsibilities and locate themselves in a position that enables the acquisition of incoming information, the coordination of design and the dissemination of information to other project actors (see also Case Study 3, Chapter 13).

Complex systems (for example, the design of a large or mega construction/ engineering project) have a tendency to self-organise (see Heylighen, 2013 and Chapter 5 above) – involving local interactions without any single agent being in control (see also Mitleton-Kelly, 2004). Networks do not call for leadership – they require enabling and facilitating as they evolve and continually adapt around the changing needs of the actors and the project itself over time. This emergent dynamic network in design (in relation to the context discussed in this chapter) provides flexibility and resilience in responding to the internal and external environments (Heylighen, 2013) in which the project sits.

The success of the design phase of a project depends on a focus on the maintenance of a network that is able to manage nonlinear and unpredictable interactions at the edge of chaos (Bertelsen, 2003). The activities of the network are facilitated by the emergence of cooperative relationships that are more complex than the relatively simple and static contractual relationships typically embedded in our procurement approaches. The difference between failure and success in the design phase of a complex project can often rest upon the ability to create an environment in which appropriate relationships can establish and thrive, without threat from the application of contractual remedies. Elsewhere in this book the need to focus upon relational and social aspects of projects has been emphasised – coupled with a move away from the technical aspects of planning, scheduling, risk analysis and project management tools and techniques (see also Winter *et al.*, 2006). Yet studies that apply network theory to the project environment have been relatively rare (Steen *et al.*, 2017).

An important feature of the concept of self-organisation is that the system is providing an environment allowing project design to be carried out effectively – a stable project network environment, yet the network needs to evolve and transform to accommodate higher levels of complexity (McMillan, 2006; Capra, 1996). Pryke *et al.* (2017) draw a comparison between the project network environment and Adam Smith's invisible hand – a reference to networks which enable supply and demand to find equilibrium in a way that is not centrally led or controlled but is a function of a very large number of independent decisions in a network environment over time. Cooke-Davies *et al.* (2008), Mahmud (2009) and Stacey (2010), cited in Pryke *et al.* (2017), suggest that self-organising within organisations has the following characteristics:

- Spontaneous and collective social[1] activity providing control, direction and some order, without prior planning.
- An emphasis upon effective and timely communications resulting in co-creation and a mutual understanding of process and common project goal.
- A recognition of the idiosyncratic and unpredictable nature of systems (reflected in the networks related to these systems) and their evolution; each system comprises a network of individual actors capable of making their own choices throughout the working day.

---

1 And here I use the word social in its broadest sense – involving human interaction, rather than using it as a reference to recreational social activity.

- An acknowledgement that the self-organised structure, by virtue of the nature of its creation, is more coherent, stable and capable of being adaptive to its environment as compared to a centrally imposed governance system.

We might also observe that actors are in an environment where they are influenced by the actions and views of other actors; similarly, an individual actor can use his or her position within the network to influence others. Individual actors in a network acquire prominence rather than have it bestowed centrally and formally. This is important because the bestowal of prominence by consensus and through individual action is more legitimate than the position power (Seidman, 1970) allocated with formal contractual relationships.

I raise the question of whether BIM systems are compatible with the transient nature of the self-organising networks associated with projects. Indeed, I question whether transient self-organising systems have been considered in the development of BIM technology.

BIM and Networks: A Research Agenda

The project is an environment where interpersonal communication and associated information exchange are vehicles for the iterative process of design and what Emmitt and Gorse (2003) refer to as 'collaborative problem-solving'. This involves a high degree of self-organisation (Pryke, 2012; Pauget and Wald, 2013; Lingard *et al.*, 2014). We need to start to understand how these self-organising networks form and evolve and how they can be maintained and their decay (where desirable) managed. Work currently being carried out at the Engineering Department at Stanford University, under the supervision of Professor Ray Levitt, involves the use of a Windows plug-in linked to the Revit software package to capture editing, saving, viewing and activities within Revit. This team, run by Reid Senescu under Professor Levitt's supervision, is gathering network path information – send and receive data by date.

In the UK at the time of writing, Bejal Mandalia, a research student working with University College London and embedded within a rail infrastructure project being delivered for Transport for London (the client and project management office for London's transport infrastructure), was carrying out a pilot study using a social media application known as 'Yammer'. Yammer is a 'freemium'[2] social networking software application designed to facilitate communications within organisations. Security is achieved through approval of email addresses prior to access being granted. Yammer was launched at the 'TechnoCrunch50' conference (Wikipedia, accessed 25 August 2016) and Microsoft acquired Yammer in 2012. Its features are in summary:

- A single destination for message, files and documents where approved users can view them
- (And therefore) an increase in connectivity for individuals working together on a project
- Informalisation of project communications.

See yammer.com.

---

2 'Freemium' involves an application that is provided free of charge to users but which provides a platform for associated services to be provided at a premium to freemium app users.

Yammer can be integrated with Twitter (see https://twitter.com/yammer?lang=en-gb) and as of 2015 Yammer has enabled its system to accommodate external project stakeholders through an 'Exchange Transport Rules' system. It is not suggested that Yammer might replace Revit or any other BIM software package. But is interesting to see how Yammer much more closely represents the systems that individuals use recreationally to exchange information and coordinate interdependent activity.

Some work has recently been completed at University College London dealing with the investigation of self-organising networks in infrastructure engineering projects (Pryke *et al.*, 2017). This work has established that the analysis of project network topography is important as we move forward to redefine how we manage projects. Pryke *et al.* (2017) looked specifically at network density and the path lengths associated with a complex project, and utilised SNA software (in this case, Gephi) to identify and classify subgroups within the design network. The research found that functional clusters of relatively high density within networks of lower density highlighted the identification of three important self-organising clusters that do not reflect the contractual governance within which the project was located. These three clusters represented 'doing', 'decision-making' and 'designing' (see also Chapter 11). It is suggested that further research needs to be carried out to understand how these clusters evolve and ultimately decay; we need to establish how best to facilitate these clusters and to design interventions that maintain the clusters and their effectiveness. Finally, in terms of recent research linking BIM and SNA, Al Hattab and Hamzeh (2015) have carried out some work looking at the topography of design information networks with a focus upon errors in design.

More broadly, in terms of carrying out social network analysis with a direct application to building information modelling, I suggest that some attention might, in the future, be given to:

- Nodal characteristics – the characteristics of individual actors in the context of the project network. Some of this is influential; some is influenced by the behaviour of other project actors.
- The classification of network roles – increasingly we are thinking about *network* roles as against *project* roles (discussion in Chapter 5 above). Some of the interventions that might be formulated to deal with network problems involve the introduction of other network actors with remedial network roles.
- Comparison of the three groups of centrality measures discussed in Chapter 4 is instructive in a project context. This partly relates to the last point.
- Network topography is becoming increasingly important, perhaps replacing more traditional views about organisation structures.
- Cluster identification enables the researcher to identify functions that are being carried out as a result of self-organising behaviour but which do not relate to formally allocated project roles.

The purpose of this chapter was to highlight the relationship between project networks and building information modelling and to suggest the links between them. I looked at the origins of BIM, referring to the trailblazing work of British Airports Authority. I then made the connection between BIM and information management and reflected upon Levitt's (2011) contention that in projects a 'bottom-up' adaptation of information management systems is needed as the project environment evolves. Next I made the connection between information management and (project) organisational structure – and specifically the structure of project relationships in the context of construction supply chains. I referred to the concept of the 'fantasy document', presenting false assumptions and effectively corrupting project information management systems.

I suggested that the BIM model might be regarded as an 'artefact' and linked this to my five dangerous assumptions in relation to projects, their planning, design, procurement and delivery. I pointed to the importance of problem-solving (refer also to case study material in Chapter 11 below). I would argue that systems integration is still largely a human function.

Finally, I refer to some interesting work being carried out at Stanford University in the USA. I also highlighted a piece of research at UCL involving the experimental use of personal IT technology to manage information exchange in projects. Recent research carried out at Cambridge University in the UK (Pritchard, 2016) suggests that there is anecdotal evidence pointing towards the fact that the majority of construction project actors do not have access to IT in fulfilling their project roles.

The intention of this chapter was to raise awareness of and help to commence the setting of an agenda associated with the application of network theory to analysis of the effects of the implementation of BIM in construction projects.

10

Introduction to the Case Studies

Technical Overview of Case Studies

The purpose of this overview is to provide context from the engineering programme for the three case studies that follow in Chapters 11, 12 and 13. A detailed understanding of context is very important to the accurate interpretation of network data. An understanding of context is, in fact, important to the accurate interpretation and analysis of all forms of research data. It is hoped that this book will be relevant to students, scholars and practitioners with a wide range of sectoral interests. Yet there can be only one context and in this case it is infrastructure engineering. For those interested in networks but not transport infrastructure engineering, the following section could be skipped; the discussion and analysis following in Chapters 11, 12 and 13 would still be valid without an understanding of the technical details of the project. For those with an interest in and understanding of the context, the following information is provided so that the case study findings can be more fully understood.

Bank Monument Station Complex: City of London, UK

Bank Monument station on the London tube system is entirely underground and covers an area between the Bank of England and the Thames river in the heart of London's financial district. The station is an important hub in the London metro system, with interchanges between the Northern, Central and Waterloo and City, District and Circle underground lines, along with the Docklands Light Railway which links to the Docklands. The station is used by an average of 340,000 passengers per day. The purpose of the Bank Station Capacity Upgrade (BSCU) project, which commenced on site in 2016, was to:

- Increase capacity of the station and provide some 'future proofing' based upon predicted growth in passenger traffic
- Reduce passenger (pedestrian) journey times and consequent crowding throughout the station complex
- Improve disability access
- Improve emergency fire and evacuation protection measures
- Improve finishings and general ambience within the complex.

Figures 10.1, 10.2 and 10.3 provide an indication of the layout of the project.

Managing Networks in Project-Based Organisations, First Edition. Stephen Pryke.
© 2017 John Wiley & Sons Ltd. Published 2017 by John Wiley & Sons Ltd.

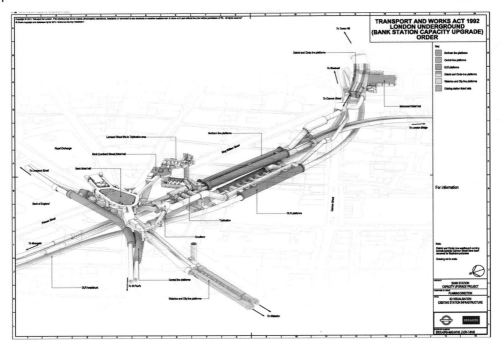

Figure 10.1 Bank Station upgrade as existing. Source: TfL.

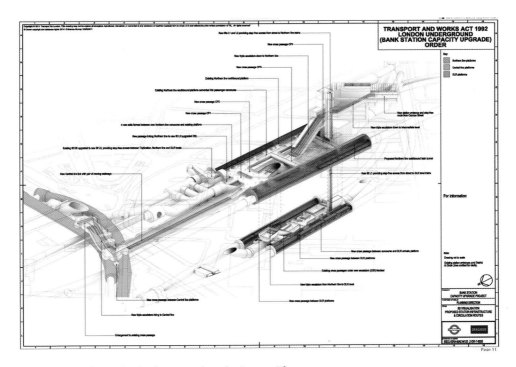

Figure 10.2 Schematic 3D of proposed works. Source: TfL.

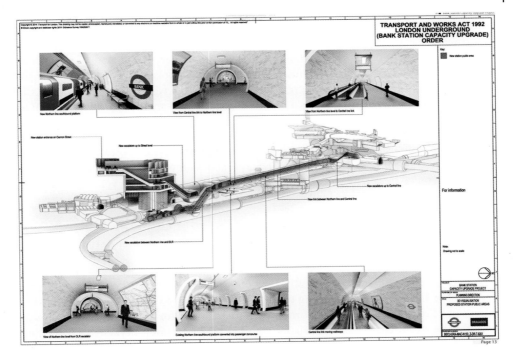

Figure 10.3 Artist's impression of final scheme. Source: TfL.

This project was highly complex because of the multitude of regulatory requirements and the difficulties of gaining access to a railway system that must remain in operation during the execution of the construction and engineering works. Also, work is limited to 'engineering hours' – principally the few hours between night-time close down of the transport system (typically between 12 midnight and 1 am) and the restart of transport services around 5 am later that same morning). There are issues associated with getting materials and equipment to underground locations in a railway system that was not designed with maintenance or upgrade in mind. Sensitivity associated with the large number of historic buildings under which much of the works had to take place was a major stakeholder management issue and possibly the single most important risk management heading for the project team. The oldest city metro railway in the world is inevitably faced with problems of compliance with current building regulations in the design of replacement systems and facilities.

The project management team for the Bank Station Capacity Upgrade project made a decision early on to co-locate the design team within the offices of Transport for London (TfL), situated a few metres from the Bank underground station in King William Street, London. The design stage involved approximately 250 'white collar' personnel representing six specialist tunnelling and other infrastructure engineering consultancies. The client employed a consultant project manager but maintained a project management office (PMO) itself to provide client functions integrated into the network of design-related actors.

The project was let using an NEC Option C Target Cost form of contract with a 50/50 pain/gain share between the client (London Underground, part of Transport for London) and the principal contractor – a Spanish contractor called Drogados. The pain/gain share was subject to a 2.5% 'shoulder' whereby the client bore the whole cost or benefit of the first 2.5% of cost changes. This was a contract with design, and provision was made to abort the construction phase and the end of the design phase subject to payment of the appropriate fees to the contractor. Interim fee accounts were paid on milestones based upon delivery of design. The project had an estimated completion cost of £563 M at the time of this book going to press (2017). Conceptual design was completed in September 2014 and detailed design in Spring 2016, and construction was due to commence during 2016. The research was carried out during the design stage of the project.

Research Funding

The research project was funded by the Technology Strategy Board, subsequently renamed Innovate UK. The research project was funded as a Knowledge Transfer Partnership (KTP), the grant being awarded to University College London with the intention of a establishing a collaboration with Transport for London over a two-year period. The Knowledge Transfer Partnership led by Dr Stephen Pryke from UCL and Simon Addyman from Transport for London contributed to the work of Infrastructure UK (IUK) through the activities of the Collaborative Project Teams Programme. The research associate was Soundararaj Balmururgan (known affectionately to the team as 'Bala'). Dr Sulafa Badi, from the Centre for Organisational Network Analysis (CONA@ UCL), completed the team from University College London.

Summary

The programme of work associated with the upgrade of Bank station was huge and highly complex both technically and organisationally. The research project had a duration of two years. The case studies that follow represent a small fragment of the data gathered. The purpose here was to provide an insight into a small part of the highlights of the findings of the overall research project.

The research project used social network analysis to map and analyse the systems used to design the engineering programme described above. The purpose of the analysis was to establish best practice, expressed in network terms, and ultimately to provide a range of appropriate interventions for future large and/or complex projects. The next three chapters present case study material related to the following issues:

- **Case Study 1: Chapter 11**: Communities in self-organising project design networks. The contrast between self-organising behaviour and the roles procured contractually is highlighted.
- **Case Study 2: Chapter 12**: A phenomenon referred to as 'dysfunctional prominence'; derived from the application and analysis of three different measures of actor centrality in the context of project information exchange.
- **Case Study 3: Chapter 13**: The potential to explore network evolution cost, leading to the identification of optimum network density in project communication networks.

11

Case Study 1: Communities in Self-Organising Project Networks

For an overview of the construction project, please refer to the previous chapter 'Introduction to the Case Studies'.

Data collection took place between January and April 2014 during the design and approvals stage of the project. The boundaries for the gathering of the network data were established using the principles set out in Pryke (2012) – principally data was gathered from those cited by others as having an involvement in the project on a 'snowball' basis. As the project was at the design and approvals stage, fewer ambiguities arose than might be the case for a project at implementation stage. The aim was to gather data about information exchange networks, and Case Study 1 focused upon three main concepts relating to the network data:

- Geodesic distance – the number of network links between any two actors in the network
- Communities – a means of identifying clusters of individuals who are particularly densely connected
- Density of the information exchange networks as a whole – also referred to as a measure of 'connectivity'.

Geodesic distance is important in studies looking at communications because we are often concerned with the number of actors through which information must flow to reach its destination. Fewer links tends to be associated with faster communications and perhaps efficiency in relation to the management of the project. Conversely, there are occasions where the involvement of more actors provides the opportunity to check and verify information before it reaches its final destination. What is important is the appropriateness of the geodesic distances given the environment in which the network is functioning. So, a large geodesic distance between two actors would indicate that there are a relatively large number of actors between the two given actors and this would result in longer periods of time for information exchange; there is potential for higher levels of confused or ambiguous communication. The geodesic distance would also usually create a lower sense of belonging and empathy between the two actors.

Communities, or 'clusters', are associated with 'networks within networks'. Communities involve higher levels of density or connectivity than exists in the networks that surround these clusters. They are of interest because they tend to indicate a focus within the

Managing Networks in Project-Based Organisations, First Edition. Stephen Pryke.
© 2017 John Wiley & Sons Ltd. Published 2017 by John Wiley & Sons Ltd.

network. Usually a number of such communities would co-exist simultaneously within a network.[1] The important point about communities is the use of those with experience within the organisation to identify the purpose or objective of each community. The research team comprised the lead for UCL (the author), the lead for Transport for London (TfL) (the research client), a research associate employed by UCL and located in the offices of BSCU/TfL and a further research associate located within UCL. Regular meetings were held between the team and one of the important functions of these meetings was to make sense of the data as gathered – including identification of community roles. Community structures are important in terms of those included within the denser community groups. They are also an important indication of those actors *not* included. In terms of applying SNA to the management of project networks, the identification of inappropriately disconnected actors in relation to the role formally allocated through contract, for example, provides the opportunity to identify interventions aimed at improving the performance of the project network. Co-location can be a factor and the effect upon network topography is important.

On the subject of density (also commonly referred to outside network analysis groups as 'connectivity'), if we are studying information exchange and other forms of communication network, density clearly must be an important measure, particularly in relation to comparisons in a longitudinal sense and between similar networks. Somewhere between the situation where all actors are linked to all other actors and where all actors are isolates lies a value that represents the optimum given the topography of the network and environment in which the network functions. Density can provide a measure for speed of diffusion. Actors who are linked to all other actors are likely to diffuse a message quickly to those other actors. These actors are able to diffuse information quickly and can react to each other easily, without obstruction from gatekeepers. But densely connected networks are not necessarily better for complex project information exchange networks. Densely connected networks are 'cohesive' but cohesion can lead to poor quality decisions, in particular where specialist knowledge is required. This is a good reason to look at communities where a number of highly specialised groups are working within a highly interdependent environment – as typically found in complex construction and engineering projects. Case Study 3 explores the issue of network cost and clearly density is a factor in considering the cost of constructing and maintaining a network.

Data Collection

Given the size and complexity of the project overall, it was decided for this first study to focus upon part of the overall scheme. The line between project and programme becomes blurred on very large projects and it was necessary to draw a boundary around a quite specific element within the scheme. Case Study 1 focused upon the design for the installation of a group of escalators serving the Central Line stations within the overall Bank Station complex. Actors were asked to identify other actors with whom

---

1 One of the important distinctions between project networks and other social networks is that the project network is 'multi-functional'. The project has a variety of functions to support including design management, risk management and financial management, among others. Each of these functions should be regarded as a classification of network within the multiple layers of networks that comprise the project. Contrast this with a network dealing with the spread of infectious diseases. In this latter case the data refers only to contacts between infectious actors – the network might be regarded as 'mono-functional'.

they communicated particularly in relation to the resolution of problems. For the purpose of this study no distinction was made between various means of communicating. Likert scale values were used for frequency of communication and the perceived quality of such a communication to the project. Frequency was allocated a low, medium or high rating. 'Importance' (in terms of valuing the linkages) was classified as quality of communication and quality of communication itself was allocated five distinct measures: importance, clarity, accuracy, timeliness, reliability and understanding. The values attributed to frequency were multiplied by the values attributed to quality (using the average overall for quality). This product was used as a proxy for tie strength, following the principles originally outlined in Pryke (2012).[2]

Data collection was initially problematic. Most of the staff working on the project had never been asked for network data relating to their own personal contacts within the project and there was some resistance. Work had to be done to explain the purpose of the study and overcome a feeling of 'big brother' watching every detail of actors' activities. A screen was installed at a busy pedestrian traffic hub within the offices of the client (where the design team was co-located). The screen showed the individual actors and their linkages and the staff could see the networks evolve as they entered their own data. Drop-in sessions were arranged to improve awareness and dispel anxieties. Over the period of the study, the staff who were the subject of the study developed a great interest in the idea of networks and their place within those networks. After completion of the study and discussion of the findings with the respondents, a number of requests for further studies relating to individual teams were received. Inviting the respondents to contribute to the interpretation of the data analysis was a factor here. Critics may point to the Hawthorne Effect. I believe that any such potential effect is outweighed by the value associated with gathering network data through an interactive process as against the analysis of data associated with, for example, email traffic or other purely quantitative data.

Data was collected through an online questionnaire from 60 project actors. Actors were asked to provide some basic information which located them in terms of their role in the project; they were then asked to identify the individuals with whom they communicated in relation to very specific boundaries. The membership of the networks was identified using a 'snowballing' method, where participants were identified progressively by those who completed the survey.

Complexity was an issue in this case study. To enter an environment where individuals are working on a technically and procedurally highly complex project and convince them of the value of completing a survey aimed at analysing their work-related social networks was a challenge. Designing a questionnaire that gathered sufficient data while not being perceived as overly complex was important. In the case of the pilot study the questionnaire format presented in Pryke (2012) was utilised. It was modified to provide some additional detail requested by the client.

---

2 The issue of tie strength is complicated, particularly in the context of projects. Tie strength is quite subjective and personal to the individual actor – strength of relationship is perceived by each individual, rather than being quantifiable. Tie strength must also be considered in the context of the environment in which the project is being delivered and the context of each network within that project environment. A lot has been written in the mainstream social network analysis literature about tie strength – see, for example the work of Granovetter (1973, 1983), Haythornthwaite (2005), Krackhardt (1992) and Wellman (1997). Yet the majority of this work and material published elsewhere does not serve social network analysis as regards projects. Consequently, a model for calculating tie strength was proposed in Pryke (2012). The work carried out with Transport for London provided an opportunity to refine this project-specific tie strength model.

Data Analysis

The data collected through the online questionnaire was uploaded to an SQL database. The data was subsequently retrieved using a PHP Hypertext Processor and combined into one network by merging the overlapping links in each survey response and calculating weights of the links (tie strength) from the frequency and quality data. The data was then analysed using igraph (see igraph.org). As previously discussed, density, diameter and average path lengths were the measures used within igraph. After analysis the graph (or network) was exported to a tabular format and visualised using Gephi (see https://gephi.org/). ForceAtlas2 (a graph algorithm designed to provide visualisation from Gephi SNA software) was used for all visualisations, apart from community detection, which was created manually.

The network analysis visualisation was taken back to the group from which data was gathered and their observations sought. In some cases their questions were valuable in terms of dealing with ambiguities in the analysis of the data. In other situations their observations in relation to the network environment were crucial in providing context for some of the analysis of the data. Once feedback and input had been sought from participants, a meeting was held between the lead for Transport for London, the lead for UCL and the research associate responsible for gathering and analysing data. Crucially for the research project, the knowledge needed to finalise the analysis of the data was shared by those three parties, as follows:

- Lead for TfL – detailed knowledge of the context; knowledge of the roles and actor titles.
- Lead for UCL – detailed knowledge of the application of SNA to the project context; previous track record of gathering data in the project context.
- Research associate – detailed knowledge of the data-gathering process and subsequent analysis.

Certain assumptions were inevitably necessary during data gathering and analysis. Data analysis was not possible without all the parties being present and this was a limiting factor in terms of speed of analysis, especially as we approached the end of the research contract.

Findings

Figure 11.1 shows the information exchange network for Case Study 1. This case study took a discrete part of the overall project (specifically the work associated with the escalators serving the Central Line). A focus was placed upon network density, distance between actors (number of linkages or path length) and the existence of communities within the network. Density will always be important when looking at information exchange and other forms of communication – density is a reflection of the extent to which the network is connected. Low density means relatively few linkages and high density means good connectivity overall. In addition to density for the network we are interested in those actors who have prominence within the network and the reasons for that prominence. We could have looked at several measures for centrality (see Pryke, 2012) but in the case of this project at design stage, the examination of communities was

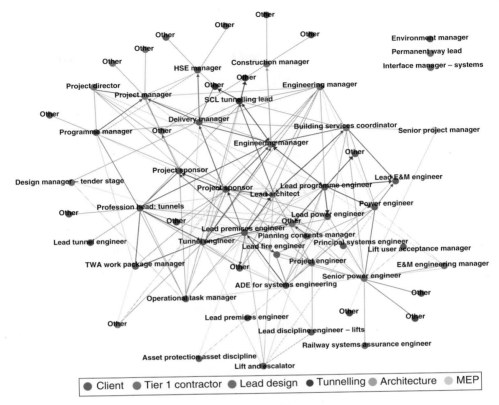

Figure 11.1 Information exchange network. Source: adapted from Pryke *et al.* (2015a).

felt to be important because of the self-organising hypothesis established. Finally, the discussion of communication involved consideration of path lengths. Paths lengths refer to the number of connections between actors. Path lengths are important because distance is a factor in speed of communication and problem resolution. Path length also relates to the potential for corruption of information and the extent to which supervision or checking and controls are necessary within information flows between given points.

The network contained 270 links and had a density of 7.6%. Figure 11.1[3] indicates a core periphery format with some properties that are referred to as 'small world',[4] in this case, particularly clustering and short average path lengths. The core in this case

---

3 In Figure 11.1, 'MEP' denotes mechanical, electrical and public health services.

4 'Small world' in SNA terms refers to the idea that an individual might randomly meet a stranger and find that the individual and the stranger have an acquaintance in common. 'It's a small world' we might declare. Of more specific relevance to this case study is the work of Watts (1999). Watts identified a particular type of small world phenomenon that helps us to understand how networks of designers might relate to each other when designing a complex engineering project. Watts looked at the coincidence of highly localised clustering and short separation across the network and concluded that these attributes were associated with sparse (low density), decentralised networks that had some degree of randomness. These factors fit well with our network environment from Case Study 1, which comprised a small number of highly specialised groups of designers working within the constraints of very high levels of interdependency, with relationship evolution driven by the need to coordinate and integrate and to solve complex problems.

comprised the managers and lead designers within the design disciplines and the client and their project managers. The network has few actors with high levels of prominence and the structure of the network is such that any two actors are connected to each other by a maximum of five links, with an average of 2.23 steps or links. Average geodesic distance is relatively short, indicating that information travels quickly between actors, with a small number of links involved in each information exchange transaction. This is an important observation in terms of the validity of the network in relation to its purpose. It indicates that there is a high level of autonomy vested in the key actors involved in design and they are able to move quickly despite the complexity of their role and the context in which their role and the network to which it relates is located.

There are three isolated actors in the network (Figure 11.1). These actors have no connections with others in the context of the precisely defined area of activity with which the network was engaged at the time of the research. If we are looking at information exchange, we must always be concerned about isolates because they are disengaged from the activities of the network. Here is a good example of why the analysis needs to be played back to the contributors of data. The isolated actors happened to have expertise that related to other aspects of the project. What is important here is the reasons for the lack of connections and whether this is a common observation over the progress of a longitudinal study. In this case the lead for TfL was not concerned about the three isolates. The three were connected in other networks operating concurrently with the network being studied.

Communities in Self-Organising Project Networks

One of the underlying themes in this research into project networks has been the relationship between roles allocated and the roles acquired by individuals during the project. Identifying communities or subgroups within the main network provides an insight into the structures evolving as a result of the self-organising behaviour of the project actors. Communities comprise clusters of actors between whom there are higher levels of density of connections than is found outside of those communities. Communities can be encouraged through the use of various interventions affecting the context of networks, for example:

- Co-location of staff who might benefit from easier communications, particularly face-to-face
- Efforts to identify team memberships
- Encouragement of arrangements for resource sharing
- The provision of 'communication brokers' (a team of individuals without project roles who are available to facilitate communications and resolve disputes within and between teams).

In this case study three distinct communities emerged. See Figure 11.2.

In Case Study 1, through the process of community detection facilitated by igraph and Gephi (see above) and validation with the actors involved, three distinct communities were identified:

- The 'doing' group. This comprised engineering design staff engaged in gathering appropriate information for their own design group to input and process, solving problems encountered day to day, and dissemination and communication. This community has three prominent actors – Lead Programme Engineer and two Engineering Managers.

- The 'designing' group. A smaller group than the 'doing' group and with actors of lower prominence. The project sponsor, Thames Water Authority (water and sewerage providers in London), and three senior tunnelling engineers have prominence in this community. The Tier 2 lead for tunnelling is particularly prominent.
- The 'decision-making' group. This is the smallest of the communities and is led by the Operational Task Manager and supported by the Lead Architect and the Lift and Escalator lead.

What is important here is that the three community roles are a function of the self-organising activities of designers faced with a complex task under pressure of time.

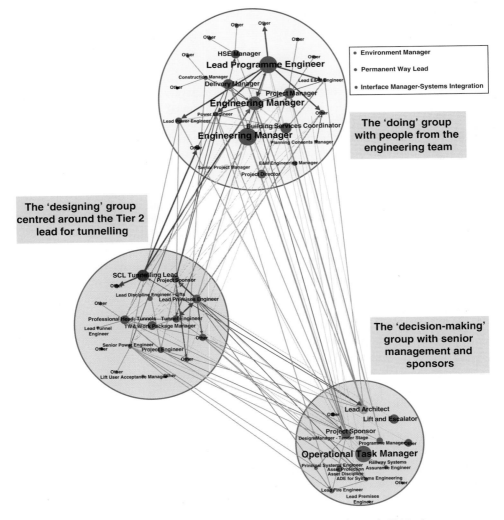

Figure 11.2 Community substructure within the network. Source: Pryke *et al.*, 2015a: 9.

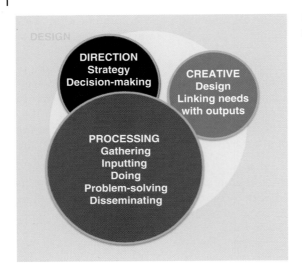

Figure 11.3 Multi-functional clusters supporting design.

The designers and client representatives tacitly separated day-to-day design from communication and information gathering and the need to make decisions. These three emergent sub-functions are not procured in a contractual sense. Now that these sub-functions of design have been identified, the potential exists to identify and manage these functions on other projects. This would be particularly important where the design phase extends over a long period.

Summary

Case Study 1 comprised a large rail infrastructure project. This type of project is characterised by technical, organisational and environmental complexity (Bosch-Rekveldt *et al.*, 2011). In this context we observe distinct communities evolving which combine actors from a range of diverse disciplines. These communities are not identified by the contracts through which the human resources for the project are procured – they are self-organised by the project actors in response to the need to identify and acquire information relating to the project and to disseminate the products of actors whose role it is to originate design material and disseminate it to other project actors.

The three main communities identified in this case study were the 'doing', 'designing' and 'decision-making' clusters. The 'doers' involved those who meet with others, seek information resources and disseminate information resources created; the 'designers' design and leave others to find information resources and disseminate completed and partially-completed design. Finally, a third community exists to make decisions and resolve problems. This 'design function trinity' comprises three self-classifying and self-organising communities and Figure 11.3 reflects this multi-functional trinity.

One important point here is that these functions might well suit quite different personality types (Chapter 7). Perhaps this is the beginning of a process of identifying revised structure and content for construction and engineering contracts. Perhaps, in identifying these key functions, we pave the way for interventions which might enable more effective allocation of tasks, both gathering and dissemination of information and improved decision-making and problem-solving. Awareness may help us to design better contracts and identify problems within the relationships that achieve design output, and may provide the knowledge to better manage the networks that support our projects.

12

Case Study 2: Dysfunctional Prominence in Self-Organising Project Networks

As with Case Study 1, data collection took place between January and April 2014 during the design and approvals stage of the project. The aim was to gather data about information exchange networks and Case Study 2 focused upon the prominence of project actors in information exchange networks.

Data Collection

Actors (individuals involved in the project) were asked to identify other actors with whom they communicated in relation to the design of the project, using a modified form of the questionnaire published in the appendix to Pryke (2012). For the purpose of this study no distinction was made between various means of communicating.[1] Likert scale values were used for frequency of communication and the perceived quality of that communication to the project. Frequency was allocated a low, medium or high rating. Importance was classified as quality of communication and this was allocated six distinct measures: importance, clarity, accuracy, timeliness, reliability and understanding (these values were discussed and agreed with the research client prior to data gathering). The values attributed to frequency were multiplied by the values attributed to quality (using the average overall for quality). This product was used as a proxy for tie strength (following the principles originally outlined in Pryke, 2012). As with Case Study 1, data was collected through an online questionnaire from 60 project actors. All actors provided some basic information about their role in the project.

---

1 SNA can provide very focused analysis of communication networks. Each network must be clearly classified to make sense of the analysis and to ensure rigour. Communications can be classified according to frequency and importance (in both cases using a Likert Scale – see, for example, Pryke, 2012: 249). It is possible to also classify by project management function served (client requirements, progress management, cost management, etc.); the analysis can distinguish between 'send' and 'receive' communications. It can also focus upon the nature of the communication – instruction, consultation, advice given or received, etc.; we could also separately classify communication by mode – meeting, one-to-one conversation, email, telephone call, etc. Unless it is essential to classify to this extent, some of the classifications can be combined and used to value the graph. The weight of the lines could be changed to indicate the frequency or importance of the communication; typically, direction is shown using arrows. Once the linkages are shown in this way, each classification is best regarded as the subject of a separate graph, leading to very large volumes of data.

Managing Networks in Project-Based Organisations, First Edition. Stephen Pryke.
© 2017 John Wiley & Sons Ltd. Published 2017 by John Wiley & Sons Ltd.

Data gathering was triangulated by asking each respondent to enter both sent and received information. An absence of reciprocity prompted the team to ask further questions to establish the reasons for the ambiguity in data.

Data Analysis

As before, the data collected through the online questionnaire was uploaded to an SQL database. The data was subsequently retrieved using a PHP Hypertext Processor and combined into one network by merging the overlapping links in each survey response and calculating the weights of the links (tie strength) from the frequency and quality data. ForceAtlas2 (a graph algorithm designed to provide visualisation from Gephi SNA software) was used for all visualisations.

An important part of the process was a period of consultation with the respondents following the analysis and graphic presentation of the data. This enabled the actors in the network to comment on the analysis. The data analysis was presented in terms of network measures; the respondents were able to explain the differences in values.

Case Study 2 deals with a particular issue of actor prominence and there were a number of measures used to value actor prominence or centrality. In order to make sense of the data analysis, a brief review of the relevant area of network theory is necessary.

Actor Prominence Measures

One of the important measures used in the analysis of organisational networks is centrality. Centrality provides a measure of the prominence which an actor has within a given network. Centrality is calculated by quantifying the number of connections that an actor has within a network. There are three important measures of centrality. These are:

- point or degree centrality
- influence or eigenvector centrality
- brokerage or betweenness centrality.

Point or Degree Centrality

Degree centrality is simply each actor's number of degrees (or links) in a non-directed graph (one without arrows showing the direction of flows):

$$C_D(n_i) = d_i / (n_i - 1)$$

where d is the number of nodes to which a given node is connected and n is the total number of nodes in the network.

Possibly the simplest format for a communication network would be the 'hub and spoke' (see Figure 12.1). The actor at the end of each spoke has the lowest possible value for point

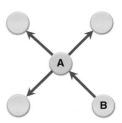

Figure 12.1 Degree centrality.

Figure 12.2 Influence or eigenvector centrality.

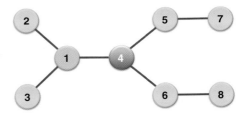

centrality in that network. Below this value (if the actor becomes detached from the hub and remains disconnected from all other actors) the actor becomes an isolate with a point centrality value of zero. The actor at the centre of the hub has the maximum centrality value for a network of that size; s/he is connected to all other actors in the network. Point centrality is the simplest measure of prominence and perhaps, therefore, power in a given network of actors.

Point centrality as a measure of prominence works quite well in the context of the 'hub and spoke' configuration. This is a network of low density (because the actors at the end of the spokes are only connected to one other actor – the central actor). The hub and spoke network configuration is frequently seen where contractual relationships are represented. In fact the construction management form of procurement is represented graphically by the hub and spoke network (for an example see Figure 7.19 in Pryke, 2012: 168). But contracts are essentially (some might say unfortunately) dyadic. Human communications are rarely if ever dyadic; complex communications need multiple communications. In human communications we might be interested in a measure of not only the number of connections an individual actor has, but also the number of secondary connections involved (eigenvector). We might also be interested in the extent to which an actor has the ability to come between communications of other actors (betweenness). There follows a discussion of these two other measures of prominence.

Influence or Eigenvector Centrality

This comprises the inverse of the sum of geodesic distances from actor i to the $g - 1$ other actors (i.e. the reciprocal of his or her 'farness' score):

$$C_C(n_i) = \left[\sum_{j=1}^{g} d(n_i, n_j) \right]^{-1}$$

Figure 12.2 shows two prominent actors who would have identical point centrality scores: actor 1 and actor 4. Each of these two actors is directly connected to two other actors. If we consider secondary connections, then it is clear that actor 4 has more influence. This actor is connected to two actors (actors 5 and 6) each of whom is connected to another actor (actors 7 and 8, respectively). If we were considering the ability of an actor to or likelihood that an actor could solve a problem or influence as many people as possible, clearly actor 4 should score more highly than actor 1. Eigenvector provides a centrality measure that reflects the extent of secondary connections and this is an important measure when dealing with complex communication networks.

Brokerage or Betweenness Centrality

Brokerage or betweenness centrality for actor i is the sum of the proportions, for all pairs of actors j and k, in which actor i is involved in a pair's geodesic(s) – a measure of distance:

$$C_B(n_i) = \sum_{j<k} \frac{g_{jk}(n_i)}{g_{jk}}$$

Referring to Figure 12.3, we can see that once again actors 1, 2 and 3 each have similar point centrality scores. Actors 2 and 3 are connected to four actors each; actor 1 is connected to three actors only. Using point centrality as a measure of prominence would represent actor 1 as of lower prominence than actors 2 and 3. If we were interested in understanding any given actor's ability to control others and act as filter or connect people with resources with those needing such resources, actor 1 clearly has the most prominent position. Uniquely, actor 1 is in a position to organise linkages between all other actors, even if through bridges (actors 2 and 3 act as bridges in Figure 12.3). In communication networks and/or those involved in the dissemination of information or coordination of effort and ideas, actor 1 is the most prominent actor. Betweenness centrality reflects the relevance of the brokerage position in a given network.

Organisational Networks

In Figure 12.4, the nodes are colour-coded to show the main groups of project actors.

Because this was an infrastructure engineering project, the lead designer was an engineer rather than an architect. Network studies produce very high volumes of data. This particular series of comparative figures (Figures 12.4, 12.5 and 12.6) were isolated from the remainder of the network data analysis following discussions with the respondents on the graphical representation of the data analysis. Here we focus upon the role of the senior power engineer (shown in a dotted circle in Figure 12.4). In Figure 12.4, where point centrality is used as a measure, the actors have similar levels of centrality (reflected in Figure 12.4 in the size of the nodes). The prominence is shared between the actor categories (as per colour coding). If we apply point centrality we conclude that no actor is relatively prominent. The network is quite dense and the prominence is evenly spread across the network.

When we apply eigenvector centrality in Figure 12.5, rather than the point centrality seen in Figure 12.4, prominence begins to polarise between the classifications (colour-coded) of actor role types. Perhaps it is not entirely surprising that the lead designer

Figure 12.3 Brokerage or betweenness centrality.

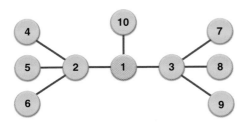

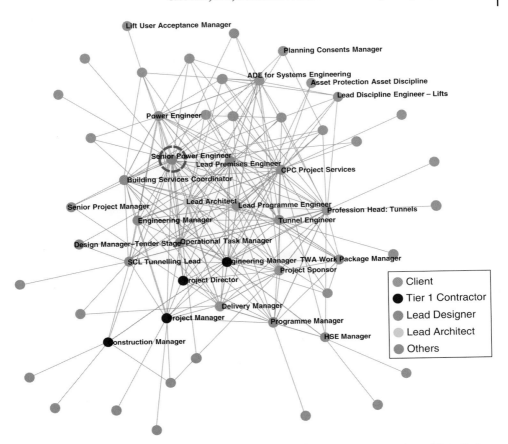

Figure 12.4 Point centrality for project design communication network. Source: adapted from Pryke *et al.* (2017).

and the contractor (whose contract included responsibility for design) were among the most prominent actors. The senior power engineer is more prominent now that eigenvector centrality is applied as a measure of centrality – the prominence reflects the relatively large number of secondary connections.

Finally, in Figure 12.6, the same data set was analysed using brokerage or betweenness as the measure of centrality. The figure illustrates that when this measure is used the prominence of the senior power engineer exceeds that of all other actors.

The findings of the research team were presented initially to the project manager acting for (and employed by) the client for this project. All of the actors for the project were co-located at the office of the client organisation, located directly above the project (which was underground for the most part). The network figures were discussed with the client's project manager, enabling an investigation into the reason for the high prominence of that actor. It was determined to be the result of an excessive display of gatekeeper/hoarder characteristics and the identification of the actor's role in unnecessarily delaying the dissemination of project information meant that action could be taken by the client's project manager to ensure information flowed more easily between design team actors.

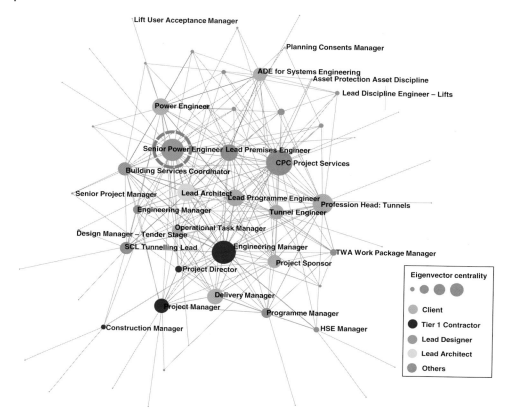

Figure 12.5 Influence or eigenvector centrality for project design communication network. Source: adapted from Pryke *et al.* (2017).

Summary

Case Study 2 involved technical, organisational and environmental complexity (Bosch–Rekveldt *et al.*, 2011), as was noted above in Case Study 1. Case Study 2 provided an insight into the organisational complexity of this project. The research looked very specifically at communications associated with design information exchange and revealed that the application of point centrality in the attempt to understand the prominence of actors in this very specific aspect of the social network environment would provide misleading findings. In an environment which focuses upon technically complex activities associated with complex (and as noted previously, self-organising) project network environments, the application of brokerage or betweenness centrality provides the opportunity to identify what is referred to here as 'dysfunctional prominence'. This is prominence that is inappropriate and undesirable. It is possibly associated with some personality types (see Chapter 7) and would inevitably be related to technical and organisational complexity also.

The research project happened to coincide with a decision to take action in relation to a particular project actor whom we found to have an excessively high level of

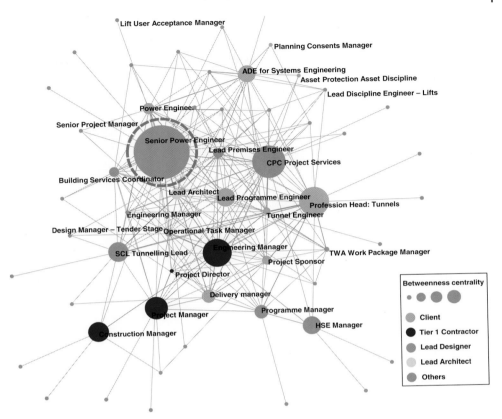

Figure 12.6 Brokerage or betweenness centrality for project design communication network. Source: adapted from Pryke *et al.* (2017).

prominence when measured by brokerage centrality. It might be argued that regular or real-time monitoring of this form of prominence in project networks involving technical and organisational complexity and in an information exchange phase could provide early warning of the development of such dysfunctional prominence. In this way, action to monitor and modify behaviour at an earlier stage might have avoided disruption to the project. Selection of a different personality type in relation to the network role might also have helped the project.

13

Case Study 3: Costing Networks

The business case for proceeding with the two-year research project from which the case studies have been drawn was based upon the premise that studying network topography could provide data analysis that would enable large complex projects to be organised more effectively and to provide organisational cost savings. The aim was to identify issues that were disruptive to the effective organisation of projects (see Case Study 2, for example), to provide a means of early detection in future projects and to establish interventions in the case of detection. Much of the governance that is established in projects is static – established at procurement stage, formalised through contract and then current for the duration of the project. In the case of large projects, this period could comprise several years, perhaps running into a decade or more.

Networks evolve as project activity increases, and decay towards the end of the project as activity reduces prior to completion. Within each specialist field and contract package, we would see the evolution of function-based networks and their decay as the next package comes onstream. The cost of a network relates to the number of actors, and the density of the network-connections manifested by some sort of interaction create a cost in terms of time expended by an individual actor. Case Study 3 pursued the feasibility of applying costs to both network initiation and maintenance. The work on costing networks was at feasibility stage at the time of writing.

Conceptual Framework

Complex networks occur in social sciences (and I am applying network science to the study and management of projects here), where the nodes in the networks are the project role-holding actors and the connections comprise the interactions between them. Barabási and Albert (1999) observed that complex networks (those with complex topography or structural configuration) were being described using random graph theory, and in particular referred to the work of Erdös and Rényi (1960). But Erdös and Rényi's work was rarely applied in the real world because of an absence of data. I argue here that although project networks are not large scale in the sense in which 'big data' networks are large scale – the sort of data that might be derived from a study of Facebook or LinkedIn, for example – the topography of project networks is evolutionary and complex as project actors seek connections to facilitate the execution of their project roles (quickly and efficiently, so as to maximise profit and under conditions of uncertainty). Barabási and Albert (1999) noted a high degree of self-organisation in

Managing Networks in Project-Based Organisations, First Edition. Stephen Pryke.
© 2017 John Wiley & Sons Ltd. Published 2017 by John Wiley & Sons Ltd.

complex networks along with what they refer to as 'preferential attachment'. In project networks we would expect preferential attachment to be driven by the needs of the project actors to discharge their project responsibilities. The point here is that project network studies might usefully provide network costing data and the analysis of such data might prove instructive for future project network analyses.

Network Costs

The cost of a given network has two elements – the 'building cost' (bc) and the 'operational cost' (oc). Barabási and Albert's (1999) model shows the network building cost for a network evolution moving from zero to 20 nodes and incrementally in 20-node stages to 100 as a straight-line graph; see Figure 13.1.

Figure 13.1 was derived from a simulation of network scaling using the work of Erdös and Rényi (1960) and Barabási and Albert (1999). The model was implemented in igraph software (http://www.inside-r.org/packages/cran/igraph/docs/random.graph.game and http://www.inside-r.org/packages/cran/igraph/docs/barabasi.game). The (network) building cost is related to the number of links in the network. It is defined as:

$$bc = e \times l$$

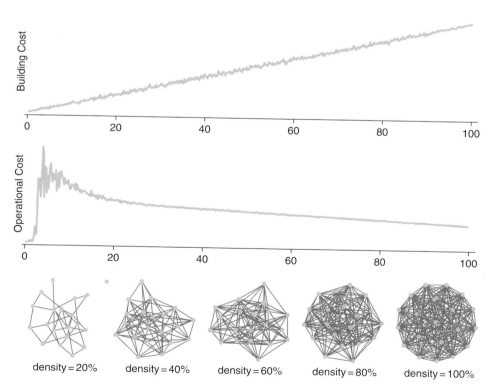

Figure 13.1 Network building and operation costs related to network density; based upon the Albert–Barabási model. Source: unpublished report (2016).

where bc is the building cost of the network, e is the number of links in the network at that point in its evolution and l is the average cost of each link. This creates a straight-line graph (see building cost part of Figure 13.1).

Building cost has an upward trend with increasing fluctuations proportionately throughout the graph (see Figure 13.1). The operational cost is measured by the total number of steps that need to be taken through the connections or links to transmit information from each actor in the network to every other actor in that network. The formula for operational cost is:

$$oc = [V_n] \times m$$

where V is the sum of all the shortest distances from each actor in the network to every other actor in the network and m is the average cost of communication between actors.[1] The operational cost, based upon the simulation, showed a slow start, then a steep upward rise as the network grew from two actors towards ten. Thereafter, there is a steep decline towards 20 nodes, followed by a gentle and consistent slope downwards beyond the 20-node threshold.

Data Analysis

Data relating to actor numbers, network density and cost were gathered longitudinally at approximately six month intervals (designated Stages 1 and 2). Both data sets involved the same project during the design phase and the purpose was to understand the evolution of the communication network relating to design communication and information exchange. Table 13.1 shows the comparison between Stage 1 and Stage 2.

The communication network associated with design and in particular coordination, negotiation and dissemination, grew by approximately 22% in terms of actor numbers. This growth was associated with the appointment by the client of a structural, civil and specialist construction engineering consultancy in the period between Stage 1 and Stage 2.

The 22% increase in actor numbers was accompanied by a 53% increase in the number of links as actors sought to make the connections they needed to make their roles viable within the evolving network. The existing actors need to adapt to the changing network topography and the incoming actors need to establish connections that facilitate their functions within the network and are compliant with the roles allocated by contract and the roles inherent in their network positions.

In consultation with the client's project manager, an average of one working day per actor was allowed as the cost of establishing links with other actors at the beginning of the self-organising process. A daily rate of £500 per day was used in this calculation,

---

1 This might seem to be a difficult figure to establish. There is, however, a useful link to the 'frequency' data gathered in order to value the links between actors (see Questionnaire in Appendix to Pryke, 2012: 249 – there are footnotes to the questionnaire illustrating this point). See also Appendix 1 to this book. By allocating an average time per communication, knowing the frequency from the network data and having access to actors' costs per hour, it is possible to calculate this cost. In Case Studies 1, 2 and 3 we had access to staff cost data. Some staff were employed under contract on an hourly rate, some were employed through a consultancy contract, others were directly employed by the client.

Table 13.1 Network size, density and cost: Stage 1 and Stage 2 comparison.

	Stage 1	Stage 2	% Change
No. of actors (n)	162	197	+22%
No. of links (1)	1440	2207	+53%
Network density $\Delta = 1/n(n-1)$	0.055	0.057	+4%[2]
Network build cost	£0.72 M	£1.10 M	+53%
Network operating cost (per project month)	£0.78 M	£1.16 M	+49%

based on an average of the cost per actor for the entire network of actors. This approximates to £1 per minute of the working day. The operating cost of the network was estimated at an average of three communications per month for each actor multiplied by the average number of connections per actor in the network. These values were once again based on an estimation made with the client's project manager. In terms of density of the evolving network, the number of linkages was increasing in order to deal with the need for a larger group of actors to establish and maintain the connections that they needed to function in their roles.

Summary

This case study outlines the approach used to establish a basis for costing the building and operational costs of project-based networks. The simulation work of Erdös and Rényi (1960) and Barabási and Albert (1999) dealt essentially with scaling in relation to network evolution and helped to establish some profiles for both network building costs and network operational costs. The data gathered was, of necessity, for a period of evolution which involved an extension of the boundaries of the initial simulation. It is not unreasonable to assume, I suggest, that trends for networks evolving to a size between 160 and 200 nodes would reflect the settled trends shown for networks greater than n = 20 in Figure 13.1. Specifically, network building costs rise upwards in relation to increasing values for n with an elevation of 6 degrees. Operational costs are variable between 0 and 20 nodes, then settle to a declining gradient of 3 degrees, flattening as n approaches infinity.

---

2 An understanding of the relationship between the changes to actor quantities, linkage quantities and network density is facilitated by inspection of the formula for density shown in the table. In this table, $n(n-1)$ approximates to n^2, especially at larger values for n, so the density varies approximately as the coefficient of the square of actor quantity. Conversely, to maintain density in a given network as it grows, the number of links needs to vary proportionately to an approximation of the square of the quantity of actors (n^2). Hence a 22% increase in the quantity of actors, accompanied by a 53% increase in the number of links, leads to a relatively small (4%) increase in density for the network.

The key points from this exploratory pilot study (in the context of a much larger research project) are as follows:

- It is possible and potentially very useful to provide figures against both network building costs and network operational costs. We were fortunate to have the client's project manager on our research team. This enabled access to costings which might not have been available to other research teams.
- Simulation based upon Erdös and Rényi (1960) and Barabási and Albert (1999) scaling indicates a high level of fluctuations in operational costs as networks evolve between values of 2 and 20 for n.
- It follows from the previous point that interventions in the management of projects are particularly important in the evolutionary cycle for value of $n = 2$ to value of $n = 20$. During this period it would be important to avoid disruptive behaviours such as gate keeping and hoarding. It would be important to encourage brokers to enable connections to be made quickly and efficiently. Temporary network enabling brokers might need to be inserted during the $n = 2–20$ evolutionary cycle. In project management organisations with large programmes of projects, a permanent team responsible for engaging with networks in this crucial evolutionary phase might be valuable.

This third case study has indicated that further research needs to be carried out in the area of project network costing, certainly in relation to project network studies. There are implications from this research for both academics and practitioners. The ability to monitor and manage network building and operation costs would be valuable in understanding the invisible, self-organising aspects of our projects.

14

Summary and Conclusions

This final chapter starts with a summary of the contents of the book, mostly for the benefit of those who, like myself, read the summary and conclusions chapter first. Following the summary is a synopsis and rationalisation of the contents of the book, and, finally, the conclusions.

Introduction

The book started with a reflection that my own experience, first in industry and latterly in academia, had provided a focus and a motivation for studying relationships in the context of managing both supply chains and projects. The book was written with the master's and doctoral student in mind, along with the reflective practitioner. It is hoped that this text has provided something for each quite different sets of needs. My experience and research interests have been principally associated with the areas of construction, property development and engineering, together with relatively brief forays into petrochemicals and housing maintenance. It is hoped that the contents of this book might generate interest beyond engineering and construction. The conceptual link between networks and projects is generic.

Chapter Summaries

Theoretical Context

In Chapter 2, I provided some conceptual and theoretical context for the discussion later in the book. I looked at project transitions – moving from procurement to placing of contract and on to delivery. I proposed that the systems supporting the project were best observed and analysed using social network analysis and, in this way, the raison-d'être for the book was established. I argued that even when the project has transitioned from procurement to delivery, the relationships established are transient, despite the assumption to the contrary in some of the standard forms of contract intended for design and construction of the built environment.

I discussed the issue of complexity and raised the question whether the contracting system has outgrown the size and complexity of projects. Briefly I turned my attention

Managing Networks in Project-Based Organisations, First Edition. Stephen Pryke.
© 2017 John Wiley & Sons Ltd. Published 2017 by John Wiley & Sons Ltd.

to the idea that procurement focuses upon dyadic, relatively inflexible, contractual relationships. But project implementation relies upon a range of activities that are essentially hidden from view – difficult to identify, difficult to quantify and therefore difficult to manage. Power, manipulation and exploitation were cited as important factors in understanding the operation of the hidden networks supporting the functional systems that design and deliver projects.

Finally, in Chapter 2, I reflected on the quasi-military and hierarchical focus in some of the management approaches to projects. We naturally focus in our recreational activities on social relationships and networks. We have in the past and in our business lives tended to assume that contract will provide systems and governance sufficient to deliver successful permanent organisational and temporary project outcomes. Perhaps we no longer need or wish to draw a distinction between what is normal in human interaction for recreational purposes and the human interaction that occurs in the course of our jobs. For networks to be useful in the project management context, they need to be precisely classified and consideration given to the fact that, unlike some other areas of social network study, the project is multi-functional and therefore complex in social network terms.

Networks and Projects

In Chapter 3, I linked social network theory back to the early work of the Gestalt theorist, Wolfgang Kohler. The development of network science gained huge momentum when information technology started to provide the computing power for individuals to carry out analysis of large network datasets on a laptop computer, together with brilliant graphical representation of the analysed data. The chapter looked at some of the problems with projects that social network analysis (SNA) has the potential to resolve. Uncertainty and its effects on individuals' behaviour within the project environment were considered and I looked at some of the criticism of SNA. Finally, although the idea that the project has served us well was conceded, the need to understand more about how procured project resources are exploited was also expressed. I argued that while the project was a useful construct by which to monitor the basic project metrics of cost, time and quality, when we turn our attention to value and innovation, for example, there is a need to understand the network topographies that enable these project functions. In fact, the application of network theory and social network analysis to projects enables the study of all the various systems that comprise project management.

Why Networks?

In Chapter 4, I made the link to my previous text in this series – *Social Network Analysis in Construction* (2012). This previous book concentrated on investigating the analysis of a large construction data set comprising four construction projects. The projects comprised two each from the public and private sectors and two using a collaborative approach to procurement. This chapter dealt with some basis concepts for the benefit of those who have not read the 2012 text. The terms network, actor, relation, mode, value, dyad, triad, subgroup, density and a number of measures of centrality are all defined in preparation for the chapters which follow and in particular Chapters 11, 12 and 13.

The chapter also looks at some actor characteristics – prominent disseminator, gatekeeper hoarder, isolate, boundary spanner, bridge. Finally, path lengths, tie strength and directed graphs were defined and explained. Rationalisation of the use of SNA in studying projects is presented and some of the most common criticisms of SNA are considered and responses offered. The chapter closes with the point that it is important to define the context for each network study – projects present a very wide range of independent variables and it is a challenge to isolate the dependent variables that will become the focus of a given network study. Classification of actors and their characteristics was also emphasised. The reader is also asked to consider carefully whether to study inter-organisational or interpersonal networks. Chapter 4 concludes with some recommendations for suitable SNA software.

Self-organising Networks in Projects

Chapter 5 takes as its theme 'five dangerous assumptions' about projects. These dangerous assumptions essentially question whether the complexity of projects, both technically and organisationally, has exceeded the capacity of the lump-sum contract approach to procurement. The importance of clearly defined roles and responsibilities were discussed, as were 'chains of command', relationships and systems in projects. I argue that the lack of early and accurate project definition is almost inevitable and there is a need to: establish flexibility in the delivery phase; understand, quantify and graphically represent that flexibility; and ultimately move towards managing flexibility alongside emergent project definition.

The chapter reflects on why networks form and begins to develop an understanding of the stimuli acting on interpersonal project networks and the effects of those stimuli on project networks. The chapter speculates about clients' needs and laments that these needs are so often not met. Project definition and the importance of the design team in responding to context are discussed. Five dangerous assumptions in relation to projects are posited, relating to: accurate and early project definition, the effects of agency on interpretation of needs, the problem of variation, the allocation of roles and the durability of roles and relationships for the duration of the project.

Finally, the chapter makes the point that projects must deal with uncertainty, and that in a sense uncertainty is partly a function of the need for individual project actors to operate profitably. The reader was encouraged to conceptualise projects as networks of relationships – and to map and interrogate those networks of relationships, to observe the structure of systems that reflect successful and unsuccessful projects and ultimately to acquire the knowledge to enable project networks to be designed and managed.

Game Theory and Networks

I started Chapter 6 with a rationalisation of game theory in the context of networks. There was reference to the 'transient nodal position' that project actors occupy and the transition to network actors that individuals joining a project need to make. So, individual actors find themselves in transient networks and their own roles within those networks are subject to negotiation with the network surrounding them; their leverage in those negotiations will depend on a range of factors. It was discussed how some knowledge of game theory might help to explain how interpersonal project networks evolve and how individual actors within networks acquire and modify roles, and, in some cases, subsequently divest themselves of roles. The chapter looked at the background to game theory and some key concepts. Attention was drawn to issues of complexity in projects in relation to the application of game theory, and the assumption of rationality made in game theory. 'Near rationality' was adopted because of the absence of incentive systems and the essentially self-organising nature of the project environment. Utility as an issue was also considered – trading off interdependent and conflicting functions in the project environment. I acknowledged the mathematical basis of game theory, yet directed the reader to the principles in the first instance. Further research is needed to exploit the potential correlation between game theory and social network analysis. The chapter closed with a discussion of the application of game theory to projects represented as social networks. Game theory was explored in relation to the five dangerous assumptions proposed in Chapter 5.

Network Roles and Personality Type

Chapter 7 builds upon the previous chapter in examining the topography of networks and the likely connections that will form between a given group of actors in a project. The rules and likely outcomes of a game (Chapter 6) are a function of the environment in which the game is set and the propensities of the players. In Chapter 7, the propensity of project actors to act in relation to other actors is explored through personality types. The chapter takes the basic actor characteristics from Chapter 4 and explores the behaviours that underpin these actor characteristics to provide a context for a discussion about personality traits. Trait or disposition theory was defined as relating to 'habitual patterns of behaviour, thought or emotion' (Kassin, 2003).

Fifteen trait classifications are identified from the personality trait literature. Some are of more immediate relevance to our analysis of project networks than others: extroversion and perfectionism look likely to prove relevant; alexithymia (inability to express emotions) might prove more difficult to apply in the project network context. Humour is proposed as a factor affecting the evolution and maintenance of networks of project relationships on the basis that socialisation is important in forming relationships in the ambiguous and uncertain environments that most projects constitute. It was noted that the ritual of humour is also a reflection of the prominence of individual actors in a network.

The main body of the chapter explores the personality traits individually and investigates the importance or otherwise of those traits to 'network person'. I then return to the network behaviours first discussed in Chapter 4 and discuss personality traits associated with each behaviour type. The intention of this chapter was to open a debate about personality, network evolution and topography.

Network Enabling

In Chapter 8 I proposed a number of 'enabling' factors for our project networks. Trust is a topic that is frequently cited as important in relationships, empathy possibly less so. Reciprocity as a concept arose out of the two-year infrastructure research project that features in Chapters 11, 12 and 13. Reciprocity was one of the contextual factors rather than an independent variable for this long-term research project. I proposed that favours are the currency of the network and that our network role is partly supported by our ability to trade in favours with others. Actors in project networks as well as in recreational networks can display a range of levels of generosity in their dealings. Set against these enabling factors are three disenabling factors: (individual) competitiveness and opportunism; narcissism; and egotism.

The chapter deals with each of these enabling and disenabling factors and discusses the effect on actors and networks of each of these behaviour types. Empathy gets a special mention, partly because so many problems occur in projects through lack of empathy. Some might argue that the seeds of this 'unempathetic'[1] behaviour are sown in the classrooms of higher education before project actors become exposed to the industry or industries within which they will ultimately work. I really would encourage all of those involved in the education of aspiring professionals to foster an empathetic attitude to the other professionals involved in projects. The chapter moves on to consider the role of psychological contracts in project networks. What do we do about project actors that engage in disenabling behaviour? What sanctions do we have? Some network (structural) responses are proposed.

The point is made that if we are considering behaviours that might be encouraged or discouraged in networks, one of the means by which a change of behaviour might be effected is contagion. Enabling behaviour is contagious and project actors look for cues from the actors around them. Actors prominent in communication networks tend to have more influence over network-enabling behaviours than those with lower levels of connectivity.

Project Networks and BIM

In Chapter 8 I deliberately 'cast the net' wider than solely construction projects. But it was difficult to ignore building information modelling in this discussion about project networks. Non-construction readers might have chosen to ignore Chapter 9 or perhaps read the contents with their own information management functions in mind.

A little context and background to BIM is provided by way of introduction. The topic of BIM is linked to information management, as one of the project management functions, that is, a system reflected within a network dedicated to the information management function. Ownership of information and intellectual property rights are referred to briefly and then information management is linked to organisational structure. The roles of fantasy documents and ritualistic behaviour are considered. The chapter moves on to consider self-organising networks in the context of design and I suggest that the BIM model might be regarded as an 'artefact', rather than a system for the delivery of a project.

Finally, the chapter moves on to propose a research agenda for building information modelling and social network analysis, citing ongoing work at University College London, UK and Stanford University, California, USA, and an interesting localisation of building information management being piloted at Transport for London, UK.

---

1 This word clearly means the *opposite* of 'empathetic' and was adopted out of frustration with the range of words offered as antonyms for empathy, including: indifference, apathy, unfeelingness, misunderstanding, uncompassionate, pitilessness, callousness, insensate and obdurate, all of which, arguably, mean something slightly different to *an inability to understand the feelings of others*. The emphasis in 'unempathetic' lies in the *inability* to feel, rather than the *disinclination to feel* implied in many of the antonyms above.

Case Study 1: Communities in Self-Organising Project Networks

A short descriptive introduction to the case studies is included in Chapter 10.

Chapter 11 demonstrates the identification of three distinct clusters within the design networks of a mega-sized infrastructure project: doing, decision-making and designing clusters. These self-organising clusters are not reflected in the roles procured by the client for the project. The chapter concluded with reference to personality traits and the better-informed decisions that might be made in relation to network creation if more knowledge was available about the network roles and function-related roles that actors have imposed upon them, or adopt, in projects.

Case Study 2: Dysfunctional Prominence in Self-Organising Project Networks

Chapter 12 looked at another aspect of a mega-sized infrastructure project for which the data was gathered at design stage in the period shortly before commencement on site. The project was procured on a 'with-design' basis and therefore the contractor had been appointed prior to scheme design. This particular case study was an exercise in studying the design information exchange network for the project outlined in the introduction to the case studies. In particular the research team was interested in looking at differences in prominence for the group of actors in the design information exchange using three measures of centrality: point or degree, influence or eigenvector, and brokerage or betweenness centrality. While degree and eigenvector indicated centrality values that were regarded as entirely appropriate by the network respondents, betweenness centrality scores were exceptionally high for one particular actor. Surrounding actors had become frustrated by the actor's habit of continually delaying information flowing through him. I conclude that in information exchange networks, and especially those involving complex design activities, high betweenness centrality scores for individual actors are disruptive to project networks. An application here would be to periodically monitor betweenness centrality in information exchange networks to look for early warnings of disruptive behaviours. In this particular case a disruption could have been avoided if network management interventions had been implemented – including actor repositioning, training and the use of network behaviour guidelines on timeliness of responses and dissemination, for example.

Case Study 3: Costing Networks

In Chapter 13, I discussed some experiments that have been carried out by the Centre for Organisational Network Analysis at UCL (CONA@UCL) as part of the two-year research project. The team started to experiment with the idea that networks could be costed and this information used to understand and manage those networks. This case study essentially dealt with the cost of scaling networks and in particular identified a relatively expensive network evolution phase for actor population growth from 2 to 20. The composition of the research team was an important factor in enabling this study because the team had access to costings for the actors in the network (time sheets were used to record time expended by each actor against a range of classifications of project functions). The research team was able to identify costs for the network in relation to both evolution and operational costs. The case study concluded that network evolution is disproportionately expensive in the earlier stages; the first 10–20% of network construction involves intensive activity in building network relationships, which is disproportionately time consuming compared to later network evolution stages. It was suggested that this calls for enabling interventions at this stage to reduce costs and provide faster network establishment times. This intervention might comprise a small team of 'brokers' whose role it is to identify linkages that are necessary for the network and facilitate these through introductions, workshops, social events and perhaps empathy-building awareness.

Conclusions

The aim of this book was to explore in some depth the links between projects and networks. The book has been partly explanatory and instructive, with the aim of involving more scholars and practitioners in the concepts and science of networks; hopefully it has raised some theoretical issues, perhaps building some theory as the discussion proceeded. It has linked subjects together in a manner that might not have been widely discussed previously, and has presented findings from a two-year research project which might suggest applications for industry. Finally, the book has identified research agendas that it is hoped others might be interested in pursuing.

Theoretical Issues

Projects are temporary and must deal with one or more transitions in order to deliver the functions essential for design and delivery. Transitions in projects are one of the causes of transience in project networks and yet I argue that the transience remains beyond transitions due to the continual evolution of relationships supporting information exchange. One of the important transitions occurs when procured resources need to establish the relationships that are necessary to function as actors in a network. I argued that the resources are procured through dyadic contractual relationships but the networks that represent the function-related project networks are essentially self-establishing and self-managing; they are self-organising in the broadest sense of the word. The existence and location of power are important in the way in which the networks evolve and sustain themselves over the life of the project.

I argue here that some of what we read and teach in relation to project management is inclined to resonate with our military past, rather than turning to face the future in our highly connected and non-hierarchical lives. One of the exciting aspects of conceptualising projects as networks is that graphical representations of functional networks have no orientation – no top and bottom. So, discussions about leadership and management seem increasingly irrelevant; we substitute enabling and facilitation. If we start to change the language used to explain what is happening and what needs to be done in our projects, then we start to think about the actors that will form our project networks – their personality traits and behaviours.

Context is, arguably, not always given the weight that it might be given, particularly where quantitative means of analysis are applied. I argued that uncertainty and its effects, both personally and organisationally, are an important contextual factor in the discussion about transience and transition in project networks. Project actors are faced with a partly unfamiliar challenge under pressure of time and in a context where the project is frequently poorly defined. I argued that in these circumstances actors form networks to facilitate the discharge of their own roles and in response to the needs of others to gather and exchange information. Project networks are complex because of: the rapid transition required of a group of actors who may not be familiar with each other; the temporariness of projects and reluctance to invest in long-term relationships; the iterative nature of project information exchange; the transience of networks as actors move between functional networks and their roles in networks evolve. Project networks are multi-functional, unlike many other forms of social network that network scientists study. Project networks are also self-instigating and self-managing (self-organising for simplicity).

One of the themes of the book is that projects suffer organisationally partly because processes and structures have not scaled up sufficiently to deal with the complex and sometimes massive projects that society demands to deal with the progress that is necessary for continued increasing personal prosperity and comfort. The five dangerous assumptions theme ran through several of the chapters and dealt with: the problems and reality of project definition; the issue of agency in projects and accuracy and completeness in representing client and user needs; the proposition that variations are beneficial to the value delivered in a project; the difficulty in defining actor roles; and finally the (contractual) assumption that roles will be static for the duration of the project. Within this is the issue that governance is strategic rather than operational and it is the actors who design and operate the systems that deliver projects. Because the networks are actor-designed, clients and perhaps their project managers are not familiar with the design and operation of these self-organising networks. Data relating to these networks is needed to enable analysis and provide the knowledge to allow project networks to be designed and managed in the future.

So, in this book I have explored some of the stimuli to which project actors respond (and the emphasis has been upon the individual as the project actor, rather than the firm as a project actor). Once we become convinced that the conceptualisation of the project as multiple layers of precisely classified networks reflecting project functions is valuable, we need to think about these layers of networks and the actors who occupy positions within them through negotiation with other actors. Negotiation between actors involves influencing the network environment and being influenced by it. And this is transient. Roles in networks evolve and change in prominence over time. Sometimes this is the environment influencing actor roles; sometimes it is the actor's own intervention. 'Near rationality' was a preferred position in my discussion of game theory and its relevance to networks. Game theory helps to explain the behaviour of actors at the various stages of the project – why we cannot all agree on project definition; why we cannot all express it in the same manner and why we do not necessarily want to reach consensus. So, project network actors are trading with each other in order to comply with their project role; in the process they might assume or have imposed a network role – those network roles may or may not suit the individual actor. Hence the discussion about personality type.

Personality affects the ability to form, survive and manipulate networks for individual and project benefit. Personality affects behaviours and there is irony in the fact that the personality and behaviour that makes an individual successful in terms of gaining employment and getting promoted within an organisation are quite contrary to the personality traits and behaviours that enable networks. Generous individuals who have empathy for colleagues and other project network actors, who take the trouble to reciprocate and show a selfless attitude, are good for our networks. Those who seek prominence may have a negative effect on the network around them. Competitiveness and opportunism, narcissism and egotism all conspire to disrupt the functioning of project networks.

Some of the research agendas proposed include further work in the area of building information modelling. The BIM movement started with the *technology* but it might have started with the *networks of relationships*. So, it is argued that there is work to do that might influence the future development of BIM. Tie strength needs to be defined in terms that are quite specific to the project network environment; the questionnaire (see Appendix) provides some insight into the framework chosen for the definition of tie strength in the case study material and this is a development of the tie strength metrics used in the previous book in this series. Case Study 1 set a research agenda in terms of understanding the clusters of actors involved in design. It revealed a discrepancy between the roles procured contractually and the roles adopted in the self-organising design networks that evolved to discharge the design function. An agenda was established in terms of the type of centrality measures that are appropriate for project networks. There is potential for a great deal of further study in this area to expand the research presented in this book. Finally, a start was made in building theory associated with the cost implications and profiling of project network establishment and operation. The material presented in this book is no more than the outline of an agenda for extensive further research in this fascinating area.

What Might Industry Learn from this Book?

Conceptualising projects as networks is valuable Whether projects are successful or unsuccessful, there is often speculation as to the cause. Procurement, culture, economic climate…the list goes on as to the source of the outcome. The reality is that so much of what happens in projects, whether at design or execution stage, is effectively invisible. The self-organising networks may work very effectively or may be quite dysfunctional, perhaps as a result of the activities of small groups of actors. But we do not gather the data, carry out the analysis, share the results with the actors or try to manage those networks, as networks. Conceptualising the project as multiple layers of functional networks is valuable and will provide knowledge that will help us all to deliver more successful projects in the future.

Network roles are quite different to project roles A better understanding of the behaviours that we need to foster and those that we need to reduce or eliminate is also valuable. We need to encourage trust, empathy, reciprocity and generosity in order to create good network actors, regardless of discipline or experience. We need to avoid those who are competitive and opportunistic, narcissistic and egotistical. We need to think about network roles as well as professional disciplinary specialisations when recruiting individuals to work in temporary project environments.

Humour might be important Humour is important in recreational social networks but the effect within project networks has yet to be fully explored. However, socialisation is as important in the assembly and operation of project networks as it is beyond the workplace.

Transient environments The project network environment is quite different to the environment envisaged in our contracts and protocols. Actors exist in an environment where they help define the systems through which the project is delivered; they influence the behaviour of other actors and are influenced themselves by the actions of other actors. The environment is not static as envisaged in the contracts procuring those resources – the environment is continually transforming and adapting to deal with the demands of the project and the systems in use.

Gaming is a factor Our actors are embedded in a network surrounded by gaming actors. Each actor needs to make a series of decisions about which games to engage with and how to position themselves in relation to those games.

Building information modelling needs humanising Some early work is being carried out to link social network analysis to Revit software to facilitate understanding of the social networks associated with BIM. I argued that it would have been better to make the social networks before building IT systems. Case Study 1, for example, points to the fact that design has three important and separate functions – creation of design, strategy (decision-making) and operations (gathering and disseminating information). It might be better to regard BIM as an information management system rather than a cure for certain perceived ills within the construction industry.

Mapping, modelling, analysing and managing networks If we are to anticipate and manage out the risk posed by, for example, dysfunctional prominence, we need to gather network data and routinely monitor networks in our projects.

Costing and financial viability of networks The discussion of the costing and financial monitoring of networks is in its infancy, particularly in relation to its impact upon industry. The UK construction industry spends approximately £30BN per annum on labour. Social network analysis is one of the few ways of quantifying and analysing the networks of functional relationships that evolve in response to the demands of the project and the actors within the network. Clearly, there is potential for the industry in understanding how its most expensive resources are being utilised and in investigating sources of disproportionate and unnecessary cost.

I hope that there is something both for the scholar and for the reflective practitioner in this book. Inevitably, many questions arise; hopefully there are some answers too. If the book stimulates discussion and debate, perhaps between those who disagree with some of what is written here, then something useful will have been achieved.

Appendix

Case Study Questionnaire

Bank - Central Line Escalators

Name	Organisation	Role
Fill in your name...	By whom are you contractually employed?	What is your job role?

Have you been involved in resolving issues concerning the Central Line Escalators (including in relation to impacts on settlements, and agreement on UMC/LMC, switchgear and maintenance spaceproofing requirements)?

yes ⬍

Approximately what percentage of your working time do you usually spend on the Bank SCU project?

in %

The aim of the following table is to capture who you communicate with to resolve issues concerning the Central Line Escalators. In the list of names presented Please tick the checkbox next to the people who you communicate with and use the sliders to indicate the quality of communication between you and them. It is important that if there are other people who you communicate with in relation to this issue who aren't shown in the list, you add their names at the end. It doesn't matter at all what organisation they work for, how senior they are or what their role is. Instructions are given below,

Frequency : Please select the appropriate number based on how often do you communicate with the person as given below,
⑥ More than once a day | ⑤ Daily | ④ Several times a week | ③ A few times a week | ② Once a week | ① Less than once a week

For the rest : Please select the appropriate number based on your level of agreement with the corresponding statements (shown by clicking the headings)
⑤ Strongly agree | ④ Agree | ③ Ambivalent | ② Disagree | ① Strongly Disagree

search	Frequency	Importance	Clarity	Accuracy	Timeliness	Understanding	Reliability
☑ Actor 1	③	⑤	②	③	③	③	③
☐ Actor 2							
☐ Actor 3							
☐ Actor 4							
☐ Actor 5							
☐ Actor 6							
☐ Actor 7							
☐ Actor 8							
☐ Actor 9							
☐ Actor 10							
☐ Actor 11							
☐ Actor 12							
☐ Actor 13							
☐ Actor 14							
☐ Actor 15							
☐ Actor 16							
☐ Actor 17							
☐ Actor 18							
☐ Actor 19							
☐ Actor 20							
☐ Actor 21							
☐ Actor 22							
☐ Actor 23							
☐							
☐							
☐							
☐							
☐							

Submit the form

Thank you :)

The explanations for each aspect (frequency, importance, etc.) are embedded in the questionnaire as interactive features (they show up as the user fills in the questionnaire), and are not shown in the text file above. These explanations are:

Frequency – How frequently do you contact this person in relation to the issue?
Importance – Information I obtain from communicating with this person is important to resolving the issue.
Clarity – Information I obtain from communicating with this person is clear.
Accuracy – Information I obtain from communicating with this person is accurate.
Timeliness – Information I obtain from communicating with this person is timely.
Understanding – I know where I stand when dealing with this person.
Reliability – I can rely on this person to share information that they have which may be of benefit to me.

References

Aish, R. (1986) Building modelling: the key to integrated construction CAD. *CIB 5th International Symposium on the Use of Computers for Environmental Engineering Related to Building*.

Al Hattab, M. and Hamzeh, F. (2015) Using social network theory and simulation to compare traditional versus BIM–lean practice for design error management. *Automation in Construction*, 52, 59–69.

Alexander, R.D. (1986) Ostracism and indirect reciprocity: the reproductive significance of humour. *Ethology and Sociobiology*, 7 (3), 253–270.

Altshuler, A. and Luberoff, D. (2003) *Mega-Projects: The Changing Politics of Urban Public Investment*. Brookings Institution Press, Washington DC.

Annamdas, K.K. and Rao, S.S. (2009) Multi-objective optimization of engineering systems using game theory and particle swarm optimization. *Engineering Optimization*, 41 (8), 737–752.

Antucheviciene, J. and Zavadskas, E.K. (2008) Modelling multidimensional redevelopment of derelict buildings. *International Journal of Environment and Pollution*, 35 (2–4), 331–344.

Aoki, M., Gustafsson, B. and Williamson, O.E. (1990) *The Firm as a Nexus of Treaties*. Sage, London.

APM (2012) *APM Body of Knowledge*. 6th edition. Association for Project Management, London.

Apte, M.L. (1985) *Humour and Laughter: An Anthropological Approach*. Cornell University Press, New York.

Atkin, R. (1974) *Mathematical Structure in Human Affairs*. Heinnemann, London.

Atkin, R. (1977) *Combinatorial Connectivities in Social Systems*. Birkhäuser, Basel.

Atkin, R. (1981) *Multidimensional Man*. Penguin, Harmondsworth.

Aumann, K., Galinsky, E. and Matos, K. (2011) *The New Male Mystique. National Study of the Changing Workforce*. Families and Work Institute, New York.

Autodesk (2002) *Building Information Modelling*. San Rafael, CA.

Badi, S.M. and Pryke, S.D. (2006) The effect of trust on the accuracy of design-development information flows in UK construction new procurement systems: a social network analysis. *Sunbelt XXVI. Annual research conference of the International Network of Social Network Analysis (INSNA), Vancouver, Canada, 24–30 April 2006*.

Managing Networks in Project-Based Organisations, First Edition. Stephen Pryke.
© 2017 John Wiley & Sons Ltd. Published 2017 by John Wiley & Sons Ltd.

Badi, S.M., Almadhoob, H. and Pryke, S.D. (2014) The influence of social networks on firm's success, survival and growth: a social network analysis investigation of SMEs in the Bahrain Construction Industry. *Sunbelt XXXIV. Annual research conference of the International Network of Social Network Analysis (INSNA), St Pete Beach, Florida, 18–23 February 2014.*

Badi, S., Li, M. and Pryke, S.D. (2016a) The influence of communication network centrality on individual popularity: a case study of a Chinese construction project. *COBRA 2016. Annual conference of the Royal Institution of Chartered Surveyors, Toronto, Canada, 19–22 September 2016.*

Badi, S., Wang, L. and Pryke, S.D. (2016b) Relationship marketing in guanxi networks: a social network analysis study of Chinese construction small and medium-sized enterprises. Industrial Marketing Management. doi:10.1016/j.indmarman.2016.03.014.

Bakker, A.B. and Leiter, M.P. (eds) (2010) *Work Engagement: A Handbook of Essential Theory and Research*. Psychology Press, Hove, East Sussex.

Banaitiene, N., Banaitis, A., Kaklauskas, A. and Zavadskas, E.K. (2008) Evaluating the life cycle of a building: a multivariant and multiple criteria approach. *Omega* 36 (3), 429–441.

Barabási, A.L. and Albert, R. (1999) Emergence of scaling in random networks. *Science*, 286 (5439), 509–512.

Baron-Cohen, S. and Wheelwright, S. (2004) The empathy quotient: an investigation of adults with Asperger syndrome or high functioning autism, and normal sex differences. *Journal of Autism and Development Disorders*, 34 (2), 163–175.

Barnes, J.A. (1974) *Social Networks, Module in Anthropology, No. 26*, Addison-Wesley, Reading, MA.

Barnes, J.A. and Harary, F. (1983) Graph theory in network analysis. *Social Networks* 5 (2), 235–244.

Barnes, M. (1988) Construction project management. *International Journal of Project Management* 6 (2), 69–79.

Barough, A.S., Shoubi, M.V. and Skardi, M.J.E. (2012) Application of game theory approach in solving the construction project conflicts. *Procedia – Social and Behavioral Sciences*, 58, 1586–1593.

Basar, T. and Olsder, G.J. (1999) *Dynamic Noncooperative Game Theory. SIAM Series in Classics in Applied Mathematics*. SIAM, Philadelphia, PA.

Bavelas, A. (1948) A mathematical model for group structures. *Human Organisation*, 7 (3), 16–30.

Bavelas, A. (1950) Communication patterns in task-orientated groups. *Journal of the Acoustical Society of America*, 22, 271–282.

Bechky, B.A. (2006) Gaffers, gofers, and grips: role-based coordination in temporary organizations. *Organization Science*, 17 (1), 3–21.

Becker, M.C. (2004) Organizational routines: a review of the literature. *Industrial and Corporate Change*, 13 (4), 643–678.

Bennigson, L.A. and Balthasas, H.V. (1974) Forecasting co-ordination problems in pharmaceutical research and development. *Proceedings of the Project Management Institute*, Paris.

Bertelsen, S. (2003) Complexity – construction in a new perspective. *IGLC-11*, Blacksburg, VA.

Biely, C., Dragosits, K. and Thurner, S. (2005) *Prisoner's dilemma on dynamic networks under perfect rationality*. 2005 e-print arXiv:physics/0504190.

Billinger, S. and Becker, M. (2014) Stability of organizational routines and the role of authority. *DRUID Society Conference*.

Bing, M.N. (1999) Hypercompetitiveness in academia: achieving criterion-related validity from item context specificity. *Journal of Personality Assessment*, 73 (1), 80–99.

Blair, H. (2001) You're only as good as your last job: the labour process and labour market in the British film industry. *Work, Employment and Society*, 15 (1), 149–169.

Blau, P.M. and Duncan, O.D. (1967) *The American Occupational Structure*. Free Press.

Blomquist, T. and Lundin, R.A. (2010) Projects – real, virtual or what? *International Journal of Managing Projects in Business*, 3 (1), 10–21.

Bonacich, P. (1972) Technique for analyzing overlapping memberships. In H. Costner (ed) *Sociological Methodology*. Jossey-Bass, San Francisco, pp. 176–185.

Bonacich, P. (1987) Power and centrality: a family of measures. *American Journal of Sociology*, 92, 1170–1182.

Bonacich, P. and McConaghy, M.J. (1980) The algebra of blockmodeling. *Sociological Methodology*, 11, 489–532.

Borel, E. (1921) *Applications aux Jeux de Hazard, Traite du Calcul des Probabilities et des ses Applications*. Gauthier-Villars, Paris.

Borg, E. and Söderlund, J. (2014) Liminality competence: an interpretative study of mobile project workers' conception of liminality at work. *Management Learning*, 1350507613516247.

Borgatti, S.P. (2005) Centrality and network flow. *Social Networks*, 27 (1), 55–71.

Borgatti, S.P. and Everett, M.G. (1989) The class of all regular equivalences: algebraic structure and computation. *Social Networks*, 11 (1), 65–88.

Borgatti, S.P. and Foster, P.C. (2003) The network paradigm in organizational research: a review and typology. *Journal of Management*, 29 (6), 991–1013.

Borgatti, S.P., Boyd, J. and Everett, M.G. (1989) Iterated roles: mathematics and applications. *Social Networks*, 11 (2), 159–172.

Bosch-Rekveldt, M., Jongkind, Y., Mooi, H., Bakker, H. and Verbraeck, A. (2011) Grasping project complexity in large engineering projects: the TOE (Technical, Organisational and Environmental) framework. *International Journal of Project Management*, 29 (6), 728–739.

Boulding, K.E. (1956) General systems theory—the skeleton of science. *Management Science*, 2 (3) 197–208.

Brady, T. and Davies, A. (2014) Managing structural and dynamic complexity: a tale of two projects. *Project Management Journal*, 45 (4), 21–38, Wiley Online Library (wileyonlinelibrary.com). doi:10.1002/pmj.21434.

Brandes, U. (2008) On variants of shortest-path betweenness centrality and their generic computation. *Social Networks*, 30 (2), 136–145.

Brandes, U., Gaertler, M. and Wagner, D. (2003) Experiments on graph clustering algorithms. *European Symposium on Algorithms*, 568–579, Springer, Berlin Heidelberg.

Brass, D.J. and Burkhardt, M.E. (1992) Centrality and power in organizations. In N. Nohria and R.G. Eccles (eds) *Networks and Organizations: Structure, Form, and Action*. Harvard Business School Press, Boston, pp. 191–215.

Brauers, W.K.M., Zavadskas, E.K., Turskis, Z. and Vilutienė, T. (2008) Multi-objective contractor's ranking by applying the MOORA method. *Journal of Business Economics and Management*, 9 (4), 245–255.

Bresnen, M., Goussevskaia, A. and Swan, J. (2005) Implementing change in construction project organisations: exploring the interplay between structure and agency. *Building Research and Information*, 33 (6), 547–560.

Brown, A.D. (1997) Narcissism, identity and legitimacy. *Academy of Management Review*, 22 (3), 643–686.

Brown, R.B. and Keegan, D. (1999) Humor in the hotel kitchen. *International Journal of Humor Research*, 12 (1), 47–70.

Buckley, W.F. (1967) *Sociology and Modern Systems Theory*. Prentice Hall, Englewood Cliffs, New Jersey.

Burger, M. and Sydow, J. (2014) How inter-organizational networks can become path-dependent: bargaining in the photonics industry. *Schmalenbach Business Review*, 66.

Burns, T. and Stalker, G.M. (2006) Mechanistic and organic systems. *Organizational Behavior 2: Essential theories of process and structure*, 2, 214.

Burt, R.S. (1976) Positions in social networks. *Social Forces*, 55 (1), 93–122.

Burt, R.S. (1977a) Positions in multiple network systems, part one: a general conception of stratification and prestige in a system of actors cast as a social topology. *Social Forces*, 56 (1), 106–131.

Burt, R.S. (1977b) Positions in multiple network systems, part two. *Social Forces*, 56 (2), 551–575.

Burt, R.S. (1979) A structural theory of interlocking corporate directorates. *Social Networks*, 1 (4), 415–435.

Burt, R.S. (1980) Models of network structure. *Annual Review of Sociology*, 6 (1), 79–141.

Burt, R.S. (1982) *Towards a Structural Theory of Action: Network Models of Social Structure, Perception and Action*. Academic Press, New York.

Burt, R.S. (1983) Studying status/role-sets using mass surveys. In R.S. Burt and M.J. Minor (eds) *Applied Network Analysis*. Sage Publications, Beverly Hills, CA.

Burt, R.S. (1987) Social contagion and innovation: cohesion versus structural equivalence. *American Journal of Sociology*, 92 (6), 1287–1335.

Burt, R.S. (1988) The stability of American markets. *American Journal of Sociology*, 94 (2), 356–395.

Burt, R.S. (2004) Structural holes and good ideas 1. *American Journal of Sociology*, 110 (2), 349–399.

Button, E.J., Loan, P., Davies, J. and Sonuga-Barke, E.J. (1997) Self-esteem, eating problems and psychological wellbeing in a cohort of schoolgirls aged 15–16: a questionnaire and interview study. *International Journal of Eating Disorders*, 21 (1), 39–47.

Camerer, C.F. (2003) *Behavioural Game Theory: Experiments in Strategic Interaction*. Princeton University Press, Princeton, NJ.

Capra, F. (1996) *The Web of Life: A New Scientific Understanding of Living Systems*. Anchor Books, New York.

Cherns, A.B. and Bryant, D.T. (1984) Studying the client's role in construction management. *Construction Management and Economics*, 2 (2), 177–184.

Chowdhury, S. (2005) The role of affect and cognition-based trust in complex knowledge sharing. *Journal of Managerial Issues*, 17 (3), 310–326.

Christin, N., Grossklags, J. and Chuang, J. (2004) Near rationality and competitive equilibria in networked systems. *Proceedings of the ACM SIGCOMM Workshop on Practice and Theory of Incentives in Networked Systems*. ACM, September, pp. 213–219.

Cicmil, S., Williams, T., Thomas, J. and Hodgson, D. (2006) Rethinking project management: researching the actuality of projects. *International Journal of Project Management*, 24 (8), 675–686.

CIOB (2014) *Code of Practice for Project Management of Construction and Development.* 4th edition. Wiley-Blackwell, Oxford.

Clarke, L. (1999) *Mission Improbable: Using Fantasy Documents to Tame Disaster.* University of Chicago Press, Chicago.

Cleland, D.I. and King, W.R. (1975) *Systems Analysis and Project Management.* 2nd edition. McGraw-Hill, New York.

Coase, R.H. (1993) The nature of the firm: influence. In O.E. Williamson and S.G. Winter (eds) *The Nature of the Firm: Origins, Evolution and Development.* Oxford University Press, Oxford.

Collet, P., Rousseau, R., Coupaye, T. and Rivierre, N. (2005) A contracting system for hierarchical components. In *International Symposium on Component-Based Software Engineering.* Springer, Berlin, Heidelberg, pp. 187–202.

Collinson, D.L. (1988) Engineering humour: masculinity, joking and conflict in shop-floor relations. *Organization Studies*, 9 (2), 181–199.

Consalvo, C.M. (1989) Humor in management: no laughing matter. *Humor*, 2 (3), 285–297.

Conway, N. and Briner, R.B. (2005) *Understanding Psychological Contracts at Work: A Critical Evaluation of Theory and Research.* Oxford University Press, Oxford.

Conway, S. (1994) *Informal Boundary-Spanning Links and Networks in Successful Technological Innovation.* PhD thesis, Aston University, Birmingham.

Conway, S. (1997) Strategic personal links in successful innovation: link-pins, bridges and liaisons. *Creativity and Innovation Management*, 6 (4), 226–233.

Cooke-Davies, T., Cicmil, S., Crawford, L. and Richardson, K. (2008) We're not in Kansas anymore, Toto: mapping the strange landscape of complexity theory, and its relationship to project management. *IEEE Engineering Management Review*, 36 (2), 5–21.

Coser, R.L. (1960) Laughter among colleagues: a study of the social functions of humor among the staff of a mental hospital. *Psychiatry*, 23 (1), 81–95.

Crawford, L.H. and Helm, J. (2009) Government and governance: the value of project management in the public sector. *Project Management Journal*, 40 (1), 73–87.

Crotty, R. (2013) *The Impact of Building Information Modelling: Transforming Construction.* Routledge, London.

Curtis, B., Ward, S. and Chapman, C. (1991) *Roles, responsibilities and risks in management contracting.* Construction Industry Research and Information Association, London.

Davies, A. and Brady, T. (2000) Organisational capabilities and learning in complex product systems: towards repeatable solutions. *Research Policy*, 29 (7), 931–953.

Davis, M.H. (1994) *Empathy: A Social Psychological Approach.* Westview Press, Boulder, CO.

DeFillippi, R.J. and Arthur, M.B. (1998) Paradox in project-based enterprise: the case of film making, *California Management Review*, 40 (2), 125–139.

Denis, J.L., Langley, A. and Sergi, V. (2012) Leadership in the plural. *The Academy of Management Annals*, 6 (1), 211–283.

Deutsch, M. and Gerard, H.B. (1955) A study of normative and informational social influences upon individual judgment. *Journal of Abnormal and Social Psychology*, 51 (3), 629.

d'Exelle, B. and Riedl, A. (2010*) Directed generosity and network formation: network dimension matters.* CESifo Working Papers. www.cesifo.org/wp.

DeYoung, C.G., Peterson, J.B. and Higgins, D.M. (2005) Sources of openness/intellect: cognitive and neuropsychological correlates of the fifth factor of personality. *Journal of Personality*, 73 (4), 825–858.

Diallo, A. and Thuillier, D. (2005) The success of international development projects, trust and communication: an African perspective. *International Journal of Project Management*, 23 (3), 237–252.

Dittrich, K., Duysters, G. and de Man, A.P. (2007) Strategic repositioning by means of alliance networks: the case of IBM. *Research Policy*, 36 (10), 1496–1511.

Doloi, H., Pryke, S. and Badi, S. (2016), *The practice of stakeholders' engagement in infrastructure projects: a comparative study of two major projects in Australia and the UK*. The Royal Institute of Chartered Surveyors (RICS), London.

Dvir, D. and Lechler, T. (2004) Plans are nothing, changing plans is everything: the impact of changes on project success. *Research Policy*, 33 (1), 1–15.

Dwyer, T. (1991) Humor, power, and change in organizations. *Human Relations*, 44 (1), 1–19.

Easley, D. and Kleinberg, J. (2010) *Networks, Crowds and Markets: Reasoning about a Highly Connected World*. Cambridge University Press, Cambridge.

Eccles, R.G. (1981) The quasifirm in the construction industry. *Journal of Economic Behaviour and Organization*, 2 (4), 337–357.

Egan Report (1998) *Rethinking Construction: The Report of the Construction Task Force to the Deputy Prime Minister, John Prescott, on the scope for improving the quality and efficiencies of UK construction*. DETR. http://www.constructingexcellence.org.uk/wp-content/uploads/2014/10/rethinking_construction_report.pdf.

Eisenberg, N. and Miller, P.A. (1987) The relation of empathy to prosocial and related behaviors. *Psychological Bulletin*, 101 (1), 91.

Elliot, A.J. and McGregor, H.A. (2001) A 2x2 achievement goal framework. *Journal of Personality and Social Psychology*, 80 (3), 501–519.

El-Sheikh, A. and Pryke, S.D. (2010) Network gaps and project success. *Construction Management and Economics*, 28 (12), 1205–1217.

Emmitt, S. and Gorse, C.A. (2003) *Construction Communication*. Blackwell Publishing, Oxford.

Engwall, M. (2003) No project is an island: linking projects to history and context. *Research Policy*, 32 (5), 789–808.

Erdös, P. and Rényi, A. (1960) On the evolution of random graphs. *Publication of the Mathematical Institute of the Hungarian Academy of Science*, 5, 17–61.

Erickson, B.H. (1978) Some problems of inference from chain data. In K.F. Schuessler (ed) *Sociological Methodology*, Jossey-Bass, San Francisco.

Erickson, B.H. and Nosanchuk, T.A. (1983) *Understanding Data*. Open University Press, Milton Keynes.

Erickson, B.H., Nosanchuk, T.A. and Lee, E. (1981) Network sampling in practice: some second steps. *Social Networks*, 3 (2), 127–136.

Everett, M.G. (1982) A graph theoretic blocking procedure for social networks. *Social Networks*, 4 (2), 147–167.

Everett, M.G. (1983a) EBLOC: a graph theoretic blocking algorithm for social networks. *Social Networks*, 5 (4), 323–346.

Everett, M.G. (1983b) An extension of EBLOC to valued graphs. *Social Networks*, 5 (4), 395–402.

Everett, M.G. (1984) An analysis of cyclically dense data using EBLOC. *Social Networks*, 6 (1), 97–102.

Eysenck, H.J. and Eysenck, S.B.G. (1977a) *Psychoticism as a Dimension of Personality*. Taylor & Francis Group, London.

Eysenck, S.B. and Eysenck, H.J. (1977b) The place of impulsiveness in a dimensional system of personality description. *British Journal of Social and Clinical Psychology*, 16 (1), 57–68.

Fayol, H. (1919) *L'Industrialisation de l'Etat*. Thomas.

Flyvberg, B., Bruzelius, N. and Rothengatter, W. (2003) *Megaprojects and risk: an anatomy of ambition*. Cambridge University Press, Cambridge.

Frank, O. (1978) Estimation of the number of connected components in a graph by using sampled subgraph. *Scandinavian Journal of Statistics*, 5, 177–188.

Frank, O. (1979a) Estimation of population totals by use of snowball samples. In P. Holland and S. Leinhardt (eds) *Perspectives on Social Networks*. Academic Press, New York.

Frank, O. (1979b) Sampling and estimation in large networks. *Social Networks*, 1 (1), 91–101.

Frank, O. (1988) Random sampling and social networks: a survey of various approaches. *Mathématiques et Sciences Humaines*, 104, 19–33.

Franken, R.E. and Brown, D.J. (1996) The need to win is not adaptive: the need to win, coping strategies, hope and self-esteem. *Personality and Individual Differences*, 20 (6), 805–808.

Franks, J. (1998*) Building Procurement Systems: A Client's Guide*. Addison Wesley Longman Ltd, Harlow, Essex and the Chartered Institute of Builders, Ascot, Berkshire.

Frederickson, B.L and Branigan, C. (2005) Positive emotions broaden the scope of attention and thought-action repertoires. *Cognition and Emotion*, 19 (3), 313–332.

Frederickson, B.L., Mancuso, R.A., Branigan, C. and Tugade, M.M. (2000) The undoing effect of positive emotions. *Motivation and Emotion*, 24 (4), 237–258.

Freeman, L.C. (1978) Centrality in social concepts conceptual clarification. *Social Networks*, 1 (3), 215–239.

Freeman, L.C. (1980) The gatekeeper, pair-dependency and structural centrality. *Quality and Quantity*, 14 (4), 585–592.

Freeman, L.C. (1983) Spheres, cubes and boxes: graph dimensionality and network structure. *Social Networks*, 5 (2), 139–156.

Freeman, L.C. (1996) Cliques, Galois lattices, and the structure of human social groups. *Social Networks*, 18 (3), 173–187.

Frewen, P.A., Pain, C., Dozois, D.J. and Lanius, R.A. (2006) Alexithymia in PTSD: psychometric and FMRI studies. *Annals of the New York Academy of Science*, 1071, 397–400.

Gajzler, M. (2008) Hybrid advisory systems and the possibilities of IT usage in the process of industrial flooring repairs. In *Proceedings of the 25th International Symposium on Automation and Robotics in Construction ISARC*, Vilnius 26–29.06.2008, 459–464.

Galbraith, J.R. (1974) Organization design: an information processing view. *Interfaces*, 4 (3), 28–36.

Gardini, S., Cloninger, C.R. and Venneri, A. (2009) Individual differences in personality traits reflect structural variance in specific brain regions. *Brain Research Bulletin*, 79 (5), 265–270.

Geertz, C. (1973) *The Interpretation of Cultures: Selected Essays*. Basic Books, New York.

Geraldi, J., Maylor, H. and Williams, T. (2011) Now, let's make it really complex (complicated). A systematic review of the complexities of projects. *International Journal of Operations and Production Management*, 31 (9), 966–990.

Giddens, A. (1984) *The Constitution of Society: Outline of the Theory of Structuration*. University of California Press, Berkley and Los Angeles.

Ginevičius, R., Podvezko, V. and Raslanas, S. (2008) Evaluating the alternative solutions of wall insulation by multicriteria methods. *Journal of Civil Engineering and Management*, 14 (4), 217–226.

Glaman, J.M., Jones, A.P. and Rozelle, R.M. (2002) Competitiveness and the similarity of preferred coworkers. *Journal of Applied Social Psychology*, 32 (1), 142–158.

Granovetter, M.S. (1973) The strength of weak ties. *American Journal of Sociology*, 78 (6), 1360–1380.

Granovetter, M. (1976) Network sampling: some first steps. *American Journal of Sociology*, 81 (6), 1287–1303.

Granovetter, M. (1977) Reply to Morgan and Rytina. *American Journal of Sociology*, 83 (3), 727–729.

Granovetter, M. (1979) The theory-gap in social network analysis. In P. Holland and S. Leinhard (eds) *Perspectives on Social Networks*. Academic Press, New York.

Granovetter, M. (1982) The strength of weak ties: a network theory revisited. In P.V. Marsden and N. Lin (eds) *Social Structure and Network Analysis*. Sage Publications, Beverly Hills, CA.

Granovetter, M. (1983) The strength of weak ties: a network theory revisited. *Sociological Theory*, 1 (1), 201–233.

Gray, C. (1996) *Value for Money*. Reading Construction Forum and the Reading Production Engineering Group, Berkshire.

Graziano, W.G., Jensen-Campbell, L.A., Shebilske, L.J. and Lundgren, S.R. (1993) Social influence, sex differences, and judgments of beauty: putting the interpersonal back in interpersonal attraction. *Journal of Personality and Social Psychology*, 65 (3), 522–531.

Green, S.D., Fernie, S. and Weller, S. (2005) Making sense of supply chain management: a comparative study of aerospace and construction. *Construction Management and Economics*, 23 (6), 579–593.

Green, S.J. (2006) The management of projects in the construction industry: context, discourse and self-identity. In D. Hodgson and S. Cicmil (eds) *Making Projects Critical*. Palgrave Macmillan, Basingstoke.

Grugulis, I. (2002) Nothing serious? Candidates' use of humour in management training. *Human Relations*, 55 (4), 387–406.

Hajdasz, M. (2008) Modelling and simulation of monolithic construction processes. *Technological and Economic Development of Economy*, 14 (4), 478–491.

Haley, K.J. and Fessler, D.M. (2005) Nobody's watching? Subtle cues affect generosity in an anonymous economic game. *Evolution and Human Behaviour*, 26 (3), 245–256.

Halmi, K.A., Tozzi, F., Thornton, L.M. and Crow, S. (2005) The relation among perfectionism, obsessive-compulsive personality disorder and obsessive-compulsive disorder in individuals with eating disorders. *International Journal of Eating Disorders*, 38 (4), 371–374.

Han, Z. and Liu, K.J. (2008) *Resource Allocation for Wireless Networks: Basics, Techniques and Applications*. Cambridge University Press, New York.

Hanisch, B. and Wald, A. (2011) A project management research framework integrating multiple theoretical perspectives and influencing factors. *Project Management Journal*, 42 (3), 4–22.

Harsanyi, J.C. (2004) Games with incomplete information played by 'Bayesian' players, I-III. part 1: the basic model. *Management Science*, 14 (3), 159–182.

Hartman, F.T. (1999) The role of trust in project management. In *Proceedings of Nordnet Conference*, Helsinki.

Hartman, F.T. (2002) The role of trust in project management. In D.P Slevin, D.I. Cleland and J.K. Pinto (eds) *The Frontiers of Project Management Research*. Project Management Institute, Newtown Square, PA, pp. 225–235.

Hatch, M.J. and Ehrlich, S.B. (1993) Spontaneous humour as an indicator of paradox and ambiguity in organizations. *Organization Studies*, 14 (4), 505–526.

Haythornthwaite, C. (2005) Social networks and internet connectivity effects. *Information, Community & Society*, 8 (2), 125–147.

Heaven, P.C., Mulligan, K., Merrilees, R., Woods, T. and Fairooz, Y. (2001) Neuroticism and conscientiousness as predictors of emotional, external, and restrained eating behaviors. *International Journal of Eating Disorders*, 30 (2), 161–166.

Heylighen, F. (2013) Self-organization in communicating groups: the emergence of coordination, shared references and collective intelligence. In A. Massip-Bonet and A. Bastardas-Boada (eds) *Complexity Perspectives on Language, Communication and Society*. Springer, Berlin, Heidelberg.

Higgin, G. and Jessop, N. (1965) *Communications in the Building Industry: The Report of a Pilot Study*. Tavistock Publications, London.

Hill, J.A., Eckerd, S., Wilson, D. and Greer, B. (2009) The effect of unethical behavior on trust in a buyer-supplier relationship: the mediating role of psychological contract violation. *Journal of Operations Management*, 27 (4), 281–293.

Hines, P., Holney, M. and Rich, N. (2004) Learning to evolve: a review of contemporary lean thinking. *International Journal of Operations and Production Management*, 24 (10), 994–1011.

HM Government (2013) *Industrial strategy: government and industry in partnership*. UK Crown.

Hobday, M. (2000) The project-based organisation: an ideal form for managing complex products and systems. *Research Policy*, 29 (7), 871–893.

Hodgson, D. (2004) Project work: the legacy of bureaucratic control in the post-bureaucratic organization. *Organization*, 11 (1), 81–100.

Hodgson, D. and Cicmil, S. (eds) (2006) *Making projects critical*. Palgrave Macmillan.

Holmes, J. and Marra, M. (2002) Over the edge? Subversive humor between colleagues and friends. *Humor: International Journal of Humor Research*, 15 (1), 65–87.

Holti, R., Nicolini, D. and Smalley, M. (2000) *Building Down Barriers: The Handbook of Supply Chain Management*. CIRIA, London.

Homans, G.C. (1961) *Social Behaviour: Its Elementary Forms*. Routledge and Kegan Paul, London.

House, R., Rousseau, D.M. and Thomas-Hunt, M. (1995) The meso paradigm: a framework for the integration of micro and macro organizational behaviour. In L.L. Cunningham and B.M. Staw (eds) *Research in Organisational Behaviour*, 17, 71–114, JAI Press, Greenwich, C.T.

Huber, G.P. (1990) A theory of the effects of advanced information technologies on organizational design, intelligence, and decision making. *Academy of Management Review*, 15 (1), 47–71.

Ika, L.A. and Hodgson, D. (2010) Towards a critical perspective in international development project management. *Proceedings of the 5th Making Projects Critical, Bristol Business School*, Bristol.

Isen, A.M. (1993) Positive affect and decision making. In M. Lewis, J.M. Haviland-Jones and L. Feldman Barrett (eds) *Handbook of Emotions*. Guilford, New York.

Isen, A.M. (2003) Positive affect as a source of human strength. In L.G. Aspinwall and U.M. Staudinger (eds) *A Psychology of Human Strengths: Fundamental Questions and Future Directions for a Positive Psychology*. American Psychological Association (APA).

Jackson, M.O. (2008) *Social and Economic Networks*, Vol. 3. Princeton University Press, Princeton.

Jacobides, M.G. and Winter, S.G. (2012) Capabilities: structure, agency and evolution. *Organizational Science*, 23 (5), 1365–1381.

Jacobsson, M., Burström, T. and Wilson, T.L. (2013) The role of transition in temporary organisations: linking the temporary to the permanent. *International Journal of Managing Projects in Business*, 6 (3), 576–586.

Janus, S.S. (1975) The great comedians: personality and other factors. *The American Journal of Psychoanalysis*, 35 (2), 169–174.

Janus, S.S., Bess, B.E. and Janus, B.R. (1978) The great comediennes: personality and other factors. *American Journal of Psychoanalysis*, 38 (4), 367.

Janusz, L. and Kapliński, O. (2006) The application of multifactor modelling LITCAC in the organization of assembly work of flexible corrugated steel structures. *Technological and Economic Development of Economy*, 12 (3), 195–199.

Jeffries, F.L. and Reed, R. (2000) Trust and adaptation in relational contracting. *Academy of Management Review*, 25 (4), 873–882.

Jensen, C., Johansson, S. and Löftström, M. (2006) Project relationships – a model for analyzing interactional uncertainty. *International Journal of Project Management*, 24 (1), 4–12.

Jeronimus, B.F., Riese, H., Sanderman, R. and Ormel, J. (2014) Mutual reinforcement between neuroticism and life experiences: a five-wave, 16-year study to test reciprocal causation. *Journal of Personality and Social Psychology*, 107 (4), 751–764.

Jones, C. and Lichtenstein, B.B. (2008) Temporary inter-organizational projects: how temporal and social embeddedness enhance coordination and manage uncertainty. In S. Cropper, C. Huxham, M. Ebers and P. Smith Ring (eds) *The Oxford Handbook of Inter-Organizational Relations*. Oxford University Press, Oxford.

Jørgensen, M. and Moløkken-Østvold, K. (2006) How large are software cost overruns? A review of the 1994 CHAOS report. *Information and Software Technology*, 48 (4), 297–301.

Kadefors, A. (2004) Trust in project relationships – inside the black box. *International Journal of Project Management*, 22 (3), 175–182.

Kaner, I., Sacks, R., Kassian, W. and Quitt, T. (2008) Case studies of BIM adoption for precast concrete design by mid-sized structural engineering firms. *Journal of Information Technology in Construction (ITcon)*, 13 (Special Issue), 303–323.

Kapliński, O. (2008) Usefulness and credibility of scoring methods in construction industry. *Journal of Civil Engineering and Management*, 14 (1), 21–28.

Karłowski, A. and Pasławski, J. (2008) Monitoring of construction processes in the variable environment. *Technological and Economic Development of Economy*, 14 (4), 503–517.

Kassin, S. (2003) *Psychology*. Prentice Hall, NJ.

Keim, S., Klärner, A. and Bernardi, L. (2013) Tie strength and family formation: which personal relationships are influential? *Personal Relationships*, 20 (3), 462–478.

Kelly, J., Male, S. and Drummond, G. (2014) *Value Management of Construction Projects*. Wiley-Blackwell, Oxford.

Kingshott, R.P.J. and Pecotich, A. (2007) The impact of psychological contracts on trust and commitment in supplier-distributor relationships. *European Journal of Marketing*, 41 (9/10), 1053–1072.

Knight, A. and Ruddock, L. (2009) *Advanced Research Methods in the Built Environment*. Wiley-Blackwell, Oxford.

Kohler, W. (1929) *Gestalt Psychology*. Liveright, New York.

Koskela, L. (1992) *Application of the new production philosophy to construction*. Technical Report 72, Center for Integrated Facility Engineering, Stanford University.

Koskela, L. (2000) *An Exploration towards a Production Theory and its Application to Construction*. Report 408. VTT Technical Research Centre of Finland, Espoo.

Krackhardt, D. (1992) The strength of strong ties: the importance of philos in organizations. In N. Nohria and R.G. Eccles (eds) *Networks and Organizations: Structure, Form, and Action*. Harvard Business School Press, Boston, MA.

Kreps, D.M., Milgrom, P., Roberts, J. and Wilson, R. (1982) *Rational Cooperation in the Finitely-Repeated Prisoners' Dilemma (No. TR-375)*. CA Institute for Mathematical Studies in the Social Sciences, Stanford University.

Kruskal, J.B. (1964a) Multidimensional scaling by optimizing goodness of fit to a nonmetric hypothesis. *Psychometrika*, 29 (1), 1–27.

Kruskal, J.B. (1964b) Nonmetric multidimensional scaling: a numerical method. *Psychometrika*, 29 (2), 115–129.

La, R. and Anantharam, V. (2003) A game theoretic look at the Gaussian multiaccess channel. *Proceedings of the DIMACS Workshop on Network Information Theory*, NJ.

Laiserin, J. (2003) Foreword to Eastman, C., Tiecholz, P., Sacks, R. and Liston, K. *BIM Handbook: A Guide to Building Information Modelling for Owners, Managers, Designers, Engineers and Contractors*. 1st edition. John Wiley & Sons, Inc., Hoboken.

Lalonde, P.L., Bourgault, M. and Findeli, A. (2012) An empirical investigation of the project situation: PM practice as an inquiry process. *International Journal of Project Management*, 30 (4), 418–431.

Larson, A. (1992) Network dyads in entrepreneurial settings: a study of the governance of exchange relationships. *Administrative Science Quarterly*, 37 (1), 76–104.

Latham Report (1994) *Constructing the Team: Joint Review of Procurement and Contractual Arrangements in the United Kingdom Construction Industry*. Chair Sir M. Latham. HMSO, London.

Laumann, E.O. (1966) *Prestige and Association in an Urban Community: An Analysis of an Urban Stratification System*. Bobbs-Merrill, Indianapolis.

Laumann, E.O. and Pappi, F.U. (1973) New directions in the study of community elites. *American Sociological Review*, 38, 212–230.

Laumann, E.O. and Pappi, U. (1976) *Networks of Collective Actions*. Academic Press, New York.

Laumann, E.O., Marsden, P.V. and Prensky, D. (1983) The boundary specification problem in network analysis. In R.S Burt and M.J. Minor (eds) *Applied Network Analysis: A Methodological Introduction*. Sage Publications, Beverly Hills.

Laumann, E.O., Marsden, P.V. and Prensky, D. (1989) The boundary specification problem in network analysis. *Research Methods in Social Network Analysis*, 61.

Leavitt, H.J (1951) Some effects of certain communication patterns on group performance. *The Journal of Abnormal and Social Psychology*, 46 (1), 38–50.

Lefcourt, H.M. (2001) *Humour: The Psychology of Living Buoyantly*. Kluwer Academic, New York.

Lefcourt, H.M. and Martin, R.A. (2012) *Humor and Life Stress: Antidote to Adversity*. Springer Science & Business Media.

Leibbrandt, A., Gneezy, U. and List, J.A. (2013) Rise and fall of competitiveness in individualistic and collectivistic societies. *Proceedings of the National Academy of Sciences*, 110 (23), 9305–9308.

Leonard, R.J. (1995) From parlor games to social science: von Neumann, Morgenstern, and the creation of game theory 1928–1944. *Journal of Economic Literature*, 33 (2), 730–761.

Levitt, R.E. (2011) Towards project management 2.0. *Engineering Project Organization Journal*, 1 (3), 197–210.

Levitt, R.E., Thomsen, J., Christiansen, T.R., Kunz, J.C., Jin, Y. and Nass, C. (1999) Simulating project work processes and organizations: toward a micro-contingency theory of organizational design. *Management Science*, 45 (11), 1479–1495.

Lewis, M. And Roehrich, J. (2010) Contacts, relationships and integration: towards a model of the procurement of complex performance. In N. Caldwell and M. Howard (eds) *Procuring Complex Performance: Studies of Innovation in Product-Service Management.* Routledge, Abingdon, Oxon.

Lin, A.C. (1998) Bridging positivist and interpretivist approaches to qualitative methods. *Policy Studies Journal*, 26 (1), 162–180.

Lin, N. (1999) Building a network theory of social capital. *Connections*, 22 (1), 28–51.

Lingard, H., Pirzadeh, P., Blismas, N., Wakefield, R. and Kleiner, B. (2014) Exploring the link between early constructor involvement in project decision-making and the efficacy of health and safety risk control. *Construction Management and Economics*, 32 (9), 918–931.

Littau, P., Jujagiri, N.J. and Adlbrecht, G. (2010) 25 years of stakeholder theory in project management literature (1984–2009). *Project Management Journal*, 41 (4), 17–29.

Long, D.L. and Graesser, A.C. (1988) Wit and humor in discourse processing. *Discourse Processes*, 11 (1), 35–60.

Loosemore, M. (1998) Social network analysis using a quantitative tool within an interpretative context to explore the management of construction crises. *Engineering, Construction and Architectural Management*, 5 (4), 315–326.

Lou, J.H., Chen, S.H., Yu, H.Y., Li, R.H., Yang, C.I. and Eng, C.J. (2010) The influence of personality traits and social support on male nursing student life stress: a cross-sectional research design. *Journal of Nursing Research*, 18 (2), 108–116.

Luce, R.D. and Raiffa, H. (1957) *Games and Decisions: Introduction and Critical Survey.* John Wiley & Sons, Inc., New York.

Lundin, R.A. and Söderholm, A. (1995) A theory of the temporary organisation. *Scandinavian Journal of Management*, 11 (4), 437–455.

Luo, X., Kranzler, H.R., Zuo, L., Zhang, H., Wang, S. and Gelernter, J. (2007) CHRM2 variation predisposes to personality traits of agreeableness and conscientiousness. *Human Molecular Genetics*, 16 (13), 1557–1568.

Mahmud, S. (2009) Framework for the role of self-organization in the handling of adaptive challenges. *E:Co*, 11(2), 1–14.

Manning, S. (2005) Managing project networks as dynamic organisational forms: learning from the TV movie industry. *International Journal of Project Management*, 23 (5), 410–414.

Manning, S. and Sydow, J. (2007) Transforming creative potential in project networks: how TV movies are produced under network-based control. *Critical Sociology*, 33 (1–2), 19–42.

Manning, S. and Sydow, J. (2011) Projects, paths, and practices: sustaining and leveraging project-based relationships. *Industrial and Corporate Change*, 20 (5), 1369–1402.

Martin, R.A. (2007) *The Psychology of Humour: An Integrative Approach.* Elsevier, Oxford.

Maslow, A.H. (1943) A theory of human motivation. *Psychological Review*, 50 (4), 370.

Masterman, J.W.E. (2003) *An Introduction to Building Procurement Systems.* E. and F.N. Spon, London.

Mathur, S., Sankar, L. and Mandayam, N.B. (2008) Coalitions in cooperative wireless networks. *IEEE Journal on Selected Areas in Communications*, 26 (7), 1104–1115.

Mayer, R.C., Davis, J.H. and Schoorman, F.D. (1995) An integrative model of organizational trust. *Academy of Management Review*, 20 (3), 709–734.

McAdams, R.H. and Nadler, J. (2005) Testing the focal point theory of legal compliance: the effect of third-party expression in an experimental hawk/dove game. *Journal of Empirical Legal Studies*, 2 (1), 87–123.

McMillan, E. (2006) *Complexity, Organizations and Change: An Essential Introduction.* Routledge, Abingdon, Oxon.

McSmythurs, A. (2011) Managing a project management division. In Hedley Smyth (ed) *Managing the Professional Practice: In the Built Environment.* Wiley Online Library, 233–248.

Mead, G.H. (1934) *Mind, Self and Society.* University of Chicago Press, Chicago.

Mehra, A., Kilduff, M. and Brass, D.J. (2001) The social networks of high and low self-monitors: implications for workplace performance. *Administrative Science Quarterly*, 46 (1), 121–146.

Merrow, E.W. (2011) *Industrial Megaprojects: Concepts, Strategies, and Practices for Success.* John Wiley & Sons, Inc., Hoboken.

Meszek, W. (2007) Uncertainty phenomenon in property valuation. *International Journal of Management and Decision Making*, 8 (5–6), 575–585.

Meyer, J.C. (1997) Humor in member narratives: uniting and dividing at work. *Western Journal of Communication (includes Communication Reports)*, 61 (2), 188–208.

Meyer, M., Zysset, S., von Cramon, D.Y. and Alter, K. (2005) Distinct fMRI responses to laughter, speech, and sounds along the human peri-sylvian cortex. *Cognitive Brain Research*, 24 (2), 291–306.

Mickaityte, A., Zavadskas, E.K., Kaklauskas, A. and Tupenaite, L. (2008) The concept model of sustainable buildings refurbishment. *International Journal of Strategic Property Management*, 12 (1), 53–68.

Milgram, S. (1967) The small world problem. *Psychology Today*, 2 (1), 60–67.

Miller, R.S. (1992) The nature and severity of self-reported embarrassing circumstances. *Personality and Social Psychology Bulletin*, 18 (2), 190–198.

Mitleton-Kelly, E. (2004) An integrated methodology to facilitate the emergence of new ways of organising. *Proceedings of the 3rd European Conference on Research Methodology for Business and Management Studies (ECRM).*

Mizruchi, M.S. (1982) *The American Corporate Network, 1904–1974.* Sage Publications, Beverly Hills, CA.

Mizruchi, M.S. (1992) *The Structure of Corporate Political Action: Interfirm Relationships and their Consequences.* Harvard University Press, Cambridge, MA.

Mizruchi, M.S. (1993) Cohesion, equivalence and similarity of behaviour: a theoretical and empirical assessment. *Social Networks*, 15 (3), 275–307.

Mizruchi, M.S. (1994) Social network analysis: recent achievements and current controversies. *Acta Sociologica*, 37 (4), 329–343.

Mizruchi, M.S. and Bunting, D. (1981) Influence in corporate networks: an examination of four measures. *Administrative Science Quarterly*, 26 (3), 475–489.

Mizruchi, M.S. and Galaskiewicz, J. (1994) Networks of Interorganizational Relations. In S. Wasserman and J. Galaskiewicz (eds) *Advances in Social Network Analysis: Research in the Social and Behavioural Sciences.* Sage Publications, Beverly Hills, CA.

Mizruchi, M.S. and Potts, B.B (1998), Centrality and power revisited: actors' success in group decision making. *Social Networks*, 20 (4), 353–387.

Mizruchi, M.S. and Schwartz, M. (eds) (1987) *Intercorporate Relations: The Structural Analysis of Business.* Cambridge University Press, New York.

Monsanto, C., Reich, J., Foster, N., Rexford, J. and Walker, D. (2013) Composing software defined networks. *Presented as part of the 10th* USENIX *Symposium on Networked Systems Design and Implementation, NSDI 13*, 1–13.

Morrison, E.W. and Robinson, S.L. (1997) When employees feel betrayed: a model of how psychological contract violation develops. *Academy of Management Review*, 22 (1), 226–256.

Morris, P.W.G. (1994) *The Management of Projects.* John Wiley & Sons, Ltd, Chichester.

Morris, P.W.G. (2013) *Reconstructing Project Management*, Wiley-Blackwell, Oxford.

Morris, P.W.G. and Hough, G.H. (1987) *The Anatomy of Major Projects: A Study of the Reality of Project Management.* John Wiley and Sons Ltd, Chichester.

Morris, P.W.G. and Pinto, J.K. (eds) (2004) *The Wiley Guide to Managing Projects.* John Wiley and Sons, Inc., Hoboken.

Mudrack, P.E., Bloodgood, J.M. and Turnley, W.H. (2012) Some ethical implications of individual competitiveness. *Journal of Business Ethics*, 108 (3), 347–359.

Müller, R., Andersen, E.S., Kvalnes, Ø., Shao, J., Sankaran, S., Rodney Turner, J., Biesenthal, C., Walker, D. and Gudergan, S. (2013) The interrelationship of governance, trust, and ethics in temporary organizations. *Project Management Journal*, 44 (4), 26–44.

Myerson, R.B. (1991) *Game Theory: Analysis of Conflict.* Harvard University Press, Cambridge, MA.

Nash, J. (1950) Equilibrium points in n-person games. *Proceedings of the National Academy of Science USA*, 36 (1), 48–49.

Nash, J. (1951) Non-cooperative games. *Annals of Mathematics*, 54 (2), 286–295.

Nohria, N. and Eccles, R.G. (eds) (1992) *Networks and Organizations: Structure Form and Action.* Harvard Business School Press, Boston, MA.

Oliver, A.L. and Liebeskind, J.P. (1998) Three levels of networking for sourcing capital in biotechnology. *International Studies of Management and Organization*, 27 (4), 76–103.

Owen, G. (1995*) Game Theory.* 3rd edition. Academic Press, London.

Pasławski, J. (2008) Flexibility approach in construction process engineering. *Technological and Economic Development of Economy*, 14 (4), 518–530.

Pauget, B. and Wald, A. (2013) Relational competence in complex temporary organizations: the case of a French hospital construction project network. *International Journal of Project Management*, 31 (2), 200–211.

Paulus, M.P., Rogalsky, C., Simmons, A., Feinstein, J.S. and Stein, M.B. (2003) Increased activation in the right insula during risk-taking decision making is related to harm avoidance and neuroticism. *Neuroimage*, 19 (4), 1439–1448.

Peldschus, F. (2008) Experience of game theory application in construction management. *Technological and Economic Development of Economy*, 14 (4), 531–545.

Peldschus, F. and Zavadskas, E.K. (2005) Fuzzy matrix games multi-criteria model for decision-making in engineering. *Informatica*, 16 (1), 107–120.

Peldschus, F., Zavadskas, E.K., Turskis, Z. and Tamosaitiene, J. (2010) Sustainable assessment of construction site by applying game theory. *Inzinerine Ekonomika-Engineering Economics*, 21 (3), 223–237.

Perrow, C. (1967) A framework for the comparative analysis of organizations. *American Sociological Review*, 32 (2), 194–208.

Peskine, A., Picq, C. and Pradat-Diehl P. (2004) Cerebral anoxia and disability. *Brain Injury*, 18 (12), 1243–1254.

Pfeffer, J. and Sutton, R.I. (2006) Evidence-based management. *Harvard Business Review*, 84 (1), 62–74.

Pinheiro, C.A.R. (2011) *Social Network Analysis in Telecommunications*. John Wiley & Sons, Inc., Hoboken.

Pinto, J.K., Slevin, D.P. and English, B. (2009) Trust in projects: an empirical assessment of owner/contractor relationships. *International Journal of Project Management*, 6 (27), 638–648.

Pitsis, T.S. and Gudergan, S. (2010) Know how? Challenges in knowledge and innovation: an introduction. *International Journal of Knowledge Management Studies* 4 (2), 109–113.

Pitsis, T.S., Clegg, S.R., Marosszeky, M. and Rura-Polley, T. (2003) Constructing the Olympic dream: a future perfect strategy of project management. *Organization Science*, 14 (5), 574–590.

Project Management Institute (PMI) (2000). *A Guide to the Project Management Body of Knowledge*. Project Management Institute, North Carolina.

PMI (2008) *A Guide to the Project Management Body of Knowledge (PMBOK guide)*. 4th edition. Project Management Institute, Newtown Square, PA.

Potts, K. and Ankrah, N. (2014) *Construction Cost Management: Learning from Case Studies*. Routledge.

Powell, W.W. (1990) Neither market nor hierarchy: network forms of organization. *Research in Organisational Behaviour*, 12, 295–336.

Powell, W.W. and Giannella, E. (2010) Collective invention and inventor networks. In B.H. Hall and N. Rosenberg (eds) *Handbook of the Economics of Innovation*, Vol. 1. Elsevier.

Prell, C. (2012) *Social Network Analysis: History, Theory and Methodology*. Sage, London.

Pritchard, A.W. (2016) *Reinventing the wheel? How knowledge transfer can benefit the delivery of major infrastructure projects*. MSc thesis submitted under the Construction Engineering Masters' programme in the Laing O'Rourke Centre for Construction Engineering and Technology.

Pryke, S.D. (2001) *UK construction in transition: developing a social network analysis approach to the evaluation of new procurement and management strategies*. PhD thesis, Bartlett School of Graduate Studies, UCL, London.

Pryke, S.D. (2004a) Analysing construction project coalitions: exploring the application of social network analysis. *Construction Management and Economics*, 22 (8), 787–797.

Pryke, S.D. (2004b) Analytical methods in construction procurement and management: a critical review. *Journal of Construction Procurement*, 10 (1), 49–67.

Pryke, S.D. (2005a) Towards a social network theory of project governance. *Construction Management and Economics*, 23 (9), 927–939.

Pryke, S.D. (2005b) *Using Social Network Analysis to Understand Innovation in Construction Procurement*. Research Paper Series, RICS, London.

Pryke, S.D. (2006) Legal issues associated with emergent actor roles in innovative UK procurement: prime contracting case study. *Journal of Professional Issues in Engineering Education and Practice*, 132 (1), 67–76.

Pryke, S.D. (2008) Social network analysis. In A. Knight and L. Ruddock (eds) *Advanced Research Methods in the Built Environment*. John Wiley & Sons, Ltd, Chichester.

Pryke, S.D. (ed) (2009) *Construction Supply Chain Management: Concepts and Case Studies*. Wiley-Blackwell, Oxford.

Pryke, S.D. (2012) *Social Network Analysis in Construction*. Wiley-Blackwell, Oxford.

Pryke, S.D. (2014) *Telling the Westfield Stratford Story*. Bartlett School of Construction and Project Management Research Publication Series, UCL, London.

Pryke, S.D. and Badi, S.M. (2013) Identifying optimal business network configurations in construction project supply chains. *Proceedings of Sunbelt XXXIII. Annual research conference of the International Network of Social Network Analysis (INSNA), Hamburg, 21–26 May 2013*.

Pryke, S.D. and Ouwerkerk, E. (2003) Post completion risk transfer audits: an analytical risk management tool using social network analysis. *Proceedings of 2003 Construction and Building Research Conference of the RICS Research Foundation (COBRA 2003)*.

Pryke, S. and Pearson, S. (2006) Project governance: case studies on financial incentives. *Building Research and Information*, 34 (6), 534–545.

Pryke, S.D. and Smyth, H.J. (2006) Introduction. In S.D. Pryke, and H.J. Smyth (eds) *The Management of Complex Projects: A Relationship Approach*. Wiley-Blackwell, Oxford, pp. 1–20.

Pryke, S.D. and Smyth, H.J. (2006) *The Management of Complex Projects: A Relationship Approach*. Wiley-Blackwell, Oxford.

Pryke, S.D., Almadhoob, H. and Badi, S.M. (2014) The influence of social networks on firm's success, survival and growth: a social network analysis investigation of SMEs in the Bahrain construction industry. *Proceedings of International Network of Social Network Analysis (INSNA) conference, Florida, 18–23 February 2014*.

Pryke, S.D., Watson, E. and Badi, S.M. (2013) Project performance and client centrality. *Proceedings of EURAM 2013. Annual Conference of the European Academy of Management, Istanbul, 26–29 Jun 2013*.

Pryke, S.D., Zagkli, G. and Kougia, I. (2011) Resource provision ego-networks in small Greek construction firms. *Building Research and Information*, 39 (6), 616–636.

Pryke, S., Badi, S.M., Soundararaj, B. and Addyman, S. (2017) Self-organising networks in complex infrastructure projects. *Project Management Journal*.

Pryke, S., Badi, S.M., Soundararaj, B., Watson, E. and Addyman, S. (2015a) Managing complex infrastructure projects: a social network perspective. *Proceedings of IRNOP 2015. Annual conference of the International Research Network on Organising by Projects, University College London, London, 22–24 June 2015*.

Pryke, S., Badi, S.M., Soundararaj, B., Watson, E. and Addyman, S. (2015b) Self-organising networks in complex projects. *Proceedings of COBRA 2015. Annual conference of the Royal Institute of Chartered Surveyors, Sydney, 8–10 July 2015*.

Reichelt, B. and Peldschus, F. (2005) The application of multi-criteria decision analysis (MCDA) in risk management of civil engineering and environmental engineering projects. *Foundations of Civil and Environmental Engineering*, 6, 159–163.

Reiss, M., Rosenfeld, P., Melburg, V. and Tedeschi, J.T. (1981) Self-serving attributions: biased private perceptions and distorted public descriptions. *Journal of Personality and Social Psychology*, 41 (2), 224–231.

RICS (2014) *Your Pathway to Qualifying in Project Management*. http://www.rics.org/uk/apc/pathway-guides/construction-pathway-guides/project-management/.

Rivkin, J.W. and Siggelkow, N. (2006) Organising to strategize in the face of interactions: preventing premature lock-in. *Long Range Planning*, 39 (6), 591–614.

Robinson, S.L. and Morrison, E.W. (2000) The development of psychological contract breach and violation: a longitudinal study. *Journal of Organizational Behaviour*, 21 (5), 525–547.

Romahn, E. and Hartman, F. (1999) Trust: a new tool for project managers. In *Project Management Institute 1999 Annual Symposium and Seminar*, 85, 1–85.

Rousseau, D.M., Sitkin, S.B., Burt, R.S. and Camerer, C. (1998) Not so different after all: a cross-discipline view of trust. *Academy of Management Review*, 23 (3), 393–404.

Ruan, X., Ochieng, D., Price, A. and Egbu, C. (2013) Time for a real shift to relations: appraisal of social network analysis applications in the UK construction industry. *Australasian Journal of Construction Economics and Building*, 13 (1), 92–105.

Ruuska, I., Ahola, T., Artto, K., Locatelli, G. and Mancini, M. (2011) A new governance approach for multi-firm projects: lessons from Olkiluoto 3 and Flamanville 3 nuclear power plant projects. *International Journal of Project Management*, 29 (6), 647–660.

Saad, W., Han, Z., Debbah, M., Hjørungnes, A. and Basar, T. (2009) Coalitional game theory for communication networks: a tutorial. *IEEE Signal Processing Magazine*, 26 (5), 77–97.

Salem, O. and Zimmer, E. (2005) Application of lean management principles to construction. *Lean Construction Journal*. Lean Construction Institute, Arlington, VA. http://www.leanconstruction.org/media/docs/lcj/LCJ_05_011.pdf.

Salkovskis, P.M., Forrester, E. and Richards, C. (1998) Cognitive-behavioural approach to understanding obsessional thinking. *British Journal of Psychiatry. Supplement*, 35, 53–63.

Šarka, V., Zavadskas, E.K., Ustinovičius, L., Šarkienė, E. and Ignatavičius, Č. (2008) System of project multicriteria decision synthesis in construction. *Technological and Economic Development of Economy*, 14 (4), 546–565.

Schlenker, B.R. (1982) Translating actions into attitudes: an identity-analytic approach to the explanation of social conduct. *Advances in Experimental Social Psychology*, 15, 193–247.

Schuessler, K.F. (ed) (1979) *Sociological Methodology*. Jossey-Bass, San Francisco, pp. 489–532.

Schwaber, K. (2004) *Agile Project Management with Scrum*. Microsoft press.

Scott, J. (1986) *Capitalist Property and Financial Power: A Comparative Study of Britain, the United States of America and Japan*. Wheatsheaf, Brighton.

Scott, J. (ed) (1990) *The Sociology of Elites*, Vol. 3. Edward Elgar Publishing, Cheltenham.

Scott, J. (1991) Networks of corporate power: a comparative assessment. *Annual Review of Sociology*, 17 (1), 181–203.

Scott, J. (1996) *Stratification and Power: Structures of Class, Status and Command*. Polity Press, Cambridge.

Scott, J. (1997) *Corporate Business and Capitalist Classes*. Oxford University Press, Oxford.

Scott, J. (2012) *Social Network Analysis: A Handbook*. SAGE Publications, London.

Seidman, H. (1970) *Politics, Position, and Power: The Dynamics of Federal Organization*. Oxford University Press, New York, pp. 110–111.

Senescu, R.R. (2011) *Design process communication methodology*. PhD thesis, Stanford University.

Shenhar, A.J. (2001) *Virtuelle Unternehmen in der IT-Branche*. Haupt, Bern.

Shepherd, R.K. and Pryke, S.D. (2014) Regional rail planning: a study of the importance of 'steering' and 'pragmatism' in stakeholder networks. *European Management Journal*, 32 (4), 616–624.

Sieber, U. (1998) *Legal aspects of computer-related crime in the information society.* University of Würzburg. COMCRIME – Study Prepared for the European Commission [Online]. http://europa.eu.int/ISPO/legal/en/com-crime/sieber.html.

Siebert, H. (1991) Konomische analyse von unternehmungnetzwerken. In W.H. Staehle and J. Sydow (eds) *Managmentforschung,* 1. DeGruyter, Berlin, New York.

Sinha, K.K. and Van de Ven, A.H. (2005) Designing work within and between organizations. *Organization Science,* 16 (4), 389–408.

Smyth, H.J. and Morris, P.W.G. (2007) An epistemological evaluation of research into projects and their management: methodological issues. *International Journal of Project Management,* 25 (4), 423–436.

Smyth, H.J. and Pryke, S.D. (eds) (2008) *Collaborative Relationships in Construction: Developing Frameworks and Networks.* Wiley-Blackwell, Oxford.

Smyth, H.J. and Pryke, S.D. (2008) Managing collaborative relationships and the management of projects. In H.J. Smyth and S.D. Pryke (eds) *Collaborative Relationships in Construction: Developing Frameworks and Networks.* Wiley-Blackwell, Oxford, pp. 1–24.

Smyth, H.J., Morris, P.W.G. and Kelsey, J.M. (2007) Critical realism and the management of projects: epistemology for understanding value creation in the face of uncertainty. *Proceedings of EURAM 2007, Paris, 16–19 May.*

Soda, G. and Usai, A. (1999) The dark side of dense networks. In A. Grandori (ed), *Interfirm Networks: Organization and Industrial Competitiveness.* Routledge, p. 276.

Söderlund, J. (2004a) Building theories of project management: past research, questions for the future. *International Journal of Project Management,* 22 (3), 183–191.

Söderlund, J. (2004b) On the broadening scope of the research on projects: a review and a model for analysis. *International Journal of Project Management,* 22 (8), 655–667.

Sorensen, O. and Waguespack, D.M. (2006) Social structure and exchange: self-confirming dynamics in Hollywood. *Administrative Science Quarterly,* 51 (4), 560–589.

Soundararaj, B., Watson, E., Pryke, S.D., Addyman, S.A. and Badi, S.M. (2015) A case study of the structure and dynamics of inter-organisational information exchange networks in large, complex infrastructure projects. *Proceedings of the Annual Research Conference of the International Network of Social Network Analysts (INSNA), Brighton, July 2015.*

Spender, J.C. (1989) *Industry Recipes: An Enquiry into the Nature and Sources of Managerial Judgement.* Basil Blackwell, Oxford.

Srivastava, V., Neel, J.O., MacKenzie, A.B., Menon, R., DaSilva, L.A., Hicks, J.E., Reed, J.H. and Gilles, R.P. (2005) Using game theory to analyze wireless ad hoc networks. *IEEE Communications Surveys and Tutorials,* 7 (1–4), 45–56.

Stacey, R.D. (2010) *Complexity and Organizational Reality: Uncertainty and the Need to Rethink Management After the Collapse of Investment Capitalism.* Routledge.

Steen, J., Pryke, S.D. and Michelfelder, I. (2017) Networks and projects. *Project Management Journal* (in press).

Stinchcombe, A.L. (1959) Bureaucratic and craft administration of production: a comparative study. *Administrative Science Quarterly,* 4 (2), 168–187.

Suitor, J.J., Wellman, B. and Morgan, D.L. (1997) It's about time: how, why and when networks change. *Social Networks,* 19 (1), 1–7.

Sydow, J. (1992) Strategische Netzwerke und Transaktionskosten. *Managementforschung,* 2 (1992), 239–212.

Sydow, J. and Staber, U. (2002) The institutional embeddedness of project networks: the case of content production in German television. *Regional Studies*, 36 (3), 215–227.

Sydow, J. and Windeler, A. (1998) Organizing and evaluating interfirm networks: a structurationist perspective on network processes and effectiveness. *Organization Science*, 9 (3), 265–284.

Sydow, J., Lindkvist, L. and DeFillippi, R.J. (2004) Project-based organisations, embeddedness and repositories of knowledge: editorial. *Organization Studies*, 25 (9), 1475–1489.

Tavistock Institute (1966) *Interdependence and Uncertainty: A Study of the Building Industry*. Tavistock Publications, London.

Taylor, F.W. (1911) The principles of management. *FO Onah Human Resource Management*.

Tetlock, P.E. (1981) The influence of self-presentation goals on attributional reports. *Social Psychology Quarterly*, 44 (4), 300–311.

Thayer, R.H. and Yourdon, E. (1997) Software engineering project management. *Software Engineering Project Management*. IEEE Computer Society, pp. 72–104.

Thiel, T. (2008) Decision aiding related to maintenance of buildings: technical, economic and environmental aspects. *International Journal of Environment and Pollution*, 35 (2–4), 158–170.

Thompson, G. (2003) *Between Hierarchies and Markets: The Logic and Limits of Network Forms of Organization*. Oxford University Press on Demand.

Thompson, J.D. (2003) *Organizations in Action: Social Science Bases of Administration*. Transaction Publishers, NJ.

Tjosvold, D., Johnson, D.W., Johnson, R.T. and Sun, H. (2006) Competitive motives and strategies: understanding constructive competition. *Group Dynamics: Theory, Research, and Practice*, 10 (2), 87–99.

Todorova, T. (2007) The Coase theorem revisited: implications for economic transition. *Atlantic Economic Journal*, 35 (2), 189–201.

Traylor, G. (1973) Joking in a bush camp. *Human Relations*, 26 (4), 479–486.

Tsvetkova, M. and Macy, M.W. (2014) The social contagion of generosity. *PloS one*, 9 (2), e87275.

Turner, J.R. (1999) *The Handbook of Project-Based Management: Improving the Processes for Achieving Strategic Objectives*. 2nd edition. McGraw-Hill, Maidenhead.

Turner, J.R. and Müller, R. (2003) On the nature of the project as a temporary organization. *International Journal of Project Management*, 21 (1), 1–8.

Turskis, Z., Zavadskas, E.K. and Peldschus, F. (2009) Multi-criteria optimization system for decision-making in construction design and management. *Engineering Economics*, 61 (1), 7–17.

Ullian, J.A. (1976) Joking at work. *Journal of Communication*, 26 (3), 129–133.

Ustinovichius, L., Zavadskas, E.K., Migilinskas, D., Malewska, A., Nowak, P. and Minasowicz, A. (2006) Verbal analysis of risk elements in construction contracts. *Lecture Notes in Computer Science*, 4101, 295–302.

Van Nederveen, G.A. and Tolman, F.P. (1992) Modelling multiple views on buildings. *Automation in Construction*, 1 (3), 215–224.

Von Bertalanffy, L. (1979) *General Systems Theory: Foundations, Development, Applications*. George Braziller, New York, NY.

Von Neumann, J. (1928) Zur Theorie der Gesellschaftsspiele. *Mathematische Annalen*, 100 (1), 295–320.

Walker, A. (2015) *Project Management in Construction.* 6th edition. Wiley-Blackwell, Oxford.

Walker, F. and Pryke, S.D. (2008) The relationship between the degree of incompleteness and loss and expense claims in construction projects. *Proceedings of the RICS Annual Construction, Building and Real Estate Research Conference (COBRA), Dublin, 4–5 September.*

Walker, F. and Pryke, S.D. (2009) Role, dimension and degrees of incompleteness in construction contract documentation. *Proceedings of the RICS Annual Construction, Building and Real Estate Research Conference (COBRA), Cape Town, 10–11 September.*

Walker, F. and Pryke, S.D. (2011) Investigating the relationship between construction contract documentation incompleteness and project transaction characteristics: the frequency characteristic. *Proceedings of the RICS Annual Construction, Building and Real Estate Research Conference (COBRA),* University of Salford, 12–13 September.

Walker, D. and Rowlinson, S. (2007) *Procurement Systems: A Cross-Industry Project Management Perspective.* Routledge.

Wasserman, S. and Faust, K. (1994*) Social Network Analysis: Methods and Applications.* Cambridge University Press, Cambridge.

Watson, T.J. (1994) *In Search of Management: Culture, Chaos and Control in Managerial Work.* Routledge, London.

Watts, D.J. (1999) Networks, dynamics, and the small-world phenomenon. *American Journal of Sociology,* 105 (2), 493–527.

Weber, M. (1946) Bureaucracy. In *From Max Weber: Essays in Sociology.* Oxford University Press, New York, pp. 196–244.

Webber, S.S. and Klimoski, R.J. (2004) Client-project manager engagements, trust, and loyalty. *Journal of Organisational Behaviour,* 25 (8), 997–1013.

Weick, K.E. (1995) *Sensemaking in Organizations.* Sage, Thousand Oaks, CA.

Wellman, B. (1982) Studying personal communities. In P.V. Marsden and N. Lin (eds) *Social Structure and Network Analysis.* Sage Publications, Beverly Hills, CA.

Wellman, B. (1985) Domestic work, paid work and network. In S. Duck and D. Perlman (eds) *Understanding Personal Relationships: An Interdisciplinary Approach.* Sage Publications, CA.

Wellman, B. (1988) Structural analysis: from method and metaphor to theory and substance. In B. Wellman and S.D Berkowitz (eds) *Social Structures: A Network Approach.* Cambridge University Press, Cambridge.

Wellman, B. (1997) An electronic group is virtually a social network. In S. Kiesler (ed) *Culture of the Internet.* Lawrence Erlbaum Associates Inc, pp. 179–205.

Wellman, B. and Berkowitz, S.D. (eds) (1988) *Social Structures: A Network Approach.* Cambridge University Press, Cambridge.

White, H.C. (1963) *An Anatomy of Kinship: Mathematical Models for Structures of Cumulated Roles.* Prentice-Hall, Englewood Cliffs, NJ.

White, H.C. (1970) *Chains of Opportunity: Systems Models of Mobility in Organisations.* Harvard University Press, Cambridge, MA.

White, H.C. (1992a) *Identity and Control: A Structural Theory of Social Action.* Princeton University Press, Princeton, NJ.

White, H.C. (1992b) Social grammar for culture: reply to Steven Brint. *Sociological Theory,* 10 (2), 209–213.

White, H.C. (1993) *Careers and Creativity: Social Forces in the Arts.* Westview Press, Boulder, CO.

White, H.C., Boorman, S.A. and Breiger, R.L. (1976) Social structure from multiple networks, I. Blockmodels of roles and positions. *American Journal of Sociology*, 81 (4), 730–780.

Whyte, J. and Levitt, R. (2011) Information management and the management of projects. In P.W.G Morris, J.K. Pinto and J. Söderlund (eds) *The Oxford Handbook of Project Management.* Oxford University Press, Oxford.

Williamson, O.E. (1975) *Markets and Hierarchies: Analysis and Antitrust Implications.* Free Press, New York.

Williamson, O.E. (1996) *The Mechanisms of Governance.* Oxford University Press, New York.

Winch, G. (1989) The construction firm and the construction project: a transaction cost approach. *Construction Management and Economics*, 7 (4), 331–345.

Winch, G. (1996) The contracting system in British construction: the rigidities of flexibility. Working Paper No. 6 from Le Group Bagnolet c/o Bartlett School, UCL.

Winch, G.M. (2000) Institutional reform in British construction: partnering and private finance. *Building Research and Information*, 28 (2), 141–155.

Winch, G.M. (2001) Governing the project process: a conceptual framework. *Construction Management and Economics*, 19 (8), 799–808.

Winch, G.M. (2010) *Managing Construction Projects.* 2nd edition. Blackwell, Oxford.

Winch, G.M. (2014) Three domains of project organising. *International Journal of Project Management*, 32 (5), 721–731.

Winch, G.M and Carr, B. (2001) Processes, maps and protocols: understanding the shape of the construction process. *Construction Management and Economics*, 19 (5), 519–531.

Windeler, A. and Sydow, J. (2001) Project networks and changing industry practices: collaborative content production in the German television industry. *Organization Studies*, 22 (6), 1035–1060.

Winter, M., Smith, C., Morris, P. and Cicmil, S. (2006) Directions for future research in project management: the main findings of a UK government funded research network. *International Journal of Project Management*, 24 (8), 638–649.

Womack, J.P. and Jones, D.T. (1996) Beyond Toyota: how to root out waste and pursue perfection. *Harvard Business Review*, 74 (5), 140–158.

Wong, P.S. and Cheung, S.O. (2004) Trust in construction partnering: views from parties of the partnering dance. *International Journal of Project Management*, 22 (6), 437–446.

Yip, J.A. and Martin, R.A. (2006) Sense of humor, emotional intelligence and social competence. *Journal of Research in Personality*, 40 (6), 1202–1208.

Young, S.E., Stallings, M.C., Corley, R.P., Krauter, K.S. and Hewitt, J.K. (2000) Genetic and environmental influences on behavioral disinhibition. *American Journal of Medical Genetics*, 96 (5), 684–695.

Zaleznik, A. (1966) *Human Dilemmas of Leadership.* Harper and Row, New York.

Zavadskas, E.K. (2008) History and evolving trends of construction colloquia on sustainability and operational research. *Technological and Economic Development of Economy*, 14 (4), 578–592.

Zavadskas, E.K. and Antucheviciene, J. (2007) Multiple criteria evaluation of rural building's regeneration alternatives. *Building and Environment*, 42 (1), 436–451.

Zavadskas, E.K. and Kaklauskas, A. (1991) *Automated multivariant design of buildings, multi-purpose comprehensive evaluation and selection of the most efficient versions.* Aalborg Universitetscenter, Aalborg.

Zavadskas, E.K. and Kaklauskas, A. (2008) Model for Lithuanian construction industry development. *Transformation in Business and Economics*, 7 (1), 152–168.

Zavadskas, E.K. and Turskis, Z. (2008) A new logarithmic normalization method in games theory. *Informatica*, 19 (2), 303–314.

Zavadskas, E.K., Peldschus, F., Ustinovičius, L. and Turskis, Z. (2004) *Game Theory in Building Technology and Management.* Technika, Vilnius (published in Lithuanian).

Zwikael, O. and Unger-Aviram, E. (2010) HRM in project groups: the effect of project duration on team development effectiveness. *International Journal of Project Management*, 28 (5), 413–421.

Further Reading

Aritua, B., Male, S. and Bower, D.A. (2009) Defining the intelligent public sector construction procurement client. *Management, Procurement and Law*, 162 (MPO), 75–82.

Baer, M. (2010) The strength-of-weak-ties perspective on creativity: a comprehensive examination and extension. *Journal of Applied Psychology*, 95 (3), 592–601.

Bergeman, C.S., Chlpuer, H.M., Plomin, R., Pedersen, N.L., McClearn, G.E., Nesselroade, J.R., Costa, P.T. and McCrae, R.R. (1993) Genetic and environmental effects on openness to experience, agreeableness, and conscientiousness: an adoption/twin study. *Journal of Personality*, 61 (2), 159–179.

Brady, T., Davies, A., Gann, D. and Rush, H. (2006) Learning to manage mega projects: the case of BAA and Heathrow Terminal 5. *Proceedings of IRNOP VII Project Research Conference, 11–13 Oct 2006, Xi'an, China.*

Burns, T. and Stalker, G.M. (2000) Mechanistic and organic systems of management. In *Technology, Organizations and Innovation: The Early Debates.* Oxford University Press, Oxford, pp. 24–50.

Burt, R.S. (2009) *Structural Holes: The Social Structure of Competition.* Harvard University Press, Cambridge, MA.

Chinowsky, P., Diekmann, J. and Galotti, V. (2008) Social network model of construction. *Journal of Construction Engineering and Management*, 134 (10), 804–812.

Conway, S. (1997a) Focal Innovation action-sets: a methodological approach for mapping innovation networks. Aston Business School Research Institute-Research Paper Series, Birmingham.

Conway, S. (1995) Informal boundary-spanning communication in the innovation process: an empirical study. *Technology Analysis and Strategic Management*, 7 (3), 327–342.

Eysenck, S.B. and Eysenck, H.J. (1977b) The place of impulsiveness in a dimensional system of personality description. *British Journal of Social and Clinical Psychology*, 16 (1), 57–68.

Fang, R., Landis, B., Zhang, Z. Anderson, M.H., Shaw, J.D. and Kilduff, M. (2015) Integrating personality and social networks: a meta-analysis of personality, network position, and work outcomes in organizations. *Organization Science*, 26 (4), 1243–1260.

Freeman, L.C. (1984) Turning a profit from mathematics: the case of social networks. *Journal of Mathematical Sociology*, 10 (3-4), 343–360.

Graziano, W.G. and Tobin, R.M. (2002) Agreeableness: dimension of personality or social desirability artifact? *Journal of Personality*, 70 (5), 695–728.

Hamlin, R.M. (1955) Review of studies in the scope and method of 'The Authoritarian Personality'. *Psychological Bulletin*, 52 (1), 83–85.

Jackson, M.O. and Watts, A. (2002) The evolution of social and economic networks. *Journal of Economic Theory*, 106 (2), 265–295.

Jünger, M. and Mutzel, P. (eds) (2012) *Graph Drawing Software*. Springer, New York, pp. 321–340.

Levitt, R.E., Fry, C., Greene, S. and Kaftan, C. (2011) Salesforce.com: the development dilemma. In *Collaboratory for Research on Global Projects* case study archive. https://gpc.stanford.edu/publications/case_studies.

Lin, N., Cook, K. and Burt, R.S. (eds) (2001) *Social Capital: Theory and Research*. 4th edition. Transaction Publishers, NJ.

Miles, G., Miles, R.E., Perrone, V. and Edvisson, L. (1998) Some conceptual and research barriers to the utilization of knowledge. *California Management Review*, 40 (3), 281–288.

Mosey, D. (2009) *Early Contractor Involvement in Building Procurement: Contracts, Partnering and Project Management*. John Wiley and Sons Ltd, Chichester.

Müller, R. and Turner, R. (2010) Leadership competency profiles of successful project managers. *International Journal of Project Management*, 28 (5), 437–448.

National Audit Office [NAO] (2009) Annual Report, HMSO.

OGC (Office of Government Commerce) (2002) Business Case Toolkit. HMSO, London.

Schlenker, B.R. (1980) *Impression Management: The Self-Concept, Social Identity and Interpersonal Relations*. Brooks/Cole, Monterey, CA.

Shenhar, A.J. and Dvir, D. (1973) *Reinventing Project Management: The Diamond Approach to Successful Growth and Innovation*. Harvard Business School Press, Boston, MA.

Soda, G., Usai, A. and Zaheer, A. (2004) Network memory: the influence of past and current networks on performance. *Academy of Management Journal*, 47 (6), 893–906.

Söderlund, J. (2004a) Building theories of project management: past research, questions for the future. *International Journal of Project Management*, 22 (3), 183–191.

Taylor, F.W. (2004) *Scientific Management*. Routledge.

Williamson, O.E. (1991) Comparative economic organization: the analysis of discrete structural alternatives. *Administrative Science Quarterly*, 269–296.

Winch, G.M. (2006) The governance of project coalitions: towards a research agenda. In D. Lowe and R. Leiringer (eds) (2006) *Commercial Management of Projects: Defining the Discipline*. Wiley-Blackwell, Oxford.

Winch, G.W. and Pinto, J. (2013) Festschrift for Professor Peter W.G. Morris, PhD. *International Journal of Project Management*, 31 (7), 937.

Zavadskas, E.K., Kaklauskas, A., Turskis, Z. and Tamošaitiene, J. (2009) Multi-attribute decision-making model by applying grey numbers. *Informatica*, 20(2), 305–320.

Index

Managing Networks in Project-Based Organisations, First Edition. Stephen Pryke.
© 2017 John Wiley & Sons Ltd. Published 2017 by John Wiley & Sons Ltd.